Domestic Violence

of related interest

Making an Impact – Children and Domestic Violence
A Reader
Marianne Hester, Chris Pearson and Nicola Harwin
ISBN 1 85302 844 4

Children and Domestic Violence
Action towards Prevention
Caroline McGee
ISBN 1 85302 827 4

Preventing Violence in Relationships
A Preventative Educational Programme for Men Who Feel They Have a Problem with their Use of Controlling and Violent Behaviour
Gerry Heery
ISBN 1 85302 816 9

Effective Ways of Working with Children and their Families
Edited by Malcolm Hill
ISBN 1 85302 619 0
Research Highlights in Social Work 35

Good Practice in Working with Victims of Violence
Edited by Hazel Kemshall and Jacki Pritchard
ISBN 1 85302 768 5

Early Experience and the Life Path
Ann Clarke and Alan Clarke
ISBN 1 85302 858 4

Child Development for Child Care and Protection Workers
Brigid Daniel, Sally Wassel and Robbie Gilligan
ISBN 1 85302 633 6

Domestic Violence

Guidelines for Research-Informed Practice

*Edited by John P. Vincent
and Ernest N. Jouriles*

Jessica Kingsley Publishers
London and Philadelphia

All rights reserved. No paragraph of this publication may be reproduced, copied or transmitted save with written permission or in accordance with the provisions of the Copyright Act 1956 (as amended), or under the terms of any licence permitting limited copying issued by the Copyright Licensing Agency, 33–34 Alfred Place, London WC1E 7DP. Any person who does any unauthorised act in relation to this publication may be liable to criminal prosecution and civil claims for damages.

The right of the contributors to be identified as authors of this work has been asserted by them in accordance with the Copyright, Designs and Patents Act 1988.

First published in the United Kingdom in 2000 by
Jessica Kingsley Publishers Ltd
116 Pentonville Road
London N1 9JB, England
and
325 Chestnut Street
Philadelphia, PA 19106, USA.

www.jkp.com

Copyright © 2000 Jessica Kingsley Publishers

Library of Congress Cataloging in Publication Data
A CIP catalog record for this book is available from the Library of Congress

British Library Cataloguing in Publication Data
A CIP catalogue record for this book is available from the British Library

ISBN 1 85302 854 1

Printed and Bound in Great Britain by
Athenaeum Press, Gateshead, Tyne and Wear

Contents

CHAPTER I

Domestic Violence

An Overview of Research that Informs Practice

Ernest N. Jouriles and John P. Vincent

Violence towards women by an intimate partner is a social problem of enormous proportion. National surveys indicate that approximately 11–14 percent of married women in the USA experience some sort of physical violence from an intimate partner each year (Schafer, Caetano and Clark 1998; Straus and Gelles 1990). Each year as many as 3 percent of married women experience very severe violence such as beatings and/or life-threatening assaults (for example, attacks with a knife or gun: Schafer *et al.* 1998; Straus and Gelles 1990). The impact of this violence is broad and substantial, with serious consequences not only for the women who are victimized, but also for their children and society at large. Women who are battered suffer physical injuries ranging from bruises and scratches to permanent bodily damage or even death (National Research Council 1996); many experience severe psychological problems including depression, anxiety, symptoms of trauma and low self-esteem (Holtzworth-Munroe *et al.* 1998; National Research Council 1996). Furthermore, men who batter also damage the children of the women they victimize. A substantial number of these children are physically injured themselves (Appel and Holden 1998; Jouriles *et al.* 2000); the psychological injury they suffer can range from severe emotional maladjustment to a repetition of the violence and aggression to which they have been exposed.

Although the most obvious and most serious consequences of intimate violence towards women are the personal suffering it causes and the long-term toll it takes on these women and their children, the social costs of this violence are substantial as well. Health care costs associated with the treatment of battered women and children, provision of shelter and services to women trying to escape violence, criminal justice system costs associated with the prosecution or incarceration of violent men, and the great loss of productivity due to physical or psychological injury of battered women are all examples of the financial burden borne by society as a result of intimate violence (National Research Council 1996). Some scholars argue that social costs do not end there; rather, we all suffer, practically and morally, by failing to stop the violence, and in effect allowing the perpetuation of a subculture that devalues women.

Given the pervasiveness and devastating consequences of violence toward women, the development of psychosocial interventions to stop the violence and help those who have already been victimized has become a national priority (National Research Council 1996). Indeed, if one uses a broad definition of intervention, the number and variety of interventions across disciplines is impressive. Interventions have been designed to address the problem from various ecological levels, from community-level efforts such as criminal justice reforms (e.g., arrest policies and police training) and governmental or quasi-governmental agencies that offer services to victims of violence (e.g., shelters, social services) to interventions targeted at individuals or families such as batterer treatment programs, support groups and advocacy programs for abused women and counseling and other programs for the children in these families. Unfortunately, empirical evidence for the effectiveness of these programs is very rare. In our haste to stop violence toward women and to offer assistance to victims of violence, very little has been done in the way of systematically evaluating the effects of these programs.

It might be asked whether there is really a need to evaluate formally interventions designed to address the problem of intimate violence and the effects that it has on victims. Is it not enough that services are being offered? We hope that the evidence and argument offered in this volume will demonstrate how *essential* it is to determine whether or not the interventions being offered are actually having the effect intended. There are just too many examples of limited resources being wasted on ineffective or only very modestly effective psychosocial interventions, and there is even some risk that what is thought to be helpful actually hurts. One particularly compelling example is provided in a review of the history of rape resistance strategies (National Research Council 1996). Such strategies involve recommendations to women about what they should do if attacked. According to this review, Storaska (1975) 'popularized among law enforcement agencies the theory that women should remain passive in the face of an attack to avoid angering the attacker and increasing her risk of serious injury or death' (pp.98–99). Although this theory was no doubt very well intentioned (as we suspect is true of most interventions), empirical evaluations of the effectiveness of various approaches to rape resistance ultimately discredited this particular approach. In fact, this review suggests that there is research indicating that 'women who actively resist attack are most likely to thwart rape completion without increasing their risk of serious injury' (p.99). Thus, advice based on unevaluated theory may have actually increased women's risk of completed rape and serious injury during an attack.

In this book we present seven chapters that illustrate how research can inform practice in the area of domestic violence. In Chapter 2, Holtzworth-Munroe describes a program of research investigating the characteristics of maritally violent men. Many cognitive-behavioral treatment programs for maritally violent men assume that these men have social skills deficits. Holtzworth-Munroe summarizes a series of studies that she conducted to test this assumption. This research compares the social information processes used by men in maritally violent relationships with those employed by men in nonviolent relationships. Her findings indicate that there are broad differences in the way violent and nonviolent men process social information, and these differences have direct implications for the design of effective interventions to curb marital violence. Specifically, Holtzworth-Munroe argues that effective treatment should teach maritally violent men how to alter the interpretations they place on their partners' behavior, their decisions regarding possible responses, and how they execute or monitor the impact of those responses.

In Chapter 3, Babcock and La Taillade review studies investigating the efficacy of interventions for domestically violent men. There are a number of obvious clinical policy implications of such research, and these authors follow their review with a discussion of a number of these issues. These authors conclude their chapter by offering ideas about promising future directions for interventions with domestically violent men.

In Chapter 4, Stephens and McDonald review research investigating the mental health correlates of domestic violence. Violence toward women is associated with a number of deleterious outcomes and this chapter describes the specific mental health needs often exhibited by victims of husbands' violence. Based on their review of the empirical literature and their clinical experience with this population, these authors provide an overview of the issues facing service providers and make recommendations for assessment of women seeking services because of violence.

In Chapter 5, Grych discusses his research on how children are affected by family conflict and violence. Specifically, he presents findings from his own and other research programs which shed light on how children perceive, interpret and remember incidents of family aggression and how these social and cognitive processes affect children's short-term and long-term emotional well-being. Grych's chapter draws heavily on the cognitive-contextual framework that he and his colleagues have been investigating during the 1990s. In addition to providing a better under-standing of how family conflict and violence affect children, Grych discusses how this understanding can inform clinical practice.

In Chapter 6, Sullivan presents a model for effectively advocating for women in abusive relationships. Her community advocacy program makes use of paraprofessional advocates who, based on a thorough assessment of client needs, help abused women mobilize community resources and learn to approach the problems they face systematically. In her chapter, Sullivan describes how the research literature on domestic violence contributed to the program's design as well as in the training of advocates who actually implement the program. In addition to presenting some case illustrations, Sullivan summarizes the results of evaluation studies that compare the community advocacy model to the standard services that are typically available to women in abusive relationships.

In Chapter 7, Ezell, McDonald and Jouriles summarize the empirical literature on children of battered women and discuss the implications of this literature for programs that serve these children. These authors also provide an overview of several approaches to intervention with children of battered women and describe the results of evaluations of these programs. The remainder of the chapter is devoted to describing in depth their own intervention program, Project SUPPORT. Project SUPPORT is designed to help families (battered women who have at least one child displaying clinical levels of conduct problems). In their description of Project SUPPORT, the authors illustrate how theory and data on the development and treatment of child conduct problems as well as knowledge about the specific needs of battered women were incorporated into the design of the intervention. These authors also summarize the results of an empirical evaluation of their program.

In Chapter 8, Vincent, Harris, Vincent, Cross and Palapattu present material that represents somewhat of a departure from the earlier chapters, which focus primarily on violence that arises within the family context. By contrast, Vincent *et al.* discuss the impact on children of violent crime perpetrated by nonfamily members. In addition to discussing the current state of knowledge concerning the psychological impact of crime on children, the authors present their own research efforts to understand the factors that impact the variability in children's trauma reactions to criminal violence. They also describe their own supportive and cognitive behavioral intervention models for facilitating children's emotional recovery from these experiences. In keeping with the book's spirit of research accountability, Vincent *et al.* also report results from their research that empirically supports the effectiveness of these interventions.

By assembling the chapters of this book, our hope was to provide readers with a greater appreciation of how research can both inform and improve practice in the field of domestic violence. We believe that such research is necessary for constructing and testing conceptual frameworks that can help guide service delivery in this area. Rigorous empirical evaluations of theory-based interventions are essential if we are to have confidence that our efforts to reduce violence and its consequences are succeeding.

References

Appel, A.E. and Holden, G.W. (1998) 'The co-occurrence of spouse and physical child abuse: a review and appraisal.' *Journal of Family Violence 2*, 139–149.

Holtzworth-Munroe, A., Jouriles, E.N., Smutzler, N. and Norwood, W. (1998) 'Victims of domestic violence.' In A.S. Bellack and M. Hersen (eds) *Comprehensive Clinical Psychology, Volume 9*. Oxford: Pergamon.

Jouriles, E.N., McDonald, R., Norwood, W.D. and Ezell, E. (2000) 'Documenting the prevalence of children's exposure to domestic violence: issues and controversies.' In S. Graham-Berman and J. Edleson (eds) *Intimate Violence in the Lives of Children: The Future of Research, Intervention, and Social Policy*. Washington DC: American Psychological Association.

National Research Council (1996) *Understanding and Preventing Violence*. N.A. Crowell and A.W. Burgess (eds) Panel on Research on Violence against Women. Washington DC: National Academy Press.

Schafer, J., Caetano, R. and Clark, C. (1998) 'Rates of intimate partner violence in the United States.' *American Journal of Public Health 88*, 1701–1704.

Storaska, F. (1975) *How to Say No to a Rapist and Survive.* New York: Random House.

Straus, M.A. and Gelles, R.J. (1990) *Physical Violence in American Families: Risk Factors and Adaptation to Violence in 8,145 Families.* New Brunswick, NJ: Transaction.

CHAPTER 2

Social Information Processing Skills Deficits in Maritally Violent Men

Summary of a Research Program

Amy Holtzworth-Munroe

Husband to wife violence is a serious problem in many countries. For example, data from US nationally representative surveys suggest that, each year, one out of every eight married men will be physically aggressive toward his wife and up to 2 million women will be severely assaulted by their male partners (Straus and Gelles 1990). Both husbands and wives engage in physical aggression, but a series of studies have demonstrated that husband violence has more negative consequences than wife violence; for example, husband violence is more likely to result in physical injury and depressive symptomatology (see review in Holtzworth-Munroe, Smutzler and Bates 1997a). In attempting to understand the correlates and potential causes of husband violence, reviewers have noted that the most fruitful efforts have focused on characteristics of the violent man, as opposed to the female partner or the dyad (Hotaling and Sugarman 1986). Thus, our research program has focused on studying violent husbands, comparing men who have been violent toward their wives to men who have not.

We believe that such work is needed to inform clinical practice with maritally violent men, as the rush to study and treat husband violence has often proceeded faster than the development or testing of theories to guide this work. The research program reviewed in this chapter is based on the premise that future research and therapy efforts would be best guided by theoretical models of husband violence. In particular, we have been interested in examining the social skills deficits of maritally violent men, as many existing treatment programs for violent men involve a behavioral/cognitive approach based on the assumption that violent men have social skills deficits (e.g., these programs often involve training in skills such as anger management, assertion, communication and conflict resolution).

Social information processing model

The social information processing model (McFall 1982) is a comprehensive model of social skills that has been applied to a variety of populations. In Holtzworth-Munroe (1991, 1992), I outlined how this model might help us to understand husband violence more effectively. The model proposes that social skills involve a series of sequential steps, each involving specific abilities that must be successfully completed if a person is to perform competently in a social interaction. Each set of tasks is necessary-but-not-sufficient for competent responding. Thus, an incompetent response in a social situation is the result of a skills deficit at one or more of the required tasks. There are three major sets of tasks involved in social interaction:

- decoding, or perceiving and interpreting the incoming social stimuli
- decision-making, or generating, evaluating and choosing a response
- enactment, or executing and monitoring the impact of the chosen response.

We have proposed that skills deficits at any of these stages may increase the risk of physical aggression (Holtzworth-Munroe 1991, 1992). To examine this notion, we have conducted a series of studies comparing the social information processing skills of violent and nonviolent husbands at each of the model stages. Before reviewing the findings from individual studies, I provide an overview of the methodological design used in many of our studies.

Methodological design of studies

First, each of the studies included one or more of three possible subject groups of maritally violent men:

- men who were beginning marital or domestic violence treatment programs, usually court-ordered to do so after legal charges were brought against them

- men who were maritally violent and maritally distressed (i.e., not satisfied with their marriage), recruited from the community (i.e., violent/distressed group)

- men who were maritally violent but not maritally distressed (i.e., violent/nondistressed group).

While it may surprise many, it is not uncommon to find couples experiencing husband violence who do not report marital distress (e.g., McLaughlin, Leonard and Senchak 1992; O'Leary *et al.* 1989).

Second, in all of the studies, we recruited two comparison samples of nonviolent men from the community. First of all, we included men who were not violent toward their wives and were not experiencing marital distress (i.e., nonviolent/nondistressed group). However, given that husband violence and marital distress are correlated (see review in Holtzworth-Munroe *et al.* 1997a), it has also been recommended that researchers include a comparison sample of men who are not violent but are maritally distressed (i.e., nonviolent/distressed group), to help distinguish effects attributable to violence from those due to marital distress and conflict (e.g., Rosenbaum and O'Leary 1981).

All study participants were recruited from a major midwestern metropolitan area in the USA. To recruit study participants, we used a variety of newspaper ads, flyers placed around town and announcements made in domestic violent treatment programs; all these methods of recruitment targeted 'husbands' for studies of 'marriage'. Interested men called our laboratory and participated in a phone interview. Thus, as discussed below, in most of our studies, men's self-reports were used to determine eligibility for the study and to place men in the appropriate subject cell. The interview included a standardized measure of marital adjustment (the Short Marital Adjustment Test or SMAT: Locke and Wallace 1959), used to place men into the maritally distressed or nondistressed groups. It also included a standardized measure of marital violence (the Conflict Tactics Scale or CTS: Straus 1979). If, on the CTS, a man reported engaging in physical aggression toward his wife in the past year (i.e., push/grab/shove or more severe violence), he was placed in the violent group(s). In some studies, we required reports of more than one husband violent act in the past year (i.e., two or three violent acts) for a man to qualify for the violent subject group(s); this was done to ensure that we had a group of moderately violent/severely violent men. If a man reported never engaging in physical aggression toward his wife (or, in a recent study, not having engaged in violence in the past five years), he was placed in the nonviolent groups.

There are potential problems with using only men's self-reports of aggression, as men tend to underreport their own use of aggression relative to their wives' reports of victimization (e.g., Moffitt *et al.* 1997). In our studies, however, the direction of this bias was conservative, making it more difficult to prove our hypotheses. In other words, our nonviolent subject groups may have included some violent men, making it more difficult to demonstrate violent–nonviolent group differences. Given concerns about husbands' self-reports, in our more recent studies (e.g., Anglin and Holtzworth-Munroe 1997; Holtzworth-Munroe *et al.* under review; Hulbert 1999), we have gathered both husband and wife reports of husband physical aggression. In these studies, to place a man in the nonviolent subject groups, we have required that neither spouse report any husband violence; if either spouse reported husband violence in the past year, then the couple was placed in one of the violent groups.

Given our geographical location, most of our study participants are Caucasian (75–80%), with the largest other group being African American (15–25%). Across studies, the average participant's age is in the young 30s. Men have had, on average, a year of college and make, on average, $2000–3000 per month. On average, men's current relationships are not short term (i.e., seven to nine years), and the men have one or two children with their partner.

In all of our studies, following the phone interview, men who were eligible for the study were scheduled for an assessment in our laboratory. In most studies, men had individual appointments (i.e., they were not assessed in groups). Men received monetary compensation for their time ($9–15 per hour). Most studies involved 1.5–2.5 hours of a participant's time.

In the majority of the studies to be presented, we assessed men's reactions to standardized marital conflict vignettes. The use of standardized stimuli allowed us to hold other factors constant. For example, researchers examining marital interactions between husbands and their wives find group differences in husband behavior (i.e., violent men engage in more negative behavior than nonviolent men) but this could be due either to group differences in skills (e.g., violent men choose less competent responses) or to differences in the situational stimuli confronted by subjects (i.e., wives in violent relationships tend to engage in more negative behavior than wives in nonviolent relationships). Thus, the use of vignettes allowed us to standard-ize the wife's behavior confronted by men in the different subject groups.

The conflict vignettes were designed to be realistic and moderately difficult to handle. They represent a range of types of marital conflict, varying both in topic (e.g., money, social plans) and theme (e.g., wife rejecting husband, wife challenging husband). Pilot research demonstrated that the situations were viewed as being realistic and moderately challenging by men in a wide variety of marriages (e.g., distressed or not, violent or not). Example vignettes include the following. 'You and your partner are at a social gathering. You notice that, for the last half-hour, she has been talking and laughing with the same attractive man. He seems to be flirting with her' (jealousy vignette). 'You've had an awful day at work and are exhausted. You are really looking forward to coming home and just relaxing. However, when you get home, the TV is blaring, the kids are running around screaming, dinner isn't made, and your wife is talking on the phone. You ask her to get off and help you deal with things, but she says, "Can't you handle it yourself?"' (wife challenge). In another vignette the wife brusquely rejects the husband's sexual advances (wife rejection). The presentation of these vig-nettes to subjects was always standardized; subjects listened to a male narrator reading the vignette and read along on a written copy of the vignette.

After the presentation of each vignette, men were asked to respond in various ways (e.g., to interpret the wife's behavior in the situation, to tell how they would respond in the situation). Responses were often later coded (e.g., for competency level). Coding was always completed by undergraduate coders who were trained to use the relevant coding system until they were reliable with a coding calibrator. Throughout each study, a random subset of responses was coded by the calibrator to check that coders remained reliable over the course of the study. In all studies, coders were masked to the participant's group placement (e.g., they did not know if the man was violent or not) and to study hypotheses.

The procedural details vary slightly from study to study, but the overall design described above fits many of the studies to be reviewed. Where there are departures from this basic design, these will be briefly discussed. This review of studies is organized by the three major social information pro-cessing steps tested in each study.

Studies of decoding skills

The first set of tasks in the social information processing model involve the decoding, or perception and interpretation, of social stimuli in a social interaction. During marital interactions, a husband perceives his wife's actions and must interpret her behaviors. Problems at this stage (e.g., inattention or misinterpretation) may result in an incompetent response in the situation. In particular, we hypothesized that violent men might perceive negative wife behavior as having been done intentionally, with negative intent. Such attributions, theoretically, would increase the probability that a husband would use violence, as violence would seem 'justified' as a 'retaliation' against a wife's hostile actions. A similar finding among aggressive boys has been labeled the 'hostile attributional bias' (e.g., Dodge and Coie 1987).

To test this hypothesis, in an early study we compared the interpretations, or attributions, of wife behavior offered by violent versus nonviolent husbands (Holtzworth-Munroe and Hutchinson 1993). Men in three subject groups (i.e., twenty-two men from domestic violence treatment programs, seventeen nonviolent/distressed men and seventeen nonviolent/nondistressed men) were presented with nine of our standardized marital conflict vignettes. Following each vignette, men completed the Negative Intentions Questionnaire (Holtzworth-Munroe and Hutchinson 1993), used to assess their hostile attributions for the wife's action in the situation (i.e., men rated how strongly they agreed with such statements as 'My wife did this to piss me off' or 'My wife did this to get my goat'). Findings revealed that violent men were more likely than both groups of nonviolent men to attribute negative intentions to the wife.

Holtzworth-Munroe and Stuart (1994a) proposed a batterer typology, suggesting that different subtypes of maritally violent men exist and differ in theoretically predictable and meaningful ways. While Holtzworth-Munroe and Stuart did not offer predictions regarding subtype differences in decoding skills, they did examine this issue in a recent study designed to test their typology (Holtzworth-Munroe in preparation; data gathered as part of the Holtzworth-Munroe *et al.* under review study). Specifically, in this study, one hundred and two violent men (falling into four subgroups) and sixty-two nonviolent men (i.e., twenty-three maritally distressed and thirty-nine non-distressed) were presented with ten hypothetical marital conflict vignettes and asked to complete the Negative Intentions Questionnaire with regard to the wife's intent in each situation. We found that, relative to nonviolent/nondistressed men, all distressed men (i.e., violent or not) evidenced a hostile attributional bias. However, the more severely violent subgroups were the only groups to differ significantly from the non-violent/nondistressed group, suggesting that the hostile attributional bias is particularly evident among more severely violent men.

In a third study, which did not address the batterer subtype issue, Holtzworth-Munroe and Smutzler (1996) recruited two violent groups of men (i.e., twenty-five beginning violence treatment and twenty-one violent/distressed men from the community) and two nonviolent comparison samples (i.e., twenty-three maritally distressed and twenty-eight nondistressed). In this study, we were interested in examining whether violent men reacted more negatively than nonviolent men only to negative/aggressive wife behavior (i.e., negative wife behavior directed at the husband, which is portrayed in most of our standardized vignettes) or whether this bias extended to other types of wife behavior. Thus, in this study, we presented men with differing types of wife behavior, using both written examples of wife statements and standardized videotaped depictions of wives engaging in various types of behavior. These included not only aggressive wife statements (i.e., negative statements directed at the husband, such as 'Keep that up and you'll be eating alone tonight'), but also distressed statements (e.g., negative statements which were not about the husband, including self-denigrating comments, such as 'I feel really fat and ugly', and complaints about the world in general, such as 'They sent me to the post office for nothing'), neutral statements (e.g., 'Political candidate B is still ahead in the polls') and even facilitation/positive statements (e.g., 'Your haircut looks nice'). In the first part of this study, husbands were asked to rate how strongly they would experience various feelings in response to each portrayed wife behavior. These included positive feelings (e.g., sympathetic, caring, supportive), angry negative feelings (e.g., irritated, angry) and nonangry negative feelings (e.g., sad, anxious). We found that, across these many types of wife behaviors, and relative to nonviolent men, violent men felt more angry and less positively/supportively; interestingly, the groups did not differ in their reported level of nonangry negative feelings. Group differences were found in response not only to aggressive wife behavior, but also to distressed and even facilitative statements, as if the violent men were not discriminating between various types of wife behavior but rather were responding negatively to almost anything their wives say!

In summary, the findings from these studies suggest that, relative to nonviolent husbands, violent men, particularly more severely violent men, attribute more hostile intent to negative wife behaviors in marital conflict situations. They also experience more anger and fewer positive/supportive feelings in response to a wide variety of wife behaviors, including behaviors that are not aggressive. One possible explanation for this finding is that violent men may have difficulty recognizing various emotions (e.g., aggressive versus distressed). If so, we do not know whether this skill deficit is limited to the recognition of emotions in their wives (i.e., intimate relationships involving strong feelings expressed in the context of personally meaningful interactions) or whether it is present with all women, or even with all or most individuals of both genders (i.e., a global skill deficit). Alternatively, these findings could indicate that violent men have interpretational skill deficits; perhaps violent husbands have negative schemas leading them to assume hostile intent from others and to perceive negativity in others without fully processing the social stimuli in each situation.

Regardless of such unresolved theoretical issues, these responses may increase the risk of a man's escalating a conflict and/or engaging in violence. As such, the findings have clinical implications. Therapists should help maritally violent men to examine both their emotional reactions and their attributions for a variety of wife behaviors, focusing on angry reactions and attributions of hostile intent. Clients should be helped to consider alternative interpretations of wife behavior. The study findings also provide indirect support for the use of anger management techniques with violent men; men should be encouraged to relax and to examine their self-statements (e.g., possible hostile attributions) when they become angered by wife behavior. The Holtzworth-Munroe and Smutzler (1996) findings suggest that this may be necessary in a wide variety of situations, not just marital conflicts where the wife is negative or aggressive. The findings also suggest that violent husbands may need training in the recognition of emotions in others and might benefit from empathy training.

As an example, consider the case of Dan, who came to a group treatment session furious and expressing concern that he might 'have to' hit his wife because she was having an affair. In the course of the group discussion, the therapist asked Dan how he found out about his wife's affair. Dan reported that two nights in a row, he had begun to make sexual advances toward his wife, but she had refused to have sex. He said that this was unusual, as their sex life was normally mutually enjoyable, and he had thus concluded that the only reason she would be uninterested in sex twice in one week was because she was sleeping with someone else. The group members helped Dan to generate other possible interpretations of his wife's behavior. Indeed, upon questioning, Dan acknowledged that on both nights, his wife had explained that she had been very busy at work and was stressed. Through this discussion, Dan was helped to see that he had jumped to only one of several possible conclusions regarding his wife's behavior.

The unclear role of a man's relationship beliefs

Given the consistent findings, across several studies, that violent men attribute more hostile intent to negative wife behavior and react more negatively to wife behavior than do nonviolent men, we hypothesized that these differing reactions might be due to violent–nonviolent group differences in the standards that men hold for wife behavior and/or in the assumptions they make about relationships. In other words, if violent men hold unrealistic standards and beliefs about relationships (e.g., 'My wife should understand my every need'; 'My wife should be available whenever I need her'; 'The fact that we disagree means that our relationship is in trouble'), they may be more likely to negatively interpret wife behavior which does not meet their standards. To test this notion, Holtzworth-Munroe and Stuart (1994b) recruited sixteen men beginning therapy for marital violence, nineteen violent and maritally distressed men from the community, twenty nonviolent/distressed men, and twenty nonviolent/nondistressed men. Each man completed standardized questionnaire measures of relationship beliefs (the Relationship Beliefs Inventory: Epstein and Eidelson 1981) and relationship standards (the Inventory of Specific Relationship Standards: Epstein et al. 1991). While significant differences emerged between the nondistressed group and the three maritally distressed groups (i.e., distressed men endorsed more dysfunctional standards and assumptions, and reported being less satisfied with how their standards were being met, and being more upset when their standards were not met), no differences emerged between the violent and nonviolent groups.

These findings do not provide support for our hypothesis that the decoding skills deficits of violent men are due to the problematic relationship standards and assumptions they bring to each marital situation. Before this hypothesis is dismissed, however, it is important to note that the two questionnaire measures used in this study were originally developed to identify the problematic relationship beliefs of maritally distressed spouses, not those of violent spouses. Thus, it is possible that violent–nonviolent group differences could emerge in a future study using a measure of relationship standards believed to be uniquely related to husband violence (e.g., a male has the right to control the female's partner behavior; relationships between men and women are innately adversarial). As, to our knowledge, no such measure yet exists, clinicians may wish to consider developing their own means of assessing the relationship standards and beliefs of batterers in treatment.

Studies of decision-making skills

After a husband interprets the situational 'task' (i.e., in the decoding stage), he must go through a series of steps to generate, evaluate and choose an appropriate response in the situation. He must think of various possible responses, consider the consequences of each and choose the one which he believes is 'best' and which he believes he can accomplish. Maritally violent men could have several skills deficits during this stage of social information processing. For example, perhaps violent men are deficient, quantitatively or qualitatively, at generating possible responses during problematic marital situations. Or perhaps, relative to nonviolent husbands, violent men view violence as more likely to produce benefits than other possible responses; if violence has been reinforced in the past, such expectations, though problematic, may be realistic.

In our first study of the decision-making stage, Holtzworth-Munroe and Anglin (1991) presented violent men (twenty-two men beginning a domestic violence program) and two nonviolent comparison groups of men (seventeen maritally distressed and seventeen nondistressed) with a series of twenty-two standardized marital conflict vignettes. Following each vignette, the man was asked what he would say or do in the situation. Responses were audiotaped and later rated for level of competency. Analyses demonstrated that the violent men provided less competent responses than the nonviolent men. As an example, in response to the party scenario (i.e., 'It appears that a man is flirting with your wife'), nonviolent men often offered responses that let the other man know, in a socially appropriate manner, that their partner was their wife (e.g., they would walk up to their wife, put their arm around her, and say, 'Honey, would you like me to get you a drink?'). In contrast, violent men often reported that they would either threaten their wife (e.g., grab her and demand that she go home immediately) or the man (e.g., threaten to fight the man if he didn't 'back off').

In this study, after each man told us what he would do in each situation, we presented a subset of the vignettes to the man again and asked him, this time, not what he would do but what he thought would be the 'best' thing to say or do in the situation. Interestingly, violent men's 'best' responses were coded as being significantly less competent than those of both groups of nonviolent men. These findings suggest that either violent men are unable to generate competent solutions (i.e., they do not know what is competent) or that they know but do not care. To further explore this, future researchers might compare violent and nonviolent men on such variables as their goals in the situation and their ideas of how effective various solutions would be.

In a study introduced on p.19, Holtzworth-Munroe and Smutzler (1996) presented men not only with negative/aggressive wife behavior but also with standardized depictions of other types of wife behavior (e.g., distressed, facilitative). In addition to asking how men would feel in response to these wife behaviors, we asked men to rate how likely they would be to engage in a variety of behavioral responses, including positive (e.g., try to comfort wife, say something supportive) and negative (e.g., argue, say something hostile, say nothing) responses. We found that, across a wide variety of wife behaviors, relative to nonviolent men, violent men were less likely to act supportively and more likely to act negatively. Given that, in this same study, violent men had more negative emotional responses than nonviolent men to these wife behaviors, it is possible that the group differences in behavioral intentions are due to differences in decoding (i.e., men's negative reactions led to more negative responses); in other words, these findings do not conclusively demonstrate decision-making stage skills deficits. Regardless of the stage of social information processing leading to these negative behavioral intentions, we have speculated that a violent man's negative reactions to a wide variety of wife behaviors make his actions unpredictable and, as others have also suggested, the fact that husband aggression is unpredictable may be exactly what makes it an effective form of male control of women (e.g., Jacobson et al. 1994).

In an extension of our work, Anglin and Holtzworth-Munroe (1997) examined whether the violent men's social skills deficits were limited only to marital situations or were also evident in nonmarital situations. For this study, we recruited twenty-five violent/distressed men and two nonviolent comparison samples of men (ten maritally distressed and twenty-three nondistressed) from the community. Men were presented with thirteen marital conflict vignettes and nine nonmarital problematic situation vignettes. The nonmarital vignettes were designed for this study and involved a range of situations or individuals (e.g., a boss asks you to stay late at work despite the fact that you told him you needed to leave on time for some special plans; a friend tells others a secret that you had asked him to keep confidential; a relative is 'freeloading' at your house and will not make serious efforts to find a job). As in our earlier study, men were asked what they would say or do in each situation; in this study, they were also asked to give a second response to each situation (i.e., 'What else could you say or do?'). Their responses were coded for competency, using a new coding system developed by asking subjects' competent peers (i.e., nonviolent, happily married community members from the same demographic groups) what would be competent or incompetent responses in each situation. We found that, relative to nonviolent men, violent men offered less competent first and second responses to both marital and nonmarital situations; however, the greatest group difference was in first responses to marital situations. These data suggest that violent men have global skills deficits (i.e., their lack of social skills is not confined to intimate relationships) but that their skills deficits are particularly pronounced in the marital situation.

It is possible that the group differences in responses to nonmarital situations were weaker than those for marital situations because (while we assume that all violent husbands have marital skills deficits) only certain subgroups of violent husbands have skills deficits outside the marriage (i.e., some of the violent men may have been offering competent responses to nonmarital situations, while others may not). Specifically, in our batterer typology (Holtzworth-Munroe and Stuart 1994a) we suggested that two subtypes of maritally violent men (i.e., family only and dysphoric/borderline) are violent primarily toward their wives and would thus evidence skill deficits in marital conflicts, while a third subtype (i.e., generally violent/antisocial) engage in extra-familial aggression and would thus evidence global social skills deficits outside of their relationship.

In a recent study attempting to validate the Holtzworth-Munroe and Stuart (1994a) batterer typology (Holtzworth-Munroe et al. under review), we compared the competency of responses offered by different subtypes of violent husbands to ten marital and five nonmarital vignettes. In this study, we asked men what they would say or do in each situation. In a new procedure for the marital situations, we also independently asked each man's wife to listen to the situation and to tell us what her husband would say or do in each situation. As pilot research had revealed that some women could not report on husband behavior outside the relationship, nonmarital situations were not presented to wives. Based on both husband and wife reports of husband responses in the marital situations, relative to the nonviolent/non-distressed comparison group, all of the violent subgroups had lower levels of response competency than nonviolent men, and the groups who engaged in more severe marital violence (e.g., dysphoric/borderline and generally violent/antisocial) offered the least competent responses. Examining men's self-reported responding to the nonmarital conflict vignettes, as predicted, generally violent/antisocial batterers (i.e., men who had engaged in the highest levels of violence outside their marriage) had the lowest levels of response competency.

Across studies, our data have clinical implications. They suggest that violent men may require social skills training to generate competent (i.e., less aggressive, more constructive) responses to marital situations. While it requires further study, the Holtzworth-Munroe and Anglin (1991) finding (i.e., that violent men could not generate competent responses even when they were asked what would be the 'best' way to respond to marital conflicts) suggests that these men either may not have competent responses in their behavioral repertoire or may choose aggressive/incompetent responses for other reasons (e.g., believing these will be the most effective way to solve a marital conflict). Clinicians need to assess both possibilities with violent clients. The Holtzworth-Munroe and Smutzler (1996) findings suggest that men may need to learn new ways of responding to a wide variety of wife behavior, not just aggressive/negative wife behavior. While the Anglin and Holtzworth-Munroe (1997) data suggest that violent men may also need help learning to respond nonaggressively in situations outside of their marriage, the Holtzworth-Munroe *et al.* (under review) findings suggest that the need for more global skill interventions may depend on the batterer subgroup to which a man belongs; consistent with common sense, violent husbands who are also aggressive outside of their intimate relationship are the most likely to evidence social skills deficits in nonmarital situations.

As examples of how clinicians might consider decision-making skills in their work with batterers, consider the cases of Tom and John. Tom lacked skills for generating alternative responses in marital conflicts. Tom and his wife had a fight in the car; Tom was driving. His wife said that she wanted to be let out of the car, and she reportedly tried to grab the steering wheel from him. Tom then hit her in the face, reporting that violence was the only option available to him, to keep her from causing an accident. The group helped

Tom to generate alternative solutions to the problem, both at earlier stages in the conflict (e.g., stopping driving while fighting) and during the most intense part of the argument (e.g., pulling over the car, blocking her from reaching the wheel without hitting her). In contrast to Tom and many of our study findings, John was often able to generate solutions, including competent solutions, to marital conflicts (indeed, he helped Tom to generate many possible competent solutions to his problem) but he tended to choose aggressive responses in his own relationship given his views regarding the most 'effective' way to meet his goals in these situations. For example, in one dispute, John's goal was to leave the argument with his girlfriend and calm down; he did not want to continue the discussion with her. He claimed that, in the situation, he had considered several possible ways to accomplish this goal (e.g., take a 'time out'; ask his girlfriend to postpone the discussion to a later time) but that he chose to slap her because he believed that this was the most efficient method to end the discussion quickly (i.e., 'I knew that would shut her up right away'). In this case, the group helped John to consider the consequences of his chosen response versus those of the other responses he had considered, paying particular attention to the long-term, versus the immediate, consequences of his actions.

Studies of enactment skills

After choosing a response to a situation (i.e., in the decision-making stage), a husband must execute that response and monitor the impact of his actions. We have hypothesized that violent men may have skills deficits at this stage of social information processing. For example, even if a man chooses an appropriate response, he may be unable to enact the response competently.

To date, we have conducted one study comparing the enactment skills of maritally violent and nonviolent men. In Hulbert (1999), we recruited twenty-one violent/distressed men and thirty-nine nonviolent men (i.e., nineteen maritally distressed and twenty nondistressed) from the community. We presented men with ten marital and five nonmarital problematic situation vignettes. In this study, men were not asked what they would think or how they would respond in each situation. Rather, they were told that 'Bob' was the man in the situation; in each situation, both the decoding and decision-making phases of social information processing were controlled across subjects (i.e., subjects were given Bob's interpretation of the situation and his feelings in the situation; subjects were also told how Bob had chosen to respond). For each situation, we chose a competent response for Bob; we used responses that were coded as competent in our coding manuals and that had been commonly given by men in prior studies (i.e., so they would not be too unusual). Then, each man in the study was asked to pretend that he was an actor and, being the best actor he could be, to enact Bob's chosen response. These enactments were videotaped and later coded for competency. Across both the marital and nonmarital situation vignettes, violent men's enactments were found to be significantly less competent than those of nonviolent men.

While violent men's enactments were less competent than those of nonviolent men (i.e., as judged by outside observers), the violent men were apparently not aware of this. Specifically, before each man enacted the given response to a situation, he was asked to predict how well he would do so; there were no significant group differences in these predictions. In addition, after all the enactments were completed, each man watched a videotape of himself engaging in the enacted responses and was asked to rate how well he had enacted each response; there were also no group differences in these judgements of performance.

The data from this study suggest that simply telling violent men the competent way to respond in various situations will be inadequate to change his behavior. Instead, violent husbands may need to practice competent responses (e.g., role-plays), receiving detailed feedback and social skills training as they do so, to help them modify the specific behaviors (e.g., voice tone, eye contact) that make their 'competent' responses incompetent. In addition, the findings suggest that men's self-reports of their competency in situations may be inaccurate. Violent men may not be able to predict their poor performance accurately and, similarly, may not be able to judge their poor performance accurately after the fact, making it difficult for them to understand the negative impact of their behavior on others.

The case of Bill provides a clinical example of the enactment skill deficits of batterers. Bill revealed that he had twice pushed and held his wife, against her will, to prevent her from leaving the room during their arguments. Bill was able to tell the therapist that his wife's threats to leave aroused his fears of abandonment and his concern that their relationship was 'over'; her leaving scared and hurt him, making him feel vulnerable. Given his ability to recognize these 'softer' feelings, the therapist encouraged Bill to tell his wife directly how he was feeling (i.e., to engage in a more competent response), rather than using physical aggression to prevent her from leaving. However, when he tried to do so, Bill was unable to adequately express his 'softer' feelings of hurt and vulnerability; instead, his message was delivered with an angry and threatening tone, making it ineffective, incompetent and scary. Thus, the therapist found it necessary to focus on more direct skills training (e.g., voice tone, facial expressions) in order to help Bill convey his message to his wife.

Generalizing from standardized stimuli to actual marital interactions

As argued above, we believed that, initially, it was important to compare the social information processing skills of violent and nonviolent husband in response to standardized vignettes, to hold wife behavior constant across groups. Having demonstrated group differences with this method, however, we then believed that it made sense to study the generalizability of our findings. In other words, we were interested in knowing whether the patterns of skills deficits demonstrated in our vignette studies were observable in the actual marital interactions of violent men and their wives. To examine this issue, we recruited a sample of a hundred couples from the community, equally divided into four subject groups: husband violent and maritally distressed, violent/nondistressed, nonviolent/distressed, and nonviolent/ nondistressed; the level of the husbands' violence in the violent/non-distressed group was less than that of the husbands in the violent/distressed group, so that these groups might also be conceptualized as representing differing severity levels of husband violence. In the laboratory, the couples engaged in a series of marital interactions which were videotaped and later coded.

In the first part of this study (Holtzworth-Munroe *et al.* 1997b), we examined the generalizability of the Holtzworth-Munroe and Smutzler (1996) finding that, relative to nonviolent men, violent men responded less supportively and more negatively to wife behaviors that were not aggressive but rather were distressed or self-denigrating (e.g., the wife is complaining about herself, not the husband). In the laboratory, the couples participated in a social support discussion, in which they discussed a personal (not a relationship) problem of the wife's, chosen by the wife (e.g., weight, career, friends). Interestingly, coding of the wives' behavior in this study revealed no significant group differences on any of the codes (e.g., positive and negative behaviors); in other words, on the coding system we used, wives in the violent groups were not more negative than wives in the nonviolent group when discussing their own problems. In contrast to this lack of group differences in wife behavior, we found that violent men engaged in less positive and more negative behavior than nonviolent men. On some codes, both groups of violent men's behavior differed significantly from both groups of nonviolent men (i.e., violent men had higher levels of belligerence/domineering, contempt/disgust and how upset/bothered the husband was by the wife's problem, and lower levels of positive behavior), while on others, the behavior of the violent men differed significantly only from the behavior of happily married men (i.e., violent men had higher levels of anger and tension and lower levels of acceptance of wife's problem definition). These findings were consistent with the Holtzworth-Munroe and Smutzler (1996) data, demonstrating that violent husbands are less supportive and more negative toward their wives even when the wife discusses her own personal problems, as opposed to during marital conflicts.

Having conducted several studies (reviewed earlier in this chapter) suggesting that violent husbands offer less competent responses than nonviolent men in marital conflict situations, we were interested in examining group differences in husband behavior during actual marital problem interactions. Thus, following the social support discussions, the couples in this study were asked to engage in two laboratory-based marital problem discussions – one regarding a change the husband wanted in the wife's behavior (i.e., husband topic) and one regarding a change the wife wanted in the husband's behavior (i.e., wife topic). As reported in Holtzworth-Munroe, Smutzler and Stuart (1998), on most codes, the violent/distressed group was the most negative (e.g., made more demands in a negative fashion, engaged in higher levels of blaming, withdraw and avoidance behavior) and the least positive (e.g., made fewer requests with neutral or positive affect, were less accepting of the partner, less likely to define the problem clearly and less likely to collaboratively focus on oneself); the nonviolent/nondistressed group was the least negative and most positive; and the violent/nondistressed and distressed/nonviolent groups fell intermediate to the two extreme groups. In the one exception, both of the violent groups (i.e., maritally distressed and not) engaged in higher levels of contempt than the nonviolent groups during the discussion of the wife's topic. These data support conclusions from our previous studies using standardized vignettes: when engaged in marital problem discussions, maritally violent men are more negative and aggressive than nonviolent men.

Overall, the findings from this sample of couples demonstrate that data previously gathered using standardized vignettes generalize to the men's actual marital interactions, as least as observed in the laboratory. One might, however, still question the generalizability of the findings to marital interactions taking place outside of the laboratory. Thus, in two studies, we have asked violent men to report on their general patterns of marital interaction, using the Communication Patterns Questionnaire (Christensen and Sullaway 1984).

First, in Holtzworth-Munroe et al. (1998), we recruited two groups of violent men (i.e., twenty-two men beginning domestic violence treatment programs and thirty-six violent/distressed men from the community) and two groups of nonviolent men (thirty-two nonviolent/distressed and twenty-nine nonviolent/nondistressed). Examining their self-reported marital interaction patterns, in general, the maritally distressed groups of men differed from the happily married men (i.e., higher levels of mutual blame and mutual avoidance/withholding, lower levels of mutual constructive communication); the two violent groups reported higher levels of husband demand/wife withdraw than both groups of nonviolent men. Second, in our recent batterer typology study (Holtzworth-Munroe et al. under review), we examined both husbands' and wives' reports of marital interaction patterns (Holtzworth-Munroe and Herron in preparation). In this study, violent–nonviolent group differences emerged. For example, relative to the nonviolent groups, couples experiencing high levels of husband violence reported higher levels of mutual blame (based on wife report) and higher levels of husband demand/wife withdraw (based on husband report).

In summary, data gathered across these studies suggest that the findings from our earlier studies using standardized vignettes (i.e., relative to nonviolent men, violent men respond more negatively and less competently to wife behavior) are generalizable to actual marital interactions, both in the laboratory and outside of it. These data demonstrate the need for clinicians to engage in conflict resolution and spousal support skills training with violent husbands. They also provide indirect support for the practice of allowing men and their partners to receive conjoint, couples therapy once the man has successfully completed a batterers' treatment program, as he may need help in generalizing the skills he learned in the group therapy setting to his actual marital interactions.

Summary of social information processing skills studies

Our studies have demonstrated *decoding* skills deficits among maritally violent men, relative to nonviolent men. Specifically, violent husbands attribute more hostile/negative intent to negative wife behavior than nonviolent men (Holtzworth-Munroe and Hutchinson 1993); in addition, violent men experience more negative feelings in reaction to a wide variety of wife behaviors (Holtzworth-Munroe and Smutzler 1996). Finally, recent batterer typology research suggests that the more severely violent men are the most likely to evidence a hostile attributional bias (Holtzworth-Munroe in preparation). As discussed earlier, at this time we do not know if violent men cannot distinguish between various wife behaviors (e.g., cannot detect differences in various wife emotional expressions) or, if they can, why they react negatively to so many wife behaviors (e.g., have generalized negative feelings about their wives). The data suggest that clinicians will need to work with violent men, helping them to examine both their emotional reactions to, and their cognitive processing (e.g., attributions) of, a variety of wife behaviors.

A series of studies also consistently demonstrated decision-making skills deficits among maritally violent men. Relative to nonviolent men, violent husbands offer less competent (e.g., more aggressive) responses to problematic marital situation vignettes (Anglin and Holtzworth-Munroe 1997; Holtzworth-Munroe and Anglin 1991; Holtzworth-Munroe et al. under review); they similarly engage in more negative behaviors (e.g., contempt, belligerence, demanding) in laboratory-based marital problem discussions and report more negative marital interaction patterns in their homes (Holtzworth-Munroe et al. 1998; Holtzworth-Munroe and Herron in preparation). Notably, violent men appear less able than nonviolent men to generate competent responses to marital situations, even when directly asked to do so (Holtzworth-Munroe and Anglin 1991), suggesting that batterers will need help in learning how to generate competent responses. In addition, violent men (Anglin and Holtzworth-Munroe 1997) or at least certain subgroups of violent men (i.e., men who engage in violence outside of their marital relationships: Holtzworth-Munroe et al. under review) provide less competent responses than nonviolent men in nonmarital relationship conflicts (e.g., boss, friends, relatives). These findings suggest that some violent men will need a broader intervention program, focusing not only on marital conflict but also on problematic interactions with other individuals.

Finally, in one study of enactment skills (Hulbert 1999), we found that even when provided with the competent responses to marital conflict vignettes, violent men were less able than nonviolent men to enact those responses competently. These findings suggest that simply telling a man the competent responses to situations will be insufficient; rather, role-plays focused on competent behavioral enactment of competent responses will be necessary.

Other issues to consider

Across studies, the findings are clear and consistent: violent men evidence a wide range of social information processing skills deficits, relative to non-violent men. Yet, there are additional issues requiring examination in future research, which are important for clinicians to consider. A few of these issues are briefly discussed here.

Batterer subtypes and individuals

Holtzworth-Munroe and Stuart (1994a) have suggested that 'violent husbands' are a heterogeneous group, made up of various subtypes of violent men. In general, subgroups of men engaging in more severe marital violence will evidence more marital social skills deficits than subgroups of men engaging in less severe marital violence, although even less severely violent men will evidence skill deficits relative to nonviolent men. In addition, Holtzworth-Munroe and Stuart (1994a) suggested that men who are also violent outside of their intimate relationships will evidence social skills deficits in nonmarital situations. As reviewed on pp.24–25, our initial tests of these hypotheses have been supportive. The Holtzworth-Munroe and Stuart (1994a) typology, however, does not specify whether the various subtypes of men will evidence differing skills deficits at each stage of social information processing (e.g., decoding versus decision-making versus enactment). Future research will need to examine such issues. The pinpointing of social skills deficits specific to each subtype of batterer could lead to the development of interventions designed to address the specific skills deficits of differing subgroups.

Moving beyond subgroups to consider individuals, Holtzworth-Munroe (1991, 1992) originally proposed that the social information processing model could be used to identify the unique skills deficits of an individual man at each stage in the model, so that treatment could be geared to that individual's skills deficits. First, a client may be asked to interpret standardized vignettes, and his decoding deficits can thus be examined. Next, one could define the situation for the subject (i.e., present the situation and the interpretation of the situation, to hold decoding constant) and examine the man's decision-making skills by asking him to generate, evaluate and choose responses to the situation. Finally, by defining a situation and selecting a competent response for the man to perform, an evaluation of his ability to do so would provide information on his enactment skills. Then, the man's particular skill deficits could be addressed in therapy.

Automaticity of social information processing

As noted by McFall (1982), the steps proposed in the social information processing model are often carried out in an 'automatic' fashion, particularly in routine or familiar situations. For example, overlearned cognitive schemata may lead to automatic interpretation of the incoming stimuli, and overlearned behavioral responses may be implemented without conscious cognitive processing. It is quite likely that much of the negative responding of batterers is due to automatic processing and that, without help to slow down the process and pay attention to their thoughts, many violent husbands will not be able to tell their therapist how they are processing situations. Instead, they may be able to report only their emotional reactions, which are often strong and negative, resulting from their cognitive processing of social stimuli. In such cases, clinicians need to help maritally violent men slow down their processing of events, to help batterers become aware of, and able to examine, their automatic thoughts, behavioral choices, and so on.

Conditions affecting social information processing

As discussed in Holtzworth-Munroe (1991, 1992), transitory factors (e.g., alcohol, drugs or anger) can influence social information processing. Such factors may inhibit 'rational' cognitive processing, resulting in skills deficits. While we have not examined this issue in our research, it has obvious implications for therapy with violent men. First, as much as possible, men should be helped to control the conditions that interfere with their cognitive processing (i.e., provided with anger management training or alcohol interventions); such techniques may allow men to handle problematic situations more competently. Most likely, however, it will not be possible to 'eliminate' all such factors (i.e., anger). Thus, after social skills are acquired during therapy, they could be practiced under conditions of arousal and various mood states, including anger.

Summary

Our program of research examining the applicability of the social information processing model to husband violence has demonstrated that, relative to nonviolent men, violent husbands evidence a wide range of social skills deficits, at every stage in the model. These findings demonstrate the fruitful application of a specific theoretical model to the study of husband violence. The data also have direct clinical implications, generating a variety of clinical assessment and intervention issues to be considered by therapists. Ultimately, however, the effectiveness of such clinical interventions can be determined only through research examining the outcomes of therapy informed by the social information processing model versus those outcomes obtained with other therapeutic approaches. Until such research is conducted, I hope that this chapter has provided the reader with new ideas to address when considering the behavior and potential skills deficits of maritally violent men.

Author Acknowledgements

Research reported in this chapter was supported by two grants (NIMH grant R29-MH-46927 and NIH grant PHS R01-MH51935), both awarded to the author. Requests for reprints can be sent to Amy Holtzworth-Munroe, PhD, Department of Psychology, 1101 East 10th Street, Indiana University, Bloomington, IN, 47405-7007, USA. I would like to thank all of the colleagues, graduate students, undergraduate students and research assistants who helped to conduct these series of studies and made this research program possible.

References

Anglin, K. and Holtzworth-Munroe, A. (1997) 'Comparing the responses of violent and nonviolent couples to problematic marital and nonmarital situations: are the skill deficits of violent couples global?' *Journal of Family Psychology 11*, 301–313.

Christensen, A. and Sullaway, M. (1984) 'Communication Patterns Questionnaire.' Unpublished questionnaire, University of California at Los Angeles.

Dodge, K.A. and Coie, J.D. (1987) 'Social-information processing factors in reactive and proactive aggression in children's peer groups.' *Journal of Personality and Social Psychology 6*, 1146–1158.

Epstein, N. and Eidelson, R.J. (1981) 'Cognition and relationship maladjustment: development of a measure of dysfunctional relationship beliefs.' *Journal of Consulting and Clinical Psychology 50*, 715–720.

Epstein, N., Baucom, D., Rankin, L. and Burnett, C. (1991) 'Relationship standards in marriage: development of a new measure of content-specific cognitions.' Paper presented at the annual meeting of the Association for the Advancement of Behavior Therapy, New York, November.

Holtzworth-Munroe, A. (1991) 'Applying the social information processing model to maritally violent men.' *Behavior Therapist 14*, 129–132.

Holtzworth-Munroe, A. (1992) 'Social skill deficits in maritally violent men: interpreting the data using a social information processing model.' *Clinical Psychology Review 12*, 605–617.

Holtzworth-Munroe, A. (in preparation) 'Subtypes of maritally violent men: differences in the hostile attributional bias across groups.'

Holtzworth-Munroe, A. and Anglin, K. (1991) 'The competency of responses given by maritally violent versus nonviolent men to problematic marital situations.' *Violence and Victims 6*, 257–269.

Holtzworth-Munroe, A. and Herron, K. (in preparation) 'Subtypes of maritally violent men: group difference in marital interaction behavior.'

Holtzworth-Munroe, A. and Hutchinson, G. (1993) 'Attributing negative intent to wife behavior: the attributions of maritally violent versus nonviolent men.' *Journal of Abnormal Psychology 102*, 206–211.

Holtzworth-Munroe, A. and Smutzler, N. (1996) 'Comparing the emotional reactions and behavioral intentions of violent and nonviolent husbands to aggressive, distressed, and other wife behaviors.' *Violence and Victims 11*, 319–339.

Holtzworth-Munroe, A. and Stuart, G.L. (1994a) 'Typologies of male batterers: three subtypes and the differences among them.' *Psychological Bulletin 116*, 476–497.

Holtzworth-Munroe, A. and Stuart, G.L. (1994b) 'The relationship standards and assumptions of violent versus nonviolent husbands.' *Cognitive Therapy and Research 18*, 87–103.

Holtzworth-Munroe, A., Smutzler, N. and Bates, L. (1997a) 'A brief review of the research on husband violence. Part III: sociodemographic factors, relationship factors, and differing consequences of husband and wife violence.' *Aggression and Violent Behavior 2*, 285–307.

Holtzworth-Munroe, A., Stuart, G.L., Sandin, E., Smutzler, N. and McLauglin, W. (1997b) 'Comparing the social support behaviors of violent and nonviolent husbands during discussions of wife personal problems.' *Personal Relationships 4*, 395–412.

Holtzworth-Munroe, A., Smutzler, N. and Stuart, G.L. (1998) 'Demand and withdraw communication among couples: experiencing husband violence.' *Journal of Consulting and Clinical Psychology 66*, 731–743.

Holtzworth-Munroe, A., Meehan, J.C., Herron, K., Rehman, U. and Stuart, G.L. (under review) 'Testing the Holtzworth-Munroe and Stuart batterer typology.'

Hotaling, G.T. and Sugarman, D.B. (1986) 'An analysis of risk markers in husband to wife violence.' *Violence and Victims 7*, 79–88.

Hulbert, D. (1999) 'The assessment of enactment skill deficits in maritally violent men.' Unpublished (doctoral) dissertation.

Jacobson, N.D., Gottman, J.M., Waltz, J., Rushe, R., Babcock, J. and Holtzworth-Munroe, A. (1994) 'Affect, verbal content, and psychophysiology in the arguments of couples with a violent husband.' *Journal of Consulting and Clinical Psychology 62*, 982–988.

Locke, H.J. and Wallace, K.M. (1959) 'Short marital adjustment and prediction tests: their reliability and validity.' *Marriage and Family Living 21*, 251–255.

McFall, R.M. (1982) 'A review and reformulation of the concept of social skills.' *Behavioral Assessment 4*, 1–33.

McLaughlin, I.G., Leonard, K.E. and Senchak, M. (1992) 'Prevalence and distribution of premarital aggression among couples applying for a marriage license.' *Journal of Family Violence 7*, 309–319.

Moffitt, T.E., Caspi, A., Krueger, R.F., Magdol, L., Margolin, G., Silva, P.A. and Sydney, R. (1997) 'Do partners agree about abuse in their relationship? A psychometric evaluation of interpartner agreement.' *Psychological Assessment 9*, 47–56.

O'Leary, K.D., Barling, J., Arias, I., Rosenbaum, A., Malone, J. and Tyree, A. (1989) 'Prevalence and stability of physical aggression between spouses: a longitudinal analysis.' *Journal of Consulting and Clinical Psychology 57*, 263–268.

Rosenbaum, A. and O'Leary, K.D. (1981) 'Marital violence: characteristics of abusive couples.' *Journal of Consulting and Clinical Psychology 49*, 63–71.

Straus, M.A. (1979) 'Measuring intrafamily conflict and violence: the Conflict Tactics (CT) Scales.' *Journal of Marriage and the Family 41*, 75–87.

Straus, M.A. and Gelles, R.J. (1990) *Physical Violence in American Families*. New Brunswick, NJ: Transaction.

CHAPTER 3

Evaluating Interventions
for Men Who Batter

Julia C. Babcock and Jaslean J. La Taillade

As an estimated 840,000 women reported assaults at the hands of an intimate in 1996 (Bureau of Justice Statistics 1998), interventions of choice designed to address this growing public health concern have focused on the perpetrators of domestic violence in the hopes of deterring further assault. Programs designed specifically to treat domestic violence offenders have grown rapidly, from just one in 1977 to over two hundred only five years later (Harrell 1991; Pirog-Good and Stets-Kealey 1985). Currently, most communities around the USA have implemented mandatory arrest policies for domestic violence, and offer or mandate some sort of batterers' intervention program (Healey, Smith and O'Sullivan 1998). However, these policy and practice guidelines have been based more on ideologies regarding the causes and course of domestic violence, rather than by empirical research. Despite declarations that arrest followed by court-ordered treatment offers 'great hope and potential for breaking the destructive cycle of violence' (US Attorney General's Office 1984, p.48), no single treatment has proven to be effective in reducing recidivism of family violence to a meaningful degree. While community activists have been effectively lobbying for changes in police response, mandatory arrest, victimless prosecution and longer sentence terms, *treatment* is the one area in the domestic violence movement that has remained at a relative standstill (Lipchik, Sirles and Kubicki 1997).

In his review of the earlier studies on marital violence treatment programs, Rosenfeld (1992) concluded that men who complete treatment have only slightly, and often non-significantly, lower recidivism rates than men who refuse treatment, drop out of treatment or remain untreated. Some have even argued that treatment programs may put women at increased risk for domestic violence, by contributing to a false sense of security among battered women whose husbands have sought treatment (Holtzworth-Munroe, Beatty and Anglin 1995). In light of the lack of solid evidence for the efficacy of marital violence treatment programs, the very existence of such programs should be questioned, as they may actually increase the wife's risk of future assaults. The idea that treatment may increase the partner's risk for further domestic violence assaults is particularly chilling when one considers that in many municipalities, batterers' treatment is ·not simply available at the perpetrator's choosing, but rather court-ordered. Little of our practice and policy has been developed and refined based on scientific evidence because, only since the 1990s has research on the effectiveness of batterers' treatment been sufficient to inform practice or policy.

Fortunately, during the 1990s several researchers conducted well-designed studies capable of shedding some light on questions and concerns regarding the efficacy of batterers' treatment. A growing body of methodologically rigorous investigations into the conceptualization, interventions and effectiveness of current programs now exists. In this chapter, we review those studies, summarize and critique existing treatment programs, and point to promising approaches that may increase the overall effectiveness of batterers' interventions. In the first section, we critically review the current treatment models and research on batterers' interventions. In the second section, we go beyond the data to discuss some clinical and policy implications of this research. Finally, we discuss promising future directions for ways to intervene effectively with perpetrators and victims of intimate violence.

Treatment models and modalities

While many batterers' treatment models and formats exist, only a few have been empirically tested with scientific rigor. These include feminist psycho-educational men's groups, cognitive-behavioral men's groups, anger management (a form of cognitive-behavioral group treatment) and couples' therapy. Noticeably absent from this list is individual therapy for abusers and insight-oriented approaches. This is not to say that these types of interventions are ineffective, only that they are yet to be studied. First, we present a brief summary and critique of the various treatment models that have been studied; second, we describe the recent outcome studies that examine the impact of these treatments on recidivism of physical abuse.

Psychoeducational model

The most prominent type of clinical intervention with batterers is a *feminist psychoeducational approach* (Pence and Paymar 1993). This intervention, originated by the Duluth Domestic Abuse Intervention Project program in Minnesota, is frequently referred to as the *Duluth model*. According to this model, the primary cause of domestic violence is patriarchal ideology and the implicit or explicit societal sanctioning of men's use of power and control over women. This program, developed by social workers, typically eschews DSM-type diagnoses (Diagnostic and Statistical Manual of Mental Disorders; APA 1984) and does not consider the intervention to be therapy. Rather, group facilitators lead consciousness-raising exercises to challenge the man's 'right' to control or dominate his partner. Didactic and confrontational approaches are used to attack the man's defenses, excuses and devaluation of his partner. A fundamental tool of the Duluth model is the 'Power and Control Wheel', which illustrates that violence is part of a pattern of behavior including intimidation, male privilege, isolation, emotional and economic abuse, rather than isolated incidents of abuse or cyclical explosions of pent-up anger, frustration or painful feelings (Pence and Paymar 1993, p.2). The treatment goals of the Duluth model are to help men change from using the behaviors on the Power and Control Wheel, which result in authoritarian and destructive relationships, to using the behaviors on the 'Equality Wheel', which form the basis for egalitarian relationships (Pence and Paymar 1993, p.7).

The feminist approach to batterers' intervention may be more theoretically compatible with a criminal justice perspective than a psychotherapeutic or couples therapy approach (Healey *et al.* 1998). First, it clearly views domestic violence as criminal behavior, not as the result of a personality disorder, or a deficit in couple communication or other relational skills. Second, the goal is accepting responsibility and becoming accountable for one's own violence, as opposed to blaming early childhood experiences or some dysfunctional interaction with the victim. Finally, because the cause of battering stems from a societal problem of misogynist and sexist attitudes rather than from individual psychopathology, batterer programs focus on re-educating men rather than providing them with therapy (Austin and Dankwort 1999). The goal of the feminist approach is to end abusive behavior rather than to heal the batterer (the psychotherapeutic goal) or improve his relationships (the couples therapy goal).

CRITIQUE OF THE FEMINIST PSYCHOEDUCATIONAL MODEL

Domestic violence researchers appear to be reluctant to criticize the feminist psychoeducational model, and as such the feminist Duluth-type model remains the unchallenged treatment of choice for most communities. In fact, the US states of Iowa and Florida mandate that all state-certified battering intervention programs must adhere to the general tenants of the Duluth model (Abel 1999; Healey *et al.* 1998). However, in a longitudinal study of graduates of the Duluth group program, results showed that completion of the feminist educational intervention had no impact on recidivism after five years (Shepard 1990, cited in Healey *et al.* 1998). Although psycho-educational interventions integrate well theoretically with criminal justice viewpoints, there are both theoretical and empirically based reasons to question the utility of a purely psychoeducational intervention for domestic violence.

First, the model suggests that all men in our patriarchal society will be violent. There is no conclusive research evidence to suggest that males with more sexist attitudes are more likely to be violent (Holtzworth-Munroe *et al.* 1997). Next, psychoeducational approaches focus primarily on cognition rather than emotion, despite the fact that spousal battery is highly emotion-ally laden. Group psychoeducational models tend to deal in generalities, not with the idiosyncratic cognitions of the individual (Wessler and Hankin-Wessler 1989). As such, the psychoeducational model can be criticized for failing to engage and connect with the men on an emotional level. In addition, many treatment programs state that the primary client of the batterers' intervention program is not the batterer sitting in group but the *victim of his abuse.* Establishing such a focus adds an additional barrier to forming an empathic connection with the abuser by refusing to hear his perspective. Clinical research findings show that low therapist empathy quite consistently predicts negative outcomes in diverse therapeutic contexts (Miller 1985). In addition, psychoeducational approaches have proven to be less effective than cognitive behavioral interventions in general in treating behavioral or psychological problems. For example, of fifteen psychosocial interventions for alcohol use disorders, confrontational interventions and educational groups were among the three least effective treatment modalities (Finney and Moos 1998). Adopting an intervention designed to change belief systems through re-education, rather than therapy designed to change some pathology of the individual, has theoretical appeal if one's agenda is to blame violence ultimately on our patriarchal society. However, given our knowledge about the general efficacy of psychoeducation as compared to cognitive-behavioral interventions, it is questionable whether a psycho-educational approach to a serious behavior problem like violence would be the most effective.

Finally, and perhaps most importantly, using a didactic, confrontational intervention with court-mandated clients may be counter-productive. Like self-help programs, psychoeducational groups work best when participants are highly motivated; some authors suggest that persons who lack motivation to work on their problems should be screened out of psychoeducational groups (Sank and Shaffer 1984; Wessler and Hankin-Wessler 1989). A well-recognized problem in domestic violence is that most clients are court-ordered or feel coerced into treatment by life circumstances and, therefore, lack motivation for treatment (Daniels and Murphy 1997). Most clinical research suggests that excessive confrontation is ineffective and that supportive strategies are better able to motivate treatment-resistant clients (Murphy and Baxter 1997). Men rarely listen to alternatives to their own beliefs unless they feel heard and understood (Harway and Evans 1996). Many batterers react against frequent and intense confrontation with vociferous counter-arguments, silence, 'phony' agreement or termination of treatment (Murphy and Baxter 1997). Additionally, teaching batterers to take responsibility for the abuse may have only limited effectiveness on its own because it tends to shame and guilt men and leads to large dropout rates among already defensive clients (Harway and Evans 1996).

Cognitive-behavioral groups

An alternative to the feminist psychoeducational group is the *cognitive-behavioral* model. Cognitive-behavioral batterers' interventions, developed primarily by psychologists, tend to make violence the primary focus of treatment. Since violence is a learned behavior, nonviolence can similarly be learned, according to the cognitive-behavioral model (Adams 1988). Violence continues because it is functional for the user, working to reduce bodily tension, achieves victim compliance, puts a temporary end to an uncomfortable situation and gives the abuser a sense of power and control (Sonkin, Martin and Walker 1985). Recognizing the functional aspects of violence, cognitive-behavioral therapists point out the pros and cons of violence. In addition, they use skills training and anger management techniques, such as time outs, relaxation training, assertiveness and social skills, and changing self-talk statements as alternatives to violence. Sexism and patriarchal beliefs are sometimes not addressed in cognitive-behavioral groups.

CRITIQUE OF THE COGNITIVE-BEHAVIORAL MODEL

Cognitive-behavioral interventions with batterers and anger management techniques specifically have been roundly criticized by influential clinicians in the areas of domestic violence (Adams 1988; Bograd 1984; Gondolf and Russell 1986). According to the developers of the Duluth model, focusing on stress, anger or an inability to express feelings is easier than addressing the societal context and issues of gender in batterers' treatment and is more palatable to the men. Additionally, they see this model as limited in scope because it fails to acknowledge the real experiences of women who live with men who batter (Pence and Paymar 1993, p.2). Advocates of the feminist approach assert that any failure to confront directly instances of victim blaming, denial or minimization amounts to collusion by the therapist with the abusive behavior (Murphy and Baxter 1997). Anger-control techniques are important, but may paradoxically become another tool by which a man can exert control over his partner (Gondolf and Russell 1986; Harway and Evans 1996). Some batterers may display an unusual degree of control over their own physiological responses to anger, and may use this skill to increase the severity and effectiveness of their violence (Jacobson and Gottman 1998, p.42). Like the feminist psychoeducational approach, cognitive-behavioral men's groups may also be criticized for failing to connect with the men on an emotional level. Focusing on cognition, problem-solving and skill acquisition without also addressing, for example, the batterer's prominent feelings of shame or fear of abandonment (Dutton 1995) misses an opportunity to engage therapeutically with the men to alter their patterns of violence.

Current group practice

Modern batterers' groups tend to incorporate different theoretical approaches and treatment interventions (Healey *et al.* 1998). Currently, most batterers' treatment programs are a fusion between the feminist psychoeducational model and utilization of cognitive-behavioral techniques. Many longer-term programs are comprised of three phases: the first is a feminist educational format to address denial of responsibility, the second utilizes cognitive-behavioral techniques for skill-building, and the third component addresses individual psychological issues in an unstructured format for those men identified as having additional related psychological problems (Healey *et al.* 1998). Such multi-component treatment packages may affect a broader range of clientele and allow flexibility in addressing individual clients' needs. Skilled facilitators, regardless of the treatment philosophy, are able to engage their group members on an emotional as well as intellectual level.

Couples therapy

CRITIQUE OF COUPLES AND FAMILY THERAPY MODEL

As the marriage constitutes both the locus and the context of domestic violence, one might expect couples therapists to be at the cutting edge of interventions with abusive families, yet this is not the case (Shamai 1996). Most court-mandated batterers' intervention programs favor the group format for theoretical and practical reasons. Most states in the USA set standards, guidelines or mandates that discourage or prohibit the funding of any program that offers couples or family counseling as a primary mode of intervention (Healey *et al.* 1998; Lipchik *et al.* 1997). Typically, couples counseling is not recommended by most practitioners because couples and family counselors, in an attempt to avoid 'triangulation' or labeling one partner as the 'identified patient' (Minuchin 1974), tend to view male and female partners as equal participants in creating the relationship problems. In cases of marital violence, this tendency to equalize the responsibility may collude with the batterer to blame the partner for his violent behavior. Even therapists who are adamant about the unacceptability of violence contradict themselves, as interventions aimed at the couple implicitly implicate the wife in the perpetuation of violence (Jacobson 1993). Couples treatment is also believed to place woman at increased risk, as the woman's disclosures in the presence of her partner may lead to later 'retribution' (Lipchik *et al.* 1997). In addition, couples therapy may focus on what the woman can do to prevent her husband's anger and violence; for example, by suggesting that he take a 'time out'. However, research has found that during the course of an argument between a batterer and his wife, her behavior had no effect on the outcome or the process of the argument (Jacobson 1993). The logic of engaging the female partner as an active participant in violence prevention is therefore questionable. Furthermore, another implicit goal of couples counseling is relationship preservation, which may be contraindicated in violent relationships where divorce or dissolution is the recommended alternative. In contrast, men's groups send a clear message about who is primarily responsible for the violence. In addition, they tend to be less costly than private couples counseling and provide the added potential benefit of hearing other battering men offer insights into their own behavioral problems.

POTENTIAL UTILITY OF COUPLES THERAPY

For these reasons, many states discourage or explicitly disallow funding for couples interventions as a primary mode of intervention with batterers (Healey *et al.* 1998). However, it is premature to dismiss all couples interventions categorically without empirically testing them. In light of the small to moderate effect sizes for pro-feminist group interventions, some in the domestic violence field are exploring alternatives to the psycho-educational groups approach. Since 50–70 percent of system-involved violent couples (Feazell, Mayers and Deschner 1984) and 62 percent of violent couples not seeking services (Jacobson *et al.* 1996) choose to remain together, couples interventions, if done safely and ethically, may be a viable alternative. Violence is quite common in couples seeking therapy, even though it is often missed in the typical pre-treatment assessment (O'Leary, Vivian and Malone 1992). Alarming as it is, therapists unwittingly treat violent couples as a matter of routine.

Clinicians suggest that couples who experience less severe and pervasive violence, where the woman still has some agency and power within the relationship and the man shows capacity to take responsibility for the violence, may be appropriate for couples therapy, and both partners wish to remain in the relationship (Holtzworth-Munroe *et al.* 1995). Others suggest that relationships in which the physical aggression has not developed into a battering dynamic as a means of control, where there have been no injuries, and the woman is not afraid of her partner, may be suitable for conjoint therapy (Jacobson 1993). Thus, it may turn out that an identifiable subset of couples experiencing domestic violence are treatable by couples therapy (Jacobson and Addis 1993).

However, it is important to discriminate between 'patriarchal terrorism' indicative of battering (M.P. Johnson 1995) and 'common couples violence'. Patriarchal terrorism is described as a product of patriarchal traditions of men's right to control 'their' women via a systematic use of violence, economic subordination, threats, isolation and other control tactics (M.P. Johnson 1995). Common couples violence is thought to be less a product of patriarchy, and more a result of conflict escalation, leading to 'minor' forms of violence by the male, female or both partners (M.P. Johnson 1995). National surveys and laboratory research on community samples of 'batterers', usually defined as having used any physical aggression towards a partner in the past year (Rosenbaum 1998), may reflect an entirely different population than the literature on victims in treatment and batterers at treatment agencies.

It may be a subset of these couples with 'common violence', who are not involved with the criminal justice system or seeking services for domestic violence, who may be best served through couples therapy. In a longitudinal comparison of relative risks and benefits of batterers' treatment groups and conjoint therapy for wife assault, O'Leary, Heyman and Neidig (1999) found that male and female participants from both treatments significantly reduced their levels of psychological and physical aggression at one year follow-up. Although about two-thirds of the husbands did not engage in severe violence in the year following treatment, only 26 percent of the husbands ceased their violent behavior. Additionally, there were no differences across treatments in wives' reports of their own safety, and in wives' ability to refrain from taking blame for their husbands' violent behavior. The only differential effects of treatment type found were improvement in marital satisfaction ratings for husbands who participated in conjoint treatment. O'Leary et al.'s (1999) findings suggest that when treatments are targeted at the cessation of violence, both conjoint and group therapies demonstrate significant improvements in, but not cessation of, violence.

Review of outcome studies

The primary question that faces policy-makers is whether treatment 'works'. However, the answer to that question depends on what one considers treatment success: if batterers report decreased violence? If partners report no violence? If the police are no longer involved? If all forms of power and control perpetrated by the batterer cease? Success criteria for outcome studies may be viewed on a continuum (Edleson 1996). At one end of the continuum, some researchers have used 'typically significant positive change' or statistically significant changes in a desired direction among participants (Neidig 1986) to claim program success. At the other end, others have advocated for nothing short of a transformation of program participants 'until men are prepared to take social action against the woman-battering culture' (Gondolf 1987, p.347) and become an 'accountable man' (Hart 1988, cited in Edleson 1996).

The use of *statistically significant* decreases in violent behavior can be problematic as criteria for success (Edleson 1996). For a finding to be statistically significant simply means that the result is unlikely to be attributable to chance. The Conflict Tactics Scales (CTS: Straus 1979) is the most commonly used instrument in batterer program evaluations. A large sample of program participants whose CTS score decreases by a point or two more than a comparison group could be considered successful under this criterion (Edleson 1996). For example, a group of men could be successful participants if they have decreased their violence from six to three beatings a week. The problem with using statistically significant change as a criterion of success is that it may have little practical significance (Bloom, Fischer and Orme 1995) or impact on the quality of life for victims (Edleson 1996).

Considering practical significance, most working in interventions with batterers agree that ending violent behavior is an important success criterion (Edleson 1996). Although most program evaluations do not examine changes in psychological abuse or sexual abuse, by using the revised and expanded CTS–2 (Straus *et al.* 1996) these behaviors can also be easily assessed. Few studies examine changes in terroristic threats, men's accountability for the violence, or in patriarchal relationship power structures, even though most treatment facilitators would see these as worthy goals. Future studies may also choose to examine the broader context of treatment success such as women's feelings of safety and relationship satisfaction, and children's experience of their own and their mother's safety. For the purposes of this review, we consider success as no instances of physical violence reported by the victims and/or no domestic violence incidents reported to the police during a follow-up period.

Methodological considerations

A number of studies in this area have employed a post-test only or a pre-post-test design, with no comparison group, to evaluate treatment effectiveness. These pre-post-test studies have been reviewed previously (Davis and Taylor 1999; Hamberger and Hastings 1993; Rosenfeld 1992). These are the weakest methodological designs, although their findings did help to lay the foundation upon which stronger designs could be built (Davis and Taylor 1999). Stronger quantitative evaluations of domestic violence interventions generally fall into two categories:

- quasi-experimental, where treatment completers are compared to treatment dropouts or to a matched comparison group

- true experimental designs, where clients are randomly assigned to treatment(s) vs no treatment.

We will summarize the findings of studies from 1988 to the present, casting a broad net to include manuscripts in press as well as data presented at national conferences. Since violence tends to be an intermittent behavior and many treatments are brief, we include only studies with at least a six month follow-up period post-treatment. Additionally, many of the earlier studies rely exclusively on batterers' self-report as an outcome measure. Such studies cannot differentiate between treatment success and batterers' tendency to underreport vastly the true incidence of abuse (Davis and Taylor 1999; Rosenfeld 1992). In light of the obvious reporting bias, only studies that use at least one independent report of recidivism, either victim report or criminal record, are included in this review.

Effect sizes

Table 3.1 presents the general design, type of treatment and recidivism or reoffense rates of all identifiable quasi-experimental designs conducted since 1992, and Table 3.2 presents the existing true experimental studies conducted since 1988. The reoffense rates reported in the studies are then recalculated into an effect size, using the g statistic on proportions (Hedges and Olkin 1985) which is then transformed in the d statistics, adjusting for sample size (B.T. Johnson 1995). An 'effect size' is an attempt to quantify the magnitude of the effect due to treatment using a shared metric that is not influenced by the size of the sample. Effect sizes less than 0.50 are considered 'small'; effect sizes that are between 0.51 and 0.79 are considered 'medium'; and effect sizes of 0.80 and above are considered large. Studies of psychotherapy outcome often have effect sizes in the medium to high medium range, with a median effect size of 0.78 (Kazdin 1994). In true experimental designs, the effect size allows us to evaluate the magnitude of the treatment effects; in quasi-experimental designs, it estimates strength of the relationship between treatment and recidivism. Previous studies (Davis and Taylor 1999; Levesque and Gelles 1998) have reported the effect size of batterers' treatment in terms of Cohen's h, which yields a comparable effect size (Cohen 1988). However, this statistic does not adjust for sample size and is more commonly used in power analysis rather than meta-analysis, the goal of which is to synthesize results across studies. Recalculating the effect sizes in terms of Cohen's h does not substantially change the conclusions of this chapter. We should note that the purpose of this chapter is not to conduct a meta-analysis on these data (for a meta-analytic review see Babcock, Green and Robie in preparation; Levesque and Gelles 1998) or to describe every available study in detail. Rather we hope to summarize and synthesize the research findings on recidivism using a common, comparable metric with some practical significance on the lives of the victims.

<table>
<caption>Table 3.1 Quasi-experimental designs</caption>
<tr><th>Study</th><th>Group design</th><th>Treatment</th><th>Outcome measures</th><th>% reoffended</th><th>effect size (d)</th></tr>
<tr>
<td>Babcock and Steiner (1999)</td>
<td>Tx[1] completers (n = 106) Tx dropouts (n = 178) Incarcerated (n = 55)</td>
<td>Multi-site, majority Duluth model, 36 weeks psycho-educational + probation</td>
<td>Police report at 2 year follow-up</td>
<td>Completers = 8% Dropouts = 23% Incarcerated = 62%</td>
<td>Tx vs dropouts = 0.40 Incarcerated vs dropouts = –0.89</td>
</tr>
<tr>
<td>Gondolf (1998)</td>
<td>Tx completers (n = 546) Tx dropouts (n = 294)</td>
<td>Multi-site Duluth model programs of different lengths (3 months to 9 months)</td>
<td>Police reports and partner report (67% of sample) at 15 months</td>
<td>*Police report* Completers = 5% Dropouts = 20%

Partner report Completers = 28% Dropouts = 40%

No significant differences by site or tx length</td>
<td>Police report = 0.51 Partner report = 0.26</td>
</tr>
<tr>
<td>Dutton et al. (1997)</td>
<td>Tx completers (n = 156) Tx dropouts and rejected (n = 290)</td>
<td>Clinical anger management (16 week) vs dropouts and rejected (for noncooperation, psychosis, etc.)</td>
<td>Police reports ranging up to 11 years (mean 5.2 years)</td>
<td>Completers = 18% Dropouts = 21%</td>
<td>0.07</td>
</tr>
<tr>
<td>Dobash et al. (1996)</td>
<td>Tx completers (n = 40) Tx dropouts (n = 80)</td>
<td>Psycho-educational group vs dropouts</td>
<td>Police and partner reports (25% of sample) at 1 year follow-up</td>
<td>*Police report* Completers = 7% Dropouts = 10%

Partner report Completers = 30% Dropouts = 62%</td>
<td>Police report = 0.11 Partner report = 0.67</td>
</tr>
</table>

[1] Note on abbreviations used

 Tx = treatment, Dv= domestic violence, AA = alcoholics anonymous,
 CBT = cognitive-behavioural therapy

Table 3.1 Quasi-experimental designs (continued)

Newell (1994)	Tx 1 = DV[1] group Completers (n = 155) Tx 1 dropouts (n = 118) Tx 2 = other tx (n = 83) No tx (n = 135)	Psycho-educational group 12 weeks) vs other tx (AA,[1] couples, individual) vs group dropouts vs no tx control	Police reports (rearrest) at 2 year follow-up	Tx 1 completers = 23% Tx 1 dropouts = 36% Tx 2 = 16% No tx = 22%	Tx 1 completers vs dropouts = 0.29 Tx 1 completers vs no tx = -0.02 Tx 2 vs no tx = 0.15
Harrell (1991)	Tx 1 (n = 81) No treatment control (n = 112)	Mandated CBT[1] group (8–12 weeks) vs no treatment mandated	Police report at 15–29 months; partner report on 90% of sample at 6 months	*Police report* Tx = 50% No tx = 30% *Partner report* Tx = 43% No tx = 12%	Police report = -0.42 Partner report = -0.76
Chen et al. (1989)	Mandated to tx (n = 120) Not mandated (n = 101)	Anger management (8 weeks)	Police reports	Completers = 5% Dropouts = 10%	0.19
Edleson and Grusznski (1988) Study 3	Tx completers (n = 84) Tx dropouts (n = 37)	Psychoeducation (8 weeks) + process oriented (16+ weeks)	Partner report at 6 month follow-up	Completers = 42% Dropouts = 49%	0.14
Hamberger and Hastings (1988)	Tx completers (n = 32) Tx dropouts (n = 36)	CBT group (15 weeks)	Combination of self + partner + police report at 1 year follow-up	Completers = 9% Dropouts = 17%	0.23
Waldo (1988)	Tx completers (n=30) Tx dropouts (n = 30) Control (n = 30)	Relationship enhancement men's group (12 weeks)	Police reports at 1 year follow-up	Completers = 0% Dropouts = 20% Controls = 20%	Completers vs dropouts = 0.70 Completers vs control = 0.70

Note on abbreviations used

    Tx = treatment, Dv= domestic violence, AA = alcoholics anonymous,

    CBT = cognitive behavioural therapy

Quasi-experimental studies

Table 3.1 presents the quasi-experimental studies, most of which compare treatment completers to dropouts. All of the quasi-experimental studies share the methodological problem of potentially 'stacking the deck' in favor of treatment. Men who choose to complete treatment are known to be different from those who drop out, for example, they are more educated, more likely to be employed, married and Caucasian, and less likely to have a criminal record (Babcock and Steiner 1999; Hamberger and Hastings 1988). Two studies did attempt to control for these preexisting group differences (Babcock and Steiner 1999; Gondolf 1997) and found that the effect attributable to treatment remained *statistically* significant. However, the percentages and effect sizes presented in Table 3.1 are not corrected for these confounds. It is difficult to estimate the effect size controlling for demographic variables because most studies do not present the data in a manner such that a reanalysis controlling for confounds would be possible, but we predict that doing so would dramatically decrease the effect size. In the Babcock and Steiner (1999) study, for example, when correcting for differences in demographic and prior criminal history, the treatment effect size dropped from a moderate 0.40 to a negligible 0.06.

Across the quasi-experimental studies, only one study reported higher recidivism rates among treatment completers (Harrell 1991) and only one study reports an effect size that approaches a large effect (Waldo 1988). The unpublished Harrell (1991) study is clearly an outlier, with its large negative effect size ($d = -0.76$), and will be excluded from the following summary statistics. Based on police reports, the average effect size for the quasi-experimental designs (mean $d = 0.32$) is about the same based on partner report (mean $d = 0.33$).

True experiments

Because of the ever-present risk of confounds among quasi-experimental studies, results of the five experimental studies should be considered a more accurate estimate of the actual effect size due to batterers' treatment. Table 3.2 presents the five studies in the period 1992–99 which employed random assignment. These five well-designed studies deserve special attention.

Feder and Forde (1999) randomly assigned batterers on probation to either a feminist-psychoeducational program or no treatment. In general, there were no statistically significant differences between the two groups on recidivism as measured by police records or by victim report. There was a small but significant effect on recidivism among the subset of men randomly assigned to group treatment who attended all 26 sessions. Data with which to calculate the overall effect size are not yet available. Given the lack of statistical significance when simply comparing men assigned to treatment and the control groups, the effect size of the treatment is assumed to be minimal.

Table 3.2 Experimental designs					
Study	**Groups**	**Treatment**	**Outcome measures**	**% reoffended**	**Effect size (d)**
Feder and Forde (1999)	Tx = Duluth (n = 174) Control (n = 230)	26 week Duluth + probation vs probation only	Police and partner report (21% of sample) at 1 year follow-up	Data not yet available	Unknown
Davis, Taylor and Maxwell (1998)	Tx 1 = long (n = 129) Tx 2 = brief (n = 61) Control (n = 186)	Duluth model 26 week vs 8 week treatment vs community service control	Police and partner report of new incident in past 2 months (50% of sample) at 1 year follow-up	*Police report* Tx 1 = 10% Tx 2 = 25% Control = 26% *Partner report* Tx 1 = 14% Tx 2 = 18% Control = 22%	*Police report* Tx 1 = 0.41 Tx 2 = 0.02 *Partner report* Tx 1 = 0.21 Tx 2 = 0.10
Dunford (1998)	Tx 1 = CBT (n = 164) Tx 2 = Couples (n = 158) Comp 1 = Monitoring (n = 155) Comp 2 (n = 145)	CBT men's group vs conjoint vs rigorous monitoring vs victims' safety planning control	Partner report on *injury* at 18 months follow-up	*Partner report* Tx 1 = 19% Tx 2 = 16% Comp 1 = 17% Comp 2 = 21%	Tx 1 vs comp 2 = 0.05 Tx 2 vs comp 2 = 0.13 Comp 1 vs comp 2 = 0.10
Ford and Regoli (1993)	Tx 1 = pretrial diversion into counseling (n = 127) Tx 2 = counseling as condition of probation (n = 114) Control = sentence without counseling (n = 106)	Counseling (unknown type) as pretrial diversion vs condition of probation vs other sentencing (e.g. fine, jail) control.	Partner report at 6 month follow-up	Tx 1 = 29% Tx 2 = 34% Control = 35%	Tx 1 = 0.13 Tx 2 = 0.02
Palmer, Brown and Barrera (1992)	Tx (n = 30) Control (n = 26)	10 week psycho-educational vs probation only	Police at 1–2 year follow-up	Tx = 10% Control = 31%	Tx = 0.54

Davis *et al.* (1998) compared a long (26 week) psychoeducational group to a brief (8 week) psychoeducational group, and to a community service control

(70 hours of clearing vacant lots, painting senior citizen centers, etc.). They found a statistically significant reduction in recidivism and a small but respectable effect size of 0.41 based on criminal records among the long treatment group only; the 8 week group was indistinguishable from the community service control ($d = 0.02$). However, when based on victim report of new incidents in the previous 2 months, neither the long nor the brief intervention had any statistically significant effect on reassault when compared to no treatment. Correspondingly, the effect sizes due to treatment based on victim report are meager.

In Dunford's (1998) large, well-designed evaluation of navy personnel, neither a 26 week cognitive-behavioral therapy (CBT) group, couples therapy nor rigorous monitoring had any meaningful effect on the number of subsequent injuries to victims, compared to arrest and victims' safety planning alone (data on the rates of subsequent physical assaults are not currently available). Neither CBT men's groups ($d = 0.05$) nor couples therapy ($d = 0.13$) had a significant impact on injury rates at 18 month follow-up compared to no treatment. It is important to note that this sample of batterers, those employed through the navy in San Diego, California, are not representative of the population of batterers court-mandated to domestic violence programs around the USA. All of the research participants were employed, had a high stake in social conformity and thus were more 'socially bonded' (Sherman et al. 1992). Any intervention, including arrest and being identified by authorities, may work to deter socially bonded individuals from repeat offenses.

Ford and Regoli (1993) designed a study which randomly assigned batterers into treatment as a pre-trial diversion (i.e., defendants' criminal records would be cleared pending treatment completion), treatment as a condition of probation post-conviction, versus alternative sentencing strategies (e.g., paying a fine or going to jail). Although this study was designed to test different sentencing options rather than the effects due to treatment, one can compare 'treated' abusers versus 'non-treated' abusers. Again, there were no significant differences or effect sizes comparing recidivism rates based on victim report between men in treatment versus those not in treatment. Neither treatment as pre-trial diversion ($d = 0.13$) nor as a condition of probation post-conviction ($d = 0.02$) was found to be superior to purely legal interventions.

Finally, Palmer et al. (1992) conducted a small-scale study in Canada of men using block random procedure: men were assigned to a 10 week psychoeducational treatment (similar to the Duluth model) if a new group was to commence within 3 weeks or, if not, to a 'probation only' control group. Based on police reports, men assigned to the treatment condition reoffended at a significantly lower rate than men assigned to probation only, yielding a medium effect size ($d = 0.54$). However, this is limited by its small sample size, and the results may not be generalizable to other samples.

Synthesis of outcome literature

Despite the discrepancies in methodology, design and follow-up intervals, we are able to draw some conclusions from these studies based on their effect sizes. Average effect sizes across both the quasi- and true experimental designs are about the same based on police reports ($d = 0.32$) but smaller among true experiments using partner reports ($d = 0.11$). When examining types of treatments, the average effect sizes based on criminal records are somewhat larger based on more recent studies of modified Duluth-type men's groups (average $d = 0.44$) (Babcock and Steiner 1999; Davis *et al.* 1998; Gondolf 1998) when compared to studies of CBT groups and anger management programs (average $d = 0.14$) (Chen *et al.* 1989; Dunford 1998; Dutton *et al.* 1997; Hamberger and Hastings 1988). This may indicate that current, multi-modal, modified Duluth curricula so predominant in the field today may be somewhat more effective than more circumscribed skills-training-based treatment packages. Overall, batterers' treatment is related to a small reduction in recidivism of domestic violence. In addition, no intervention, psychoeducational groups, CBT groups or couples therapy has been shown to be differentially more effective than the other within the same sample. Furthermore, length of treatment does not seem to be clearly related to recidivism. With the exception of Davis *et al.*'s (1998) study, shorter programs appear to be as 'effective' as the longer, more comprehensive programs (Gondolf 1997, 1998).

Attrition

Compounding the problem of small treatment effects when clients do participate in treatment are the high rates of treatment dropouts, even when the intervention is court-ordered. Many studies find that only about one-third of batterers assigned to treatment, in fact, complete the program (Babcock and Steiner 1999; Edleson and Syers 1990; see Eisikovits and Edleson 1989 for a review of attrition rates). Consistent with these findings are the results of 2 national surveys of batterers' programs. Feazell *et al.*

(1984) reported in their survey of 90 programs that one-third to one-half of the men dropped out after the first session of treatment. Similarly, Pirog-Good and Stets-Kealey (1985) reported data based on a survey of 59 batterers' programs where they found that 48 percent of the men starting a program did not complete it. A major obstacle of the coordinated community response is that the majority of batterers mandated to attend treatment do not complete it, and those who do complete treatment may not be a prototypic set of batterers. Batterers who complete domestic violence (DV) treatment are likely to be first-time offenders, older, report a higher income, be more educated and more likely to be married and have children than DV treatment dropouts. These demographic differences may indicate that DV treatment completers have more to lose, economically and socially, than do treatment dropouts. To use Sherman *et al.*'s (1992) terminology, they were more 'socially bonded' and have a higher stake in conforming to the mores of dominant society. Treatment non-completers and incarcerated batterers were more likely to be unemployed and criminally entrenched; they may represent a socially disenfranchised subset of the batterer population who are not subject to the same informal social controls as others (Babcock and Steiner 1999).

Community response to noncompliance

Unfortunately, men who drop out are also likely to be at greatest risk of recidivism. If batterers' interventions do not help the criminally entrenched or socially disenfranchised batterer, can we conclude that they are effective? Since most treatment programs are offered or court-mandated by a coordinated community response, a problem with attrition indicates a problem not only with treatment but rather with the intervention system as a whole. Few program evaluations examine the broader coordinated community response, for example, the response from probation and the criminal justice system to those men who drop out of treatment. One study that did (Babcock and Steiner 1999) found that more than one-half of the treatment non-completers did not attend any group domestic violence sessions at all, yet only 37 percent of those had their probation revoked. The majority (63%) of noncompliant cases were not legally punished despite the fact that they did not attend even one court-mandated treatment session. Perhaps the blame does not lie in treatment inefficacy but rather a system that allows for unsanctioned attrition from court-mandated treatment programs.

Although the focus of this chapter is on batterers' treatment, treatment is just one small part of the equation in domestic violence intervention. With court-mandated populations, treatment is likely to be effective only when supported by a strong, swift and consistent legal response to treatment noncompliance and reoffense. Unfortunately, in most jurisdictions the probability is low that the courts will rigorously enforce sanctions unless there is rigorous and continuous oversight by communities to hold systems accountable for enforcement (Edleson 1996). Not sanctioning men for treatment noncompliance implicitly excuses domestic violence and colludes with batterers in minimizing the seriousness of the crime. As Murphy, Musser and Maton (1998) contend, prosecution, probation and treatment may each have a small, additive effect on the reduction in recidivism. Therefore, a more intensive treatment program, in conjunction with a stronger legal response in sanctioning men who fail to comply with treatment, may be required to have a meaningful impact on reducing further domestic assault (Babcock and Steiner 1999).

Due to a combination of factors system-wide, batterers' programs as they currently exist appear to be successful in achieving behavior change with only some men. The question remains as to what to do with those batterers whose history indicates that treatment is not likely to be effective. Some may argue that these 'at risk' men should be excluded from our current batterers' treatment services in order to maximize our limited resource, and be criminally sanctioned instead. Jacobson and Gottman (1998) assert that batterers' treatment should never be court-mandated and should be offered only on voluntary basis, in addition to – not instead of – jail time. When counseling is offered as an alternative to prison, batterers are not being held accountable and those who are forced into counseling are less likely to benefit (Jacobson and Gottman 1998, p.225). Those who voluntarily chose treatment would most likely be the treatable ones, and the unmotivated, criminal types who are 'currently clogging the system' would be excluded (Jacobson and Gottman 1998, p.275).

Prison remains a sentencing option for felony cases of family violence, but the question remains as to when incarceration is likely to deter subsequent abuse. One study examining the relationship between recidivism and incarceration in lieu of batterers' intervention found that incarcerated batterers were three times more likely to reoffend than treatment dropouts, and this difference remained significant after controlling for between-group differences in prior criminal record and demographics (Babcock and Steiner

1999). In addition, attrition rates are even higher among voluntary batterers who are not court-mandated to attend (Gondolf 1997). Would there be a widespread need for batterers' treatment if it were purely voluntary?

Alternatively, targeted intensive treatments may be tailored specifically for these at risk populations. Currently, pilot tests are under way at Des Moines Domestic Abuse Intervention Services to test a more therapeutic model with high-risk offenders (Healey *et al.* 1998). Perhaps future research will be able to tailor specific interventions, be they rehabilitative, punitive or a combination of both, to specific, high-risk populations of batterers.

Cultural issues and batterers' interventions

There is little information regarding the effects of treatment on batterers in ethnic minority groups. The handful of studies available suggests that the approaches utilized by treatment programs to address abusive behavior have limited success with ethnic minorities. Studies find that ethnic minority men who abuse their partners participate less, have lower completion rates and are reported to be less successful than their white counterparts (Babcock and Steiner 1999; Saunders and Parker 1989; Tolman and Bennett 1990). However, given that socioeconomic status (SES) and race are confounded, it is unclear that there is a racial difference in rates of domestic violence. Straus, Gelles and Steinmetz's (1980) survey of rates of domestic violence found that wife abuse was 400 percent greater among African American couples than white couples (Campbell *et al.* 1994). However, when Casenave and Straus (1979) re-examined the data collected by Straus *et al.* (1980) to assess for differences in levels of violence across racial groups and income, they found that, after controlling for income, black husbands were less likely to have been violent towards their wives than white men across almost all income levels. Similarly, when Straus and Gelles (1990) reanalyzed their 1980 results, after controlling for socioeconomic status, they instead found a *lower* rate of husband to wife violence towards black women (Hampton, Gelles and Harrop 1989; Straus and Gelles 1990). Therefore, the differences in response to treatment among people of minority cultures may be attributable to differences in SES.

Batterer treatment programs, as they are currently being offered, assume that their interventions will be equally effective across all offenders, regardless of SES, individual or ethnic background. As such, treatment providers fail to measure or consider environmental conditions that potentially exacerbate couple and family distress, thus rendering treatment potentially inapplicable to 'all but the most assimilated people of color' (Cross *et al.* 1989, p.23). In fact, a national survey of batterer treatment programs demonstrated that, of the 142 programs surveyed, less than half made some special effort to accommodate the needs of ethnic minority populations (e.g., providing outreach services, adding or tailoring interventions to encourage participation by ethnic minority groups), and only 24 percent made 3 or more such interventions (Williams and Becker 1994). In short, the conventional wisdom that ethnic minorities are not likely to benefit from treatment is misleading (Williams and Becker 1994).

SUGGESTIONS FOR FUTURE RESEARCH AND CLINICAL INTERVENTIONS

The general methodological problems surrounding domestic violence research with minority populations – inappropriate use of 'control groups', lack of self-report and observational data on relevant psychological, inter-actional and contextual variables, inconsistencies in definitions of ethnic minority samples, absence of within-group studies – must be addressed so that researchers can close the many gaps in our present knowledge base (Hampton and Yung 1996). More research with large, culturally diverse samples will allow exploration of differences within and between different ethnic groups.

However, there are some general policies which may improve treatment utility for ethnic minorities:

- employing staff who are not only culturally diverse in composition, but also knowledgeable of and comfortable with differences among and within ethnic groups and cultures

- amending current 'color-blind' interventions with communities of color to be more appropriate to the concerns and needs of this population (e.g., including kinship and family networks as part of treatment, where appropriate; incorporating traditional cultural practices that are antithetical to use of violence)

- developing community-based approaches to primary prevention.

Women arrested for domestic violence

Female perpetrators are generally excluded from outcome studies of domestic violence interventions. As we know, individuals most likely to hurt others in the home are usually men, and men are also the most likely initiators of violence in the home (Jacobson 1993). However, data from non-clinical, representative samples consistently find that women reported initiating both minor and severe violence about as frequently as men (Straus and Gelles 1990), although the injury rate among men is lower (Cantos, Neidig and O'Leary 1994). Women are also increasingly becoming identified as perpetrators of criminal domestic assault. It has been argued that clinical samples or samples derived from law enforcement settings may not be relevant to the general population because they can represent extremes (McNeely and Robinson-Simpson 1987). Nevertheless, such identified populations are of interest in their own right (Hamberger 1997).

Studying women arrested for domestic violence remains a controversial topic. However, with the prevailing view being that the fundamental cause of domestic violence is patriarchal attitudes (Pence and Paymar 1993), it begs the question of why women are sometimes domestically violent in our society. In many communities, police officers on the scene of a family violence call must establish probable cause and arrest the partner established to be the primary aggressor. While many domestic violence calls involve violence from both partners, police on the scene may arrest one, both or neither party based on their investigation of the scene. Following the implementation of a mandatory arrest policy, a community may find that the number of women arrested for domestic violence increases 10- or 12-fold (Hamberger 1997). Currently, approximately 5 percent of batterers referred to treatment agencies by the courts are female (Healey *et al.* 1998). Communities, especially those committed to a feminist, Duluth-model intervention, may find themselves without adequate programs to treat these newly identified abusive females. Thus, despite the controversy surrounding the topic, there is a practical and clinical need to examine domestically violent women.

Women who are violent are usually a former victim of some type of violence – child abuse, domestic violence or sexual crimes – and often engage in violent behavior in order to deter future victimization (Healey *et al.* 1998). In one of the few controlled studies of women arrested for being abusive toward their partners, Abel (1999) found that women arrested for domestic violence experienced more exposure to violence in the family of origin than male batterers but less than women seeking victims' services. In this study, women arrested for domestic violence, unlike males, showed a significant degree of trauma symptoms subsequent to this past abuse, albeit to a lesser degree than the women seeking victims' services. Clinical implications of this research are that treatment for abusive women explicitly address past victimization and current trauma symptoms as part of the intervention program – treatment components not common among programs for domestically violent men.

Meaning of the outcome literature

The answer to the question 'Does batterers' treatment work?' appears to be, 'Somewhat, for some people, but the overall effect size is small.' Nonetheless, treatment effect sizes, regardless of orientation, remain clearly in the 'small' range. Davis and Taylor (1999) compared a small treatment effect size of 0.41 to the effect size of an early clinical trial on the effect of aspirin on heart attacks, which was only 0.068. Compared to this standard, they conclude that 'the effect sizes seen in batterers' treatment studies are quite substantial' (Davis and Taylor 1999, p.85). However, the average effect size across psychotherapy studies, comparing a treated group to a no-treatment control, is approximately 0.78 (Kazdin 1994), in the high–medium range. Compared to *this* standard, there is great room for improvement in our batterers' treatment interventions. Surely battering intervention programs are instrumental in helping many men change or cease violence, and at least in reducing their other non-violent abusive behavior. However, in general this does not have a large, meaningful impact in terms of cessation of violence on the majority of batterers as a group.

This is not to say that we need to give up on battering interventions as they exist and disband our battering intervention agencies. Ethical and safe ways of intervening with batterers have been developed based on 20 years of collective clinical experience and rational thinking, a strong foundation to any legitimate intervention. Rather, we need to examine critically the strengths and weakness of our existing programs and strive to improve upon them. Programs need to identify the special needs of minority, female and homosexual perpetrators. Now that there is a body of well-designed research examining the efficacy of existing treatment, perhaps we can move beyond the question 'Does batterers' treatment work?' to, 'How can we improve batterers' treatment?'

Promising new approaches

Currently, no one treatment stands out above all others as the clearly most efficacious route to follow. Moreover, the domestic violence treatment field is hindered by problems of high rates of attrition, inconsistencies in the legal response and inattention to cultural and gender issues. Despite these problems, there is great potential to improve batterers' interventions and policies in the future. With the current research knowledge base, we can finally move beyond the question of whether treatment 'works'. There are several exciting, new directions we can explore as alternative interventions or as additive components to existing treatments. While none of these new approaches has clearly demonstrated empirical efficacy in treating partner assaultive men, some have preliminary data indicating their clinical utility and others have been proven to be useful in the treatment of other disorders related to domestic violence. Some of these approaches we deem to be 'promising' by analogy; that is, by drawing parallels between domestic violence and other areas of research. Whether or not these 'promising' new directions will in fact improve the efficacy of batterers' treatment remains to be seen pending rigorous, applied research.

Matching treatment to batterer type

In the light of what we now know about the small effect size due to treatment, high attrition rates and ethnic and cultural differences in response to treatment, it becomes clear that a one-size-fits-all intervention cannot accommodate the diverse population of batterers entering the criminal justice system (Healey et al. 1998). Basic research has established that batterers are a heterogeneous group. The difficulty lies, however, in the lack of consensus of how best to delimit this heterogeneity into a useful typology. Many typologies exist in the literature based on psychopathology (Holtz-worth-Munroe and Stuart 1994), physiological reactivity (Gottman et al. 1995), attachment classification (Babcock et al. 2000) or criminal history (Goldkamp 1996, cited in Healey et al. 1998). Typologies using cumbersome or time-consuming assessment techniques, like psychophysiological record-ing or the Adult Attachment Interview (Main and Goldwyn 1994), are not likely to have widespread utility. Those based on batterers' self-report and/or criminal records, however, do show potential to aid informing sentencing or treatment decisions.

Holtzworth-Munroe and Stuart (1994) created a typology of batterers based on three descriptive dimensions – severity of relationship violence, use of violence both in and outside the relationship and the batterer's degree of psychopathology or personality disorder – which have been consistently found to distinguish between batterers. They delineated three major sub-types of batterers: family-only, dysphoric/borderline and generally violent/ antisocial. Family-only batterers are expected to engage in more low-severity violent behaviors, and be the least likely to engage in psychological or sexual abuse. As their violence is restricted to family members, they are least likely to incur legal problems related to other forms of antisocial behavior. Additionally, they are expected to exhibit the lowest levels of psychopathology, and to comprise about half of all men in the larger community who are violent towards their partner. Dysphoric/borderline types are expected to engage in moderate to severe violence (including psychological and sexual aggression), demonstrate the highest levels of emotional volatility, dysphoria, borderline personality traits and psychological distress, particularly regarding their relationship with their partners, and may engage in extra-familial violence and substance abuse behaviors. They are likely to view marital conflicts as threats to their relationship stability, and are likely to use desperate means, including violence, to prevent their wives from leaving. Generally violent/antisocial batterers are characterized by engaging moderate to severe violence, both in and outside of the home, and are likely to have the most extensive history of criminal behavior. Additionally, they are likely to have an antisocial personality disorder, and display problems with substance abuse. Consistent with their antisocial features, they are likely to use violence as a means of controlling or subjugating their partner, and endorse the utilization of aggression as a general response to conflict.

Research into patterns of violent episodes suggests that certain behaviors are triggers for violence for different types of batterers. Babcock *et al.* (2000) found that one subtype of batterer was more likely to respond with violence to his wife's attempts to withdraw. This type was 'preoccupied with respect to attachment', thought to correspond to Holtzworth-Munroe and Stuart's (1994) dysphoric/borderline type. The 'dismissing' batterers, thought to correspond to the generally violent/antisocial type (Holtzworth-Munroe and Stuart 1994), were likely to respond with violence immediately after their wife being verbally defensive. These findings are tentative as they based on a small sample and have not yet been replicated. However, we speculate that these different behavioral antecedents reflect different functions of violence across various subtypes of batterers. Understanding these different antecedents and functions of violence may help in tailoring treatment curricula to different batterer profiles allowing for more contextual treatments.

Saunders (1996) has demonstrated the clinical utility of taking personality disorder characteristics into account in predicting treatment outcome.

'Antisocial' batterers showed better outcomes in feminist-cognitive-behavioral group, whereas 'dependent' batterers – thought to be roughly parallel with Holtzworth-Munroe and Stuart's (1994) borderline/dysphoric type – showed more positive outcomes in a psychodynamic-process group treatment. Gondolf (1998), however, conducted a factor analysis of scores on the Millon Multiaxial Clinical Inventory (MCMI; Millon 1994) subscales to generate four types that reflect the prevailing personality types for batterers. He characterized types as

- little psychopathology
- antisocial/narcissistic
- avoidant/dependent
- severe pathology.

Results showed no evidence that one 'type' of batterer did better in one program approach or another (i.e., didactic vs process). Further investigations into the influence of batterer subtypes, batterer characteristics and treatment effectiveness are warranted.

While intellectually stimulating and clinically relevant to psychologists, a typology of batterers based on personality disorders has limited appeal in the criminal justice arena. Judges and probation officers have limited knowledge about personality disorders, but routinely make decisions concerning the dangerousness of offenders based on the defendant's history. Goldkamp (1996, cited in Healey *et al.* 1998) has developed a practical typology based on demographic information, criminal histories, and substance abuse data to assist in the disposition of batterers (Healey *et al.* 1998). In a study of 350 batterers entering treatment, Goldkamp (1996) classified men in 1 of 5 risk categories based on indication of prior drug involvement, prior convictions and prior assault or battery arrests; 68 percent of men in the highest risk category were rearrested within 7 months. Goldkamp's approach is particularly practical from a criminal justice perspective because such information used to predict recidivism is already available to most prosecutors, probation officers and judges in rap sheets and probation reports (Healey *et al.* 1998). However, this classification system needs to be validated on a different sample to truly determine its predictive validity and potential clinical utility.

Alcohol abuse

Co-morbid substance abuse problems, especially alcohol abuse, are common among batterers in treatment. One possible way of increasing the efficacy of batterers' intervention may involve concurrent treatment of substance abuse. Husband-to-wife violence is about three times higher among frequent binge drinkers than among men abstaining from alcohol (Kantor and Straus 1987). High proportions of male alcoholics seeking treatment have been violent toward their wives (O'Farrell and Murphy 1995). In a large, multi-site program evaluation conducted by Gondolf (1998), the only substantial predictor of outcome was a man being drunk during the follow-up. Men who were reportedly 'drunk' during the follow-up were three times more likely to reassault than those who were not inebriated.

Although there is considerable debate as to whether or not alcohol causes violence (Gelles 1993), there is no doubt that alcohol abuse is a risk factor for domestic violence. The relationship between alcohol, violence and treatment needs to be examined scientifically. O'Farrell and Murphy (1995) studied violence among men in a behavioral marital therapy alcohol treatment program that included their spouses. Overall, the prevalence and frequency of marital violence declined significantly from the year before to the year after alcohol treatment. Those who were successful at maintaining sobriety were also successful in refraining from violence, whereas those who relapsed to a problem drinking showed elevated post-treatment violence (O'Farrell and Murphy 1995). Although alcohol interventions are no substitution for batterers' treatment (Babcock and Steiner 1999), adding a substance abuse component may increase the efficacy of batterers' treatment for the relatively common subtype of batterer with a chemical dependency problem.

Relationship enhancement groups

As shown in Table 3.1, the intervention with the largest effect size was based not on the predominant Duluth model or CBT groups, but instead on a study employing 12 week, relationship enhancement skills training groups. This finding can be either dismissed as an 'outlier' among scientific treatment studies, or viewed as a harbinger of a potentially powerful, new intervention. The goals of relationship enhancement, developed by Bernard Guerney (1977), as applied to battering, are to help the men develop interpersonal skills that enhance relationships and enable them to stop their use of violence (Waldo 1988). Interventions include role-plays and assigned homework targeted to improve expressive skills, empathy, communication with the partner and the identification and management of their emotions (see Waldo 1985).

Although, like the cognitive-behavioral therapies, relationship enhancement may be criticized for not directly addressing sexist belief systems, its focus on empathy, communication and emotional regulation may be important additions to domestic violence treatment. However, these treatment components are not theoretically discordant with the feminist model and may be useful additions to existing treatment groups. Of course, the results of any single, small, unreplicated study should not be overgeneralized. This large effect size could represent a spurious finding rather than a meaningful treatment effect. More research is needed on the effectiveness of relationship enhancement skills training as a mode of treatment or as an additive component to batterers' intervention groups.

Dialectical behavior therapy

Two factors that both the psychoeducational and CBT models of batterers' interventions tend to overlook are batterers' difficulty with affect regulation and their tendency to be reactive to direct therapist confrontation. Therapies shown to be effective in treating other emotionally labile and reactive clients, such as individuals with borderline personality disorder, may provide a model for working with batterers. *Dialectical Behavior Therapy* (DBT: Linehan 1993) has demonstrated empirical efficacy and has been placed on the 'empirically supported treatment' list for Borderline Personality Disorder (Chambless *et al.* 1996). DBT posits that people with borderline personality disorder experience biologically based emotion dysregulation. Emotion dysregulation is characterized by increased sensitivity to emotional stimuli, more intense reactivity, difficulty modulating or changing intense emotional reactions, and slow return to a baseline or neutral emotional state (Waltz 1999). There are theoretical reasons to believe that DBT may be a useful approach with batterers (Waltz 1999). Specifically, borderline personality characteristics differentiate batterers from non-violent men (Hamberger and Hastings 1991) and seem to be prominent in at least of subgroup of men who are abusive to partners (Dutton 1995; Holtzworth-Munroe and Stuart 1994). Both borderline personality-disordered clients and many batterers display difficulty regulating their emotions, especially when confronted with real or imagined rejection or abandonment by an intimate. For example, Dutton and Browning (1988) showed videotapes depicting 'engulfment' (the wife demanding more time with her husband) versus 'abandonment' (the wife threatening to spend time away with a friend) to a sample of batterers. Study participants responded to the abandonment scenario with more intense anger than did a control group of nonviolent men. Failure to modulate affect in such situations may lead to escalation of the emotion, and ultimately to acting upon it in an inappropriate way, such as being violent (Waltz 1999). Therefore, therapeutic approaches that are effective in teaching affect regulation for clients with borderline personality disorder may also be effective with at least some batterers (Waltz 1999).

DBT as applied to batterers may be subject to the same criticism as anger control treatment in that it may 'psychologize' or, in this case, even 'biologize' the abuse and let the batterer and the community 'off the hook' (Gondolf and Russell 1986). The treatment, therefore, would have to be modified to address patriarchal issues of power and control and to ensure that batterers are clearly held accountable for their own behavior. DBT is currently being adapted and applied to batterers' treatment. Future research may elucidate whether a DBT treatment package or specific components of the treatment may be efficacious in reducing batterers' violence and psychological abuse of their partners.

Attachment abuse

Other batterers' programs also seek to enhance the batterers' ability to regulate their own emotions and to generate compassion and empathy using cognitive-behavioral techniques designed to interrupt the batterers' violent emotional response to guilt, shame and fear of abandonment. For example, the Compassion Workshop (Stosny 1995, 1996) is a 12 week cognitive-behavioral intervention, based on attachment theory, which locates the origin of battering in the abuser's use of anger to avoid feeling 'core hurts' of shame, rejection, powerlessness or perceptions of being unlovable. Its focus on developing compassion for oneself and others is decidedly non-confrontational in tone. Preliminary evidence shows that the Compassion Workshop outperforms feminist psychoeducational groups on victims' report of recidivism of violence and psychological abuse at 1 year follow-up (Stosny 1996). However, rigorous clinical trials are needed to ascertain the efficacy of these novel approaches to batterers' treatment.

Stage of Change

Another theoretical model and clinical strategy that may increase the efficacy of batterers' treatment is the *Stage of Change model* (DiClemente and Prochaska 1985). Developed within the context of the Transtheoretical Model of Change (Prochaska and DiClemente 1984), clients with a variety of behavioral problems are thought to progress systematically through a series of five stages:

- the *precontemplation* stage, in which individuals either are unconvinced that they have a problem or are unwilling to consider change

- the *contemplation stage*, in which a person is actively considering the possibility of change

- the *preparation* stage, in which individuals have a more proximal goal to change and make a commitment as well as initiate plans to change their behavior

- the *action* stage, in which someone takes active steps to make change, and adopts strategies to prevent relapse and return to the problem behavior

- the *maintenance* stage, in which the individual consolidates the change and integrates it into his or her lifestyle.

(Prochaska, DiClemente and Norcross 1992)

Since the batterers are primarily court-mandated or otherwise pressured into treatment, the majority of abusers are assumed to start therapy in the precontemplation stage. Pence and Paymar (1993) describe a common clinical presentation of male abusers characterized by minimization and denial of abuse and its consequences. Although external pressures such as threatened loss of the relationship and legal involvement may get a client into treatment and prompt him to think about the consequences of his behavior, a client is most likely to engage in the change process if he takes ownership of his abusive behavior, and desires change for himself, rather than to avoid punishment (Daniels and Murphy 1997). The Duluth model assumes that the average batterer has not thought much about changing, is stuck in the precontemplation stage and must be jolted into action (Murphy and Baxter 1997). However, as discussed earlier, confrontational approaches are not likely to be effective with reactive clients. Moreover, the majority of curricula for both the psychoeducational and CBT groups focus on changing clients' attitudes and behavior, and thus are designed to address clients in the action stage.

Motivational Interviewing (Miller and Rolnick 1991) is a preparatory program designed to move men from denial and minimization to readiness for change (Edleson 1996). It involves feedback from an expert on the results of an individual structured assessment, and discussion among group members who are contemplating or preparing for change of the pros and cons of changing abusive behavior. The therapeutic stance of motivational interviewing differs from that of confrontational or purely didactic approaches. It attempts to empower the individual and reinforce his sense of personal control without resorting to abusive tactics (Roffman *et al.* 1994, cited in Edleson 1996). These techniques may be incorporated into standard orientation and intake procedures.

Other intervention techniques, as detailed by Daniels and Murphy (1997), could be tailored to clients in various stages of the change process. For example, with the average 24 percent post-treatment recidivism rate based on partner report (see Tables 3.1 and 3.2), maintenance of behavior change is a significant problem among abusers. The *Relapse Prevention model* (Marlatt and Gordon 1985) may provide a useful framework for developing techniques to help men maintain abuse-free relationships. Relapse prevention is generally applied in the maintenance stage and has two primary goals: first, to help clients prevent relapse and maintain treatment goals (in this case cessation of abusive behavior) by assessing high-risk situations for relapse, recognizing and coping with early warning signals, and establishing lifestyle balance, and second, to help clients who have relapsed to get 'back on track' without viewing themselves as personal failures (Marlatt and Gordon 1985). For batterers who made treatment gains over the course of the intervention, such strategies may be useful to incorporate post-treatment in the form of 'booster sessions' or extended follow-up care. However, research into the applicability of the Transtheoretical Model to domestic violence and the utility of these therapeutic techniques in batterers' treatment is in its infancy. Although theoretically promising, there are currently no data indicating that these approaches will improve the efficacy of batterers' treatment.

Basic research applied to batterers' intervention

As in many fields, there is a schism between basic laboratory research and applied clinical practice. Many researchers conduct rather esoteric studies of the differences between violent and nonviolent men without taking into account their potential clinical application. Similarly many treatment providers do not read the basic research studies on domestic violence, perhaps because they fear that these studies are bereft of any clinical utility or relevance. However, bridging this gap between researchers and practitioners is another promising direction on the path to improving the efficacy of batterers' interventions.

CLINICAL IMPLICATIONS FROM RECENT RESEARCH FINDINGS

Researchers have discovered some robust patterns of domestic violence that have potential clinical utility. For example, communication patterns have been found to differ between violent and distressed but nonviolent couples. Specifically, the demand–withdraw interaction pattern (Christensen and Heavey 1990) characterizes many distressed couples. In this pattern, the demanding partner tries to get the withdrawing partner to change, whereas the withdrawing partner retreats from these pressures through avoidance, passive inaction or stonewalling (Christensen and Heavey 1990). The demand–withdraw pattern is an index of desired levels of intimacy (Jacobson 1989) and power (Babcock *et al.* 1993) in a relationship. Specifically, the partner demanding change (usually the wife) is requesting more intimacy and is in the less powerful position than the withdrawing partner, who is presumably more comfortable with the status quo (usually the husband). One unique communication pattern reported by maritally violent couples is high rates of husband demand–wife withdraw (Babcock *et al.* 1993). This finding has been replicated twice using different observational methodologies (Berns, Jacobson and Gottman 1999; Holtzworth-Munroe, Smutzler and Stuart 1998) so we are quite confident that the husband demand–wife withdraw is a phenomenon, at least among community samples of couples with a violent husband.

These findings may indicate that despite the power and control tactics used by batterers, batterers may not experience themselves as powerful or as trying to maintain status quo (Berns *et al.* 1999). The first line of intervention may focus on stopping abusive behaviors, followed by helping couples to modulate their emotional reactions so that they can remain involved in constructive discussion rather than withdrawing before resolution is reached

(Holtzworth-Munroe *et al.* 1998). Clinically addressing feelings of power-lessness, along with education about the ineffectiveness of using demanding communication tactics, may be helpful to at least some batterers and may ultimately improve the efficacy of the batterers' intervention.

PROVIDING EMPIRICAL DATA TO GUIDE TREATMENT

Often, treatment providers design and implement new therapeutic tech-niques in the absence of empirical data or clearly formulated theoretical rationale. This is not the fault of treatment providers, however. If treatment providers were to wait for hard, empirical evidence before implementing any change, the field would have progressed little during the 1980s and 1990s. Yet basic research can help to guide clinical practice. For example, increasing empathy is a focus of many treatment programs (e.g. Compassion Workshop: Stosny 1995, 1996). However, to our knowledge, there are no hard data indicating that batterers have less empathy than unhappily married but nonviolent men. In addition, the construct of empathy has multiple subtypes (Davis 1983). Researchers may be able to uncover specifically which aspects of empathy, if any, are deficient among batterers in order to clarify approp-riate intervention strategies. Similarly, treatment providers are currently implementing specific curricula, teaching how to label facial affect displays accurately (J. Fredrickson, personal communication, 13 October 1999). Basic research on testing whether batterers do in fact show deficits in facial affect recognition as compared to nonviolent men would provide initial evidence into the utility of this technique. Other clinicians are teaching batterers how to apply distraction techniques to de-escalate negative affect (N. Hightower, personal communication, 2 November 1999). Basic labora-tory research on the psychophysiology of batterers can test whether batterers actually show greater decreases in autonomic arousal when distracting rather than ruminating while in negative affect states. Researchers, in collaboration with treatment providers, can first evaluate the potential utility of new intervention components with basic research and ultimately assess their effectiveness in treatment with applied research.

Conclusion: Beyond the status quo

Given what we now know about the overall small effect size of batterers' treatment, the energies of treatment providers, advocates and researchers alike may best be directed at ways to improve batterers' treatment. Because no one treatment model or modality has demonstrated superiority over the others, it is premature for states in the USA to issue mandates limiting the range of treatment options for batterers. Battering intervention agencies are more likely to improve their services by adding components or tailoring their treatments to specific clientele, rather than by rigidly adhering to any one curriculum in the absence of empirical evidence of its efficacy. Promising directions for improving treatment efficacy include targeting treatments to different ethnic minority groups, batterers who are chemically dependent, batterers at different motivational stages, different types of batterers and women arrested for domestic violence. Developing and incorporating therapeutic techniques that are less confrontational and more affect focused may also help to improve the overall efficacy of batterers' treatment. Treatment providers should develop alternative techniques and collaborate with researchers to evaluate their efficacy in an effort to develop an evidence-based practice. To this end, researchers need to become an integral part of the coordinated community response to domestic violence.

Of course, batterers' treatment is just one component of the coordinated community response to domestic violence. Police response, prosecution and probation, as well as treatment, all affect recidivism of domestic violence. Even the best court-mandated treatment programs are likely to be ineffective in the absence of a strong legal response in initial sentencing and in sanctioning offenders who fail to comply with treatment. Even then, treatment may not be the best intervention for all batterers. Alternative sanctions should be developed and empirically tested along with alternative treatments. At the start of the new millennium, coordinated domestic violence programs will benefit from a spirit of cooperation and experimentation with multiple modes of intervention informed by research.

References

Abel, E.M. (1999) 'Comparing women in batterer intervention programs with male batterers and female victims.' Paper presented at the International Family Violence Research Conference, Durham, NH, July.

Adams, D.A. (1988) 'Counseling men who batter: a profeminist analysis of five treatment models.' In M. Bograd and K. Yllö (eds) *Feminist Perspectives on Wife Abuse*. Newbury Park, CA: Sage.

American Psychiatric Association (1994) *Diagnostic Statistical Manual of Mental Disorders* (4th edition). Washington, DC: APA.

Austin, J.B. and Dankwort, J. (1999) 'Standards for batterer programs: a review and analysis.' *Journal of Interpersonal Violence 14*, 152–168.

Babcock, J.C. and Steiner, R. (1999) 'The relationship between treatment, incarceration, and recidivism of battering: a program evaluation of Seattle's coordinated community response to domestic violence.' *Journal of Family Psychology 13*, 46–59.

Babcock, J.C., Waltz, J., Jacobson, N.S. and Gottman, J.M. (1993) 'Power and violence: the relation between communication patterns, power discrepancies, and domestic violence.' *Journal of Consulting and Clinical Psychology 61*, 40–50.

Babcock, J.C., Green, C.E. and Robie, C. (in preparation) 'Does batterers' treatment work? A meta-analytic review of domestic violence treatment outcome research.'

Babcock, J.C., Gottman, J.M., Jacobson, N.S. and Yerington, T.P. (2000) 'Attachment and marital violence: differences between secure, preoccupied and dismissing violent and nonviolent husbands.' *Journal of Family Violence.*

Berns, S.B., Jacobson, N.S. and Gottman, J.M. (1999) 'Demand–withdraw interaction in couples with a violent husband.' *Journal of Consulting and Clinical Psychology 67*, 666–674.

Bloom, M., Fischer, J. and Orme, J.G. (1995) *Evaluating Practice Guidelines for the Accountable Professional* (second edition). Boston: Allyn and Bacon.

Bograd, M. (1984) 'Family systems approaches to wife battering: a feminist critique.' *American Journal of Orthopsychiatry 54*, 558–568.

Bureau of Justice Statistics (1998) *Violence by Intimates: Analysis of Data on Crimes by Current or Former Spouses, Boyfriends, and Girlfriends* (NCJ–167237). Washington DC: US Department of Justice.

Campbell, D.W., Campbell, J., King, C., Parker, B. and Ryan, J. (1994) 'The reliability and factor structure of the Index of Spouse Abuse with African American women.' *Violence and Victims 9*, 259–274.

Cantos, A.L., Neidig, P.L. and O'Leary, K.D. (1994) 'Injuries of women and men in a treatment program for domestic violence.' *Journal of Family Violence 9*, 113–124.

Casenave, N. and Straus, M. (1979) 'Race, class, network embeddedness and family violence: a search for potent support systems.' *Journal of Comparative Family Studies 10*, 281–299.

Chambless, D.L., Sanderson, W.C., Shoham, V., Johnson, S.B., Pope, K.S., Crits-Cristoph, P., Baker, M., Johnson, B., Woody, S.R., Sue, S., Beutler, L., Williams, D.A. and McCurry, S. (1996) 'An update on empirically validated therapies.' *Clinical Psychologist 49*, 5–18.

Chen, H., Bersani, S., Myers, S.C. and Denton, T. (1989) 'Evaluating the effectiveness of a court-sponsored abuser treatment program.' *Journal of Family Violence 4*, 309–322.

Christensen, A. and Heavey, C.L. (1990) 'Gender and social structure in the demand/withdraw pattern of marital conflict.' *Journal of Personality and Social Psychology 59*, 73–81.

Cohen, J. (1988) *Statistical Power Analysis for the Behavioral Sciences.* Hillsdale, NJ: Erlbaum.

Cross, T., Bazron, B., Dennis, K. and Isaacs, M. (1989) 'Towards a culturally competent system of care.' Washington DC: CASSP Technical Assistance Center.

Daniels, J.W. and Murphy, C.M. (1997) 'Stages and processes of change in batterers' treatment.' *Cognitive and Behavioral Practice 4*, 123–145.

Davis, M.H. (1983) 'Measuring individual differences in empathy: evidence for a multidimentional approach.' *Journal of Personality and Social Psychology 44*, 1, 113–126.

Davis, R.C. and Taylor, B.G. (1999) 'Does batterer treatment reduce violence? A synthesis of the literature.' *Women and Criminal Justice 10*, 69–93.

Davis, R.C., Taylor, B.G. and Maxwell, C.D. (1998) 'Does batterer treatment reduce violence? A randomized experiment in Brooklyn.' Unpublished manuscript, Victim Services Research, New York.

DiClemente, C.C. and Prochaska, J.O. (1984) 'Processes and stages of change: coping and competence in smoking behavior change.' In S. Shiffman and T. Wills (eds) *Coping and Substance Abuse.* New York: Academic Press.

Dobash, R., Dobash, R.E., Cavanagh, K. and Lewis, R. (1996) 'Reeducation programs for violent men: an evaluation.' *Research Findings 46*, 309–322.

Dunford, F.W. (1998) 'Experimental design and program evaluation.' Paper presented at the Program Evaluation and Family Violence Research: An International Conference, Durham, NH, July.

Dutton, D.G. (1995) *The Batterer: A Psychological Profile.* New York: Basic Books.

Dutton, D.G. and Browning, T.J. (1988) 'Concern for power, fear of intimacy, and aversive stimuli for wife assault.' In G. Hotaling, D. Finkelhor, J.T. Kirkpatrick and M.A. Straus (eds) *Family Abuse and its Consequences: New Directions in Research.* Newbury Park, CA: Sage.

Dutton, D.G., Bodnarchuk, M., Kropp, R. and Hart, S.D. (1997) 'Wife assault treatment and criminal recidivism: an 11-year follow-up.' *International Journal of Offender Therapy and Comparative Criminology 41*, 1, 9–23.

Edleson, J. (1996) 'Controversy and change in batterers' programs.' In J.L. Edleson and Z.C. Eisikovits (eds) *Future Interventions with Battered Women and their Families.* Thousand Oaks, CA: Sage.

Edleson, J. and Grusznski, R. (1988) 'Treating men who batter: four years of outcome data from the Domestic Abuse Project.' *Journal of Social Service Research 12*, 1/2, 3–22.

Edleson, J. and Syers, M. (1990) 'Relative effectiveness of group treatments for men who batter.' *Social Work Research and Abstracts 26*, 2, 10–17.

Eisikovits, Z.C. and Edleson, J.L. (1989) 'Intervening with men who batter: a critical review of the literature.' *Social Service Review 37*, 384–414.

Feazell, C.S., Mayers, R.S. and Deschner, J. (1984) 'Services for men who batter: implications for programs and policies.' *Family Relations 33*, 217–233.

Feder, L. and Forde, D. (1999) 'A test of the efficacy of court-mandated counseling for convicted misdemeanor domestic violence offenders: results from the Broward Experiment.' Paper presented at the International Family Violence Research Conference, Durham, NH, July.

Finney, J.W. and Moos, R.H. (1998) 'Psychosocial treatments for alcohol use disorders.' In P.E. Nathan and J.M. Gorman (eds) *A Guide to Treatments that Work.* New York: Oxford.

Ford, D.A. and Regoli, M.J. (1993) 'The criminal prosecution of wife batterers: process, problems, and effects.' In N.Z. Hilton (ed) *Legal Responses to Wife Assault.* Newbury Park, CA: Sage.

Gelles, R.J. (1993) 'Alcohol and other drugs are associated with violence: they are not its cause. In R.J. Gelles and D.R. Loseke (eds) *Current Controversies on Family Violence.* Newbury Park, CA: Sage.

Goldkamp, J. (1996) *The Role of Drugs and Alcohol in Domestic Violence and its Treatment: Dade County's Domestic Violence Court Experiment.* Final report. Philadelphia, PA: Crime and Justice Research Institute.

Gondolf, E.W. (1987) 'Changing men who batter: a developmental model for integrated interventions.' *Journal of Family Violence 2*, 335–349.

Gondolf, E.W. (1997) 'Patterns of reassault in batterer programs.' *Violence and Victims 12*, 373–387.

Gondolf, E. (1998) 'Do batterer programs work? A 15 month follow-up of a multi-site evaluation.' *Domestic Violence Report 3*, June/July, 64–65, 78–79.

Gondolf, E.W. and Russell, D. (1986) 'The case against anger control treatment programs for batterers.' *Response 9*, 2–5.

Gottman, J.M., Jacobson, N.S., Rushe, R.H., Shortt, J.W., Babcock, J.C., La Taillade, J.J. and Waltz, J. (1995) 'The relationship between heart rate reactivity, emotionally aggressive behavior, and general violence in batterers.' *Journal of Family Psychology 9*, 3, 227–248.

Guerney, B.G. (1997) *Relationship Enhancement: Skill Training Programs for Therapy, Problem Prevention and Enrichment.* San Francisco: Jossey Bass.

Hamberger, K. (1997) 'Female offenders in domestic violence: a look at actions in their context.' In R. Geffner, S.B. Sorenson and P.K. Lundberg-Love (eds) *Violence and Sexual Abuse at Home: Current Issues in Spousal Battering and Child Maltreatment.* New York: Haworth.

Hamberger, K. and Hastings, J. (1988) 'Skills training for treatment of spouse abusers: an outcome study.' *Journal of Family Violence 3*, 2, 121–130.

Hamberger, K. and Hastings, J. (1991) 'Personality correlates of men who batter and nonviolenve men: some continuities and discontinuities.' *Journal of Family Violence 6*, 131–147.

Hamberger, K. and Hastings, J. (1993) 'Court-mandated treatment of men who assault their partner: issues, controversies, and outcomes.' In N.Z. Hilton (ed) *Legal Responses to Wife Assault.* Newbury Park, CA: Sage.

Hampton, R.L., Gelles, R.J. and Harrop, J. (1989) 'Is violence in black families increasing? A comparison of 1975 and 1985 national survey rates.' *Journal of Marriage and the Family 51*, 969–980.

Harrell, A. (1991) 'Evaluation of court ordered treatment for domestic violence offenders.' Unpublished final report. Washington DC: Urban Institute.

Hart, B. (1988) *Safety for Women: Monitoring Batterers' Programs.* Harrisburg: Pennsylvania Coalition Against Domestic Violence.

Harway, M. and Evans, K. (1996) 'Working in groups with men who batter.' In M.P. Andronico (ed) *Men in Groups: Insights, Interventions, and Psychoeducational Work.* Washington DC: American Psychological Association.

Healey, K., Smith, C. and O'Sullivan, C. (1998) *Batterer Intervention: Program Approaches and Criminal Justice Strategies.* Report. Washington DC: National Institute of Justice.

Hedges, L.V. and Olkin, I. (1985) *Statistical Methods for Meta-analysis.* Orlando, FL: Academic Press.

Holtzworth-Munroe, A. and Stuart, G.L. (1994) 'Typologies of male batterers: three subtypes and the differences among them.' *Psychological Bulletin 116*, 476–497.

Holtzworth-Munroe, A., Beatty, S.B. and Anglin, K. (1995) 'The assessment and treatment of marital violence: an introduction for the marital therapist.' In N.S. Jacobson and A.S. Gurman (eds) *Clinical Handbook of Couple Therapy.* New York: Guilford.

Holtzworth-Munroe, A., Bates, L., Smutzler, N. and Sandin, E. (1997) 'A brief review of the research on husband violence. Part I: maritally violent versus nonviolent men.' *Aggression and Violent Behavior 2*, 65–99.

Holtzworth-Munroe, A., Smutzler, N. and Stuart, G.L. (1998) 'Demand and withdraw communication among couples experiencing husband violence.' *Journal of Consulting and Clinical Psychology 66*, 731–743.

Jacobson, N.S. (1989) 'The politics of intimacy.' *Behavior Therapist 12*, 29–32.

Jacobson, N.S. (1993) 'Domestic violence: what are the marriages like?' Plenary delivered at the American Association of Marriage and Family Therapy annual meeting, Anaheim, CA, October.

Jacobson, N.S. and Addis, M.E. (1993) 'Research on couples and couples therapy: what do we know? Where are we going?' *Journal of Consulting and Clinical Psychology 61*, 85–93.

Jacobson, N.S. and Gottman, J.M. (1998) *When Men Batter Women: New Insights into Ending Abusive Relationships.* New York: Simon & Schuster.

Jacobson, N.S., Gottman, J.M., Gortner, E., Berns, S. and Short, J.W. (1996) 'Psychological factors in the longitudinal course of battering: when do the couples split up? When does the abuse decrease?' *Violence and Victims 11*, 371–392.

Johnson, B.T. (1995) *D-Stat: Software for the Meta-analytic Review of Research Literatures (Version 1.11)*. Hillsdale, NJ: Erlbaum.

Johnson, M.P. (1995) 'Patriarchal terrorism and common couple violence: two forms of violence against women.' *Journal of Marriage and the Family 57*, 283–294.

Kantor, G.K. and Strauss, M.A. (1987) 'The "drunken bum" theory of wife beating.' *Social Problems 34*, 213–230.

Kazdin, A.E. (1994) 'Methodology, design, and evaluation in psychotherapy research.' In A.E. Bergin and S.L. Garfield (eds) *Handbook of Psychotherapy and Behavior Change*. New York: Wiley.

Levesque, D.A. and Gelles, R.J. (1998) 'Does treatment reduce recidivism in men who batter? A meta-analytic evaluation of treatment outcome.' Paper presented at the Program Evaluation and Family Violence Research: an International Conference, Durham, NH, July.

Linehan, M.M. (1993) *Cognitive Behavioral Therapy of Borderline Personality Disorder*. New York: Guilford.

Lipchik, E., Sirles, E.A. and Kubicki, A.D. (1997) 'Multifaceted approaches in spouse abuse treatment.' In R. Geffner, S.B. Sorenson, and P.K. Lundberg-Love (eds) *Violence and Sexual Abuse at Home: Current Issues in Spousal Battering and Child Maltreatment*. New York: Haworth.

McNeely, R.L. and Robinson-Simpson, G. (1987) 'The truth about domestic violence: a falsely framed issue.' *Social Work 32*, 485–490.

Main, M. and Goldwyn, R. (1994) 'An adult attachment classification system.' Unpublished scoring manual, Department of Psychology, University of California at Berkeley.

Marlatt, G.A. and Gordon, J.R. (eds) (1985) *Relapse Prevention: Maintenance Strategies in the Treatment of Addictive Behaviors*. New York: Guilford.

Miller, W.R. (1985) 'Motivation for treatment: A review with special emphasis on alcoholism.' *Psychological Bulletin 98*, 84–107.

Miller, W.R. and Rolnick, S. (1991) *Motivational Interviewing: Preparing People to Change Addictive Behavior*. New York: Guilford.

Millon, T. (1994) *Manual for the MCMI-III* (third edition). Minneapolis, MN: National Computer Systems.

Minuchin, S. (1974) *Families and Family Therapy*. Cambridge, MA: Harvard University Press.

Murphy, C.M. and Baxter, V.A. (1997) 'Motivating batterers to change in the treatment context.' *Journal of Interpersonal Violence 12*, 607–619.

Murphy, C.M., Musser, P.H. and Maton, K.I. (1998) 'Coordinated community intervention for domestic abusers: intervention system involvement and criminal recidivism.' *Journal of Family Violence 13*, 263–284.

Neidig, P.H. (1986) 'The development and evaluation of a spouse abuse treatment program in a military setting.' *Evaluation and Program Planning 9*, 275–280.

Newell, R.G. (1994) 'The effectiveness of court-mandated counseling for domestic violence: an outcome study.' *Dissertation Abstracts International Section A: Humanities and Social-Sciences 55*, 5-A, 1193.

O'Farrell, T.J. and Murphy, C.M. (1995) 'Marital violence before and after alcoholism treatment.' *Journal of Consulting and Clinical Psychology 63*, 256–262.

O'Leary, K.D., Vivian, D. and Malone, J. (1992) 'Assessment of physical aggression in marriage: the need for a multimodal method.' *Behavioral Assessment 14*, 5–14.

O'Leary, K.D., Heyman, R.E. and Neidig, P.H. (1999) 'Treatment of wife abuse: a comparison of gender-specific and conjoint approaches.' *Behavior Therapy 30*, 475–506.

Palmer, S.E., Brown, R.A. and Barrera, M.E. (1992) 'Group treatment program for abusive husbands: long-term evaluation.' *American Journal of Orthopsychiatry 62*, 276–283.

Pence, E. and Paymar, M. (1993) *Education Groups for Men who Batter: The Duluth Model.* New York: Springer.

Pirog-Good, M. and Stets-Kealey, J. (1985) 'Male batterers and battering prevention programs: a national survey.' *Response to the Victimization of Women and Children 2*, 223–233.

Prochaska, J.O. and DiClemente, C.C. (1984) *The Transtheoretical Approach: Crossing Traditional Boundaries of Therapy.* Homewood, IL: Dow Jones Irwin.

Prochaska, J.O., DiClemente, C.C. and Norcross, J.C. (1992) 'In search of how people change: applications to addictive behaviors.' *American Psychologist 47*, 1102–1114.

Roffman, R. (1994) 'Motivating abusers to seek domestic violence counseling.' Proposal submitted for funding to the National Institute of Mental Health, October.

Rosenbaum, A. (1998) 'Sampling issues and measures in outcome research with batterers.' Paper presented at the Program Evaluation and Family Violence Research: an International Conference, Durham, NH, July.

Rosenfeld, B.D. (1992) 'Court-ordered treatment of spouse abuse.' *Clinical Psychology Review 12*, 205–226.

Sank, L.I. and Shaffer, C.S. (1984) *A Therapist's Manual for Cognitive Behavior Therapy in Groups.* New York: Plenum.

Saunders, D.G. (1996) 'Feminist-cognitive-behavioral and process-psychodynamic treatments for men who batter: interaction of abuser traits and treatment model.' *Violence and Victims 11*, 393–414.

Saunders, D.G. and Parker, J.C. (1989) 'Legal sanctions and treatment follow-through among men who batter: a multivariate analysis.' *Social Work Research and Abstracts*, September, 21–29.

Shamai, M. (1996) 'Couple therapy with battered women and abusive men: does it have a future?' In J.L. Edleson and Z.C. Eisikovits (eds) *Future Interventions with Battered Women and their Families.* Thousand Oaks, CA: Sage.

Shepard, M. (1990) 'Predicting batterer recidivism five years after community intervention.' Unpublished report. Duluth, MN: Duluth Domestic Abuse Intervention Project.

Sherman, L.W., Smith, D., Schmidt, J.D. and Rogan, D.P. (1992) 'Crime, punishment, and stake in conformity: legal and informal control of domestic violence.' *American Sociological Review 57,* 680–690.

Sonkin, D.J., Martin, D. and Walker, L.E.A. (1985) *The Male Batterer: A Treatment Approach.* New York: Springer.

Stosny, S. (1995) *Treating Attachment Abuse: A Compassionate Approach.* New York: Springer.

Stosny, S. (1996) 'Treating attachment abuse: the Compassion Workshop.' In D. Dutton (ed) *Treating Abusiveness.* New York: Guilford.

Straus, M.A. (1979) 'Measuring intrafamily conflict and violence: the conflict tactics (CT) scale.' *Journal of Marriage and the Family 41,* 75–88.

Straus, M.A. and Gelles, R.J. (1990) 'Societal change and change in family violence from 1975–1985 as revealed by two national surveys.' In M.A. Straus and R.J. Gelles (eds) *Physical Violence in American Families.* New Brunswick, NJ: Transaction.

Straus, M.A., Gelles, R.J. and Steinmetz, S. (1980) *Behind Closed Doors: Violence in the American Family.* Garden City, NY: Anchor/Doubleday.

Straus, M.A., Hamby, S.L., Boney-McCoy, S. and Sugarman, D.B. (1996) 'The revised Conflict Tactics Scales (CTS–2).' *Journal of Family Issues 17,* 283–316.

Tolman, R.T. and Bennett, L. (1990) 'A review of quantitative research on men who batter.' *Journal of Interpersonal Violence 5,* 87–118.

US Attorney General's Office (1984) *Report of the Attorney General's Task Force on Family Violence.* Washington DC: US Department of Justice.

Waldo, M. (1985) 'A curative factor framework for conceptualizing group counseling.' *Journal of Counseling and Development 64,* 52–58.

Waldo, M. (1988) 'Relationship enhancement counseling groups for wife abusers.' *Journal of Mental Health Counseling 10,* 1, 37–45.

Waltz, J. (1999) 'Dialectical Behavior Therapy in the treatment of abusive behavior.' Unpublished manuscript. Missoula, MT: University of Montana.

Wessler, R.L. and Hankin-Wessler, S. (1989) 'Cognitive group therapy.' In A. Freeman, K. Simon, L. Beutler and H. Arkowitz (eds) *Comprehensive Handbook of Cognitive Therapy.* New York: Plenum.

Williams, O.J. and Becker, R.L. (1994) 'Domestic partner abuse programs and cultural competence: the results of a national survey.' *Violence and Victims 9,* 287–296.

CHAPTER 4

Assessment of Women Who Seek Shelter from Abusing Partners

Nanette Stephens and Renee McDonald

One of the most common forms of violence in the USA is domestic violence; that is, acts of aggression intended to result in harm or injury committed by one family member toward another (Murphy and Cascardi 1993). For many years, domestic violence was often ignored or condoned because it was a 'private matter' committed within the sanctity of the home. However, during the 1990s, physical abuse of women by their intimate male partners became an issue of national and international concern. Findings from the National Family Violence Surveys (Straus and Gelles 1990) indicate that in the USA one out of every eight women (or more than 6 million) will experience male partner violence in a given year, with three out of every hundred (or 1.8 million) of these women being severely beaten by their male partners. Over the course of a lifetime, 21–34 percent of women in the USA will be assaulted by a male partner (Browne 1993).

Although some studies have indicated that the rates of violence committed by men and women against their partners are similar (e.g., Gelles and Straus 1988; Straus, Gelles and Steinmetz 1980), critics have noted that such findings do not consider important elements of the violence, such as intent (e.g., self-defense, control, retaliation) and consequences (see Straus and Gelles 1988). For example, it is now widely acknowledged that men's partner violence, as compared to women's partner violence, is often more severe and more likely to result in physical injuries and psychological difficulties (Cantos, Neidig and O'Leary 1994; Cascardi and Vivian 1995; Cascardi, Langhinrichsen and Vivian 1992; Christian, O'Leary and Vivian 1994; Dobash *et al.* 1992; Holtzworth-Munroe, Smutzler and Bates 1997; Langhinrichsen-Rohling, Neidig and Thorn 1995; Stets and Straus 1990;

Vivian and Langhinrichsen-Rohling 1994). The deleterious consequences of male partner violence (referred to hereafter as 'husband violence' or 'wife abuse') for many women include injuries and other physical health problems, social isolation, homelessness and psychological symptoms and distress.

Although the physical and psychological outcomes associated with husband violence have been well documented, little has been written about how to assess the violence, its correlates and its sequelae (although see O'Leary and Murphy 1999 for a discussion of domestic abuse assessment issues). This chapter focuses on the psychological correlates of husband violence and on assessment strategies that can be utilized in battered women's shelters to identify the specific mental health needs of victims of husband violence. After reviewing psychological problems and needs that are experienced by many victims of husband violence, we discuss other types of difficulties that confront many battered women. Next, we describe several issues that complicate assessment endeavors, and we offer suggestions for shelter-based assessment procedures to help identify the specific needs of a battered woman so that appropriate services can be provided. Finally, we discuss issues for future consideration.

Common problems and needs of battered women: Methodological comments and caveats

Numerous studies have documented a number of difficulties that are shared by many battered women. These problems are best described as correlates of husband violence. The inherent limitations of much research (e.g., ethical restrictions on random assignment to 'violent' versus 'nonviolent' conditions, cross-sectional study designs) in the field of domestic violence restrict the ability to make causal statements about the negative consequences of husband violence. Thus, although it is clear that many battered women experience multiple and serious problems (e.g., depression, posttraumatic stress symptomatology), existing research does not allow us to conclude that it is the physical violence *per se* that is solely responsible for these problems.

Many physically abused women are also subjected to psychological abuse (Follingstad *et al.* 1990; Hudson and McIntosh 1981; O'Leary 1999; Stets 1990). Indeed, several researchers have found that psychological aggression is often a precursor of physical aggression (e.g., Malamuth *et al.* 1995; Murphy and O'Leary 1989; Stets 1990). Because this type of 'non-physical' abuse often occurs more frequently, and in some cases more chronically, than episodes of physical violence, the effects of psychological aggression may be even more pernicious than the effects of physical aggression (Follingstad *et al.* 1990). Thus, although this chapter focuses on the needs of women who have been physically battered by their intimate partners, it should be remembered that the well-being of many women is negatively affected by their partners' psychological aggression as well (Murphy and Cascardi 1993). In addition to psychological aggression, there are many other factors (e.g., social isolation, substance abuse, poverty) that may influence the well-being of women whose partners are domestically violent. Researchers and service providers will need to work together to meet the challenge of understanding the causal links between husband violence and the psychological adjustment of battered women.

It is also important to keep in mind that much research in this field is conducted with samples recruited from battered women's shelters. Although battered women who seek shelter are the focus of this chapter, it is important to recognize that they may differ in significant ways from abused women in the community. First, the abuse that battered women in shelters have experienced may be qualitatively and quantitatively different from the abuse that has been documented in national samples. For example, research indicates that women in battered women's shelters have experienced, on average, over 60 acts of husband violence per year, and violence involving the threat or use of knives or guns is experienced by more than 50 percent of sheltered battered women (Jouriles *et al.* 1998). This type of extreme wife abuse, which has been referred to as 'patriarchal terrorism' (Johnson 1995), is contrasted to the 'ordinary' (Straus 1990) or 'common couple' violence (Johnson 1995) which is more often reported in national or community surveys (e.g., Straus and Gelles 1986). This type of 'everyday' violence, which is thought to occur when conflicts occasionally get 'out of hand' (Johnson 1995), typically involves infrequent acts of pushing, grabbing or shoving. Although little is known about the effects on women of low levels of domestic violence, these 'milder' forms of violence may be of as much concern as the more serious forms of abuse, not only because all types of abuse are problematic but also because less intense forms of aggression can, in some cases, give rise to more extreme acts of aggression (Dobash, Dobash and Cavanagh 1985; Johnson 1995).

A second factor that may differentiate sheltered battered women from battered women in the community is related to the stressful process of seeking refuge at a shelter. By going to a shelter to escape her abusive partner, a woman leaves her home and neighborhood to go to an unfamiliar environment which is often crowded and chaotic. Because a shelter is generally a 'last resort' solution, most women in shelters are often those who have the fewest resources (e.g., money, employment, family and friends who are able to provide temporary housing) and are in the greatest need of refuge and support. In addition, when these women have children, they often have to contend with helping their children adjust to their loss of home, belongings, friends, neighbors and school. Furthermore, anecdotal reports indicate that some women are blamed by their children for the family's having to leave their home and go to a shelter.

In addition to experiencing more extreme violence and high levels of stress that are associated with shelter living, women who seek refuge at battered women's shelters are often different from many of their community peers in that they have all recently separated from their abusive partners. In other words, women in shelters are facing the types of difficulties that are associated with leaving a relationship, albeit an abusive one. Feelings of loneliness, uncertainty about the future, financial concerns and becoming a single parent are among the issues that face newly single women. Indeed, many of these concerns are those cited by women as reasons that they eventually return to their partners (Dobash and Dobash 1979; Sullivan 1991; Sullivan and Bybee 1999). While some abused women in community samples may have separated from their partners, all women in shelters, by the nature of their shelter status, have done so.

These distinctions between victims of husband violence in the community and those in shelters are not meant to imply that abused women in the community necessarily have few problems or needs. In fact, one of the most serious concerns for these women is that they are 'invisible' – that is, they are often not identified (e.g., by marital counselors, health care workers) as victims of husband violence – and therefore their needs may go unrecognized and unaddressed. In addition, in some cases, abused women in the community and in shelters may have some of the same needs. However, given that much research on battered women is derived from samples of battered women in shelters and given that shelters are often the primary setting where battered women's needs are systematically assessed, this chapter's discussion of assessment issues focuses on shelter-based services.

Mental health correlates of husband violence

Several researchers (e.g., Browne 1993; Holtzworth-Munroe *et al.* 2000; Koss 1990; Walker 1979) have provided general discussions of the mental health correlates and consequences of husband violence. In addition, a number of studies focusing on battered women who sought medical services have also documented high rates of psychological difficulties (e.g., Abbott *et al.* 1995; Amaro *et al.* 1990; Bergman and Brismar 1991b; Roberts *et al.* 1998). Thus, it is now widely recognized that wife abuse is associated with a variety of adverse psychological outcomes, including depression, suicidality, anxiety and related posttraumatic stress symptomatology, low self-esteem and substance abuse.

Depression

Depressed mood, sleep problems, loss of energy, inappropriate guilt, problems with concentration, feelings of worthlessness and other associated symptoms of depression are reported by a large proportion of battered women. This is true for samples of battered women recruited from the community as well as from shelters. For example, studies comparing community samples of battered versus non-battered women document an association between husband violence and women's depression (Andrews and Brown 1988; Bland and Orn 1986; Campbell 1989a; Jaffe *et al.* 1986; Ratner 1993; Stets and Straus 1990; Zlotnick *et al.* 1998). Regarding the temporal relationship between husband violence and the onset of depression in community samples, Andrews and Brown (1988) found that out of fourteen depressed women in maritally violent relationships, only one woman indicated that the depression had preceded the violence. Mitchell and Hodson (1983) found that sheltered women had a mean depression score two standard deviations above the norm. Other researchers have also documented depression in large percentages of battered women in shelters or receiving non-residential services for battered women (Cascardi and O'Leary 1992; Follingstad *et al.* 1990; Gleason 1993; Jaffe *et al.* 1986; Sato and Heiby 1992), with rates ranging from 47 percent to 81 percent. It is also important to note, as pointed out by the National Research Council and the Institute of Medicine (Chalk and King 1998), that dimensions of violence (e.g., frequency, severity), other stressors and self-efficacy (i.e., feeling able to take care of one's needs) are more strongly related to abused women's level of depression than other variables such as their history of mental illness, childhood characteristics and demographic or cultural factors (Campbell *et al.* 1997; Cascardi and O'Leary 1992).

Low self-esteem

Low self-esteem, which is closely related to and often co-occurs with depression (American Psychiatric Association 1994), is generally referred to as an overall negative evaluation of self. Anecdotal reports have described ways in which many batterers vilify, blame and verbally attack their female partners, and clinical reports describe ways that violence can degrade self-esteem (e.g., Nicarthy 1986; Walker 1979).

Several researchers have examined different types of 'non-battering' abuse. Some examples of such abuse include psychological, verbal and sexual abuse (Rodenburg and Fantuzzo 1993); social isolation, threats, use of male privilege and economic control (Shepard and Campbell 1992); emotional-verbal abuse and dominance-isolation (Tolman 1989); attempts to control or dominate (Murphy and Cascardi 1993); and ridiculing traits, criticizing behavior, ignoring and jealous control (Sackett and Saunders 1999). Given that these types of emotional abuse are thought to occur frequently in the context of wife battering, it is understandable that victims of husband violence may come to doubt their self-worth and question their personal adequacy.

The relationship between wife abuse and women's self-esteem may therefore be due in part to the men's psychological maltreatment of their wives (Murphy and Cascadi 1993). For example, in an examination of types of abuse in battered women, psychological abuse was rated as being more detrimental than physical abuse. When the women were asked to rate the 'worst' type of psychological abuse, 51 percent rated ridicule and harassment as the 'worst', compared to 20 percent for threats of abuse (Follingstead *et al.* 1990), 17 percent for jealousy, 13 percent for restriction, 12 percent for threats to change the marriage and 8 percent for damage to property. Similarly, Sackett and Saunders (1999) found that battered women rated ridiculing of traits as the severest form of psychological abuse, compared to other types of psychological abuse (e.g., criticizing behavior, jealous control, ignoring), with ignoring being the strongest predictor of low self-esteem.

As suggested by findings described above, several studies have found lower levels of self-esteem in battered versus non-battered women (e.g., Aguilar and Nightingale 1994; Andrews and Brown 1988; Perilla, Bakeman and Norris 1994). Other studies have documented the association between depression and low self-esteem within samples of battered women (Campbell 1989a; Cascardi and O'Leary 1992; Rhodes 1992; Sato and Heiby 1992; Walker 1984). For example, Mitchell and Hodson (1983) found that husband violence was associated with depression and low self-esteem in a sample of women seeking services from a battered women's shelter. Results also indicated that in addition to level of violence, decreased personal resources (e.g., less education, fewer job skills, unemployment) and lack of social support and institutional support (e.g., legal services, mental health services) were associated with higher levels of depression and lower levels of self-esteem. These authors suggest that husband violence not only has direct effects on women's functioning and self-esteem, but also may indirectly affect women's well-being by interfering with their ability to use effective coping strategies and to have positive social contacts (i.e., contact with friends and families unaccompanied by their batterer).

Posttraumatic Stress Disorder

It should not be surprising that many battered women exhibit symptoms such as anxiety, hypervigilance, sleep difficulties, problems with concentration, irritability, feelings of detachment and intrusive thoughts of the abuse. This cluster of symptoms is a hallmark of Posttraumatic Stress Disorder (PTSD), which has been observed to develop among individuals who have been exposed to an event that embodies a threat of injury or death (American Psychiatric Association 1994). Browne (1993) has observed that PTSD may be the most appropriate diagnosis for many battered women.

Several researchers have found higher levels of posttraumatic stress symptomatology in women receiving services from domestic violence shelters compared to other groups of women (Gleason 1993; Woods and Campbell 1993). For example, in a study of battered women in shelters and non-battered but verbally abused women in the community, Kemp *et al.* (1995) found that 81 percent of battered women and 63 percent of women who were verbally abused met criteria for a diagnosis of PTSD. Moreover, over 80 percent of the women who had ended their relationships with their abusive partners still met diagnostic criteria for PTSD one year, on average, after the breakup. This result suggests that PTSD symptomatology does not necessarily dissipate on its own over time, nor does it abate just because the woman leaves the violent relationship. It should also be noted that a high percentage of women in this study had histories of previous abuse or trauma that could also lead to PTSD symptomatology. For example, 71 percent of physically abused women and 96 percent of verbally abused women had histories of childhood physical abuse, and 50 percent of the physically abused women and 21 percent of the verbally abused women reported being raped as an adult. Kemp *et al.* (1995) also found disengaging coping strategies (e.g., wishful thinking, social withdrawal, self-criticism) to be the best predictor of PTSD, followed by other life stressors, physical violence and lack of positive social support.

Other researchers have found high rates of PTSD symptomatology in samples of abused women, with rates ranging from approximately 40 percent to 60 percent (e.g., Astin, Lawrence and Foy 1993; Gleason 1993; Saunders 1994). Regarding the relationship between intensity of violence and PTSD symptoms, Houskamp and Foy (1991) found that 60 percent of battered women who experienced 'high exposure' to husband violence (i.e., three or more times in the last year of being injured, fearing for her life or having her partner use a knife or gun) met diagnostic criteria for PTSD in comparison to 14 percent of battered women who experienced 'low exposure' to husband violence (i.e., at least one act of husband violence during the last year, without experiencing the full criteria for 'high exposure').

Substance abuse

Although it is unclear whether problems with substance abuse arise before, during or as a result of domestic violence, it appears that at least for some women this issue warrants attention and services (Jaffe *et al.* 1986; Miller, Downs and Gondoli 1989). A group of studies that document a relationship between husband violence and substance abuse in women are derived from samples of women seeking medical services. For example, in a sample of women receiving emergency medical services, 23 percent of battered women had a history of alcoholism, whereas no women in the non-abused comparison group did (Bergman and Brismar 1991). Other researchers found that 71 percent of women patients at emergency clinics who tested positive for excessive alcohol use had histories of male partner violence (e.g. being injured, threatened or made to feel afraid by their partners) compared to 52 percent of those who did not test positive for excessive alcohol use (Abbott *et al.* 1995). In a study which reviewed medical records, battered women were found to have a higher risk for prescription and non-prescription drug and/or alcohol abuse than non-battered women did, and the women's drug and alcohol use often followed the first incident of violence (Stark *et al.* 1981). Furthermore, estimates that 16 percent of battered women will eventually develop alcohol problems (Stark and Flitcraft 1988), and observations that almost half of women in alcohol treatment program 'started out as battered women' (Flitcraft 1990, p.943) suggest that the links between domestic violence and substance abuse warrants careful consideration. In addition, findings that husband violence predicts the development of alcohol problems in women, after controlling for income, having an alcoholic partner and family of origin violence (Miller 1990), point to the need to understand more clearly the relationship between domestic violence and substance abuse.

Suicidality

Because many battered women experience high levels of depression, and because depression increases the risk of suicidal ideation or behavior, it is not surprising that several studies indicate that compared to non-battered women, battered women are at increased risk of suicide (e.g., Amaro *et al.* 1990; Bergman and Brismar 1991; Kaplan *et al.* 1995; Roberts *et al.* 1997; Stark and Flitcraft 1996). In fact, Stark and Flitcraft (1991) estimate that battered women are five times more likely to attempt suicide than non-battered women. In a sample of 648 female emergency clinic patients, 81 percent of women with histories of attempted suicide had experienced male partner violence at some time in their life versus 19 percent of those with no history of attempted suicide (Abbott *et al.* 1995). Similarly, one study found that African-American hospitalized women who had been hospitalized after attempting suicide experienced more physical and non-physical abuse by intimate partners than African-American hospitalized women with no history of suicide attempts (Kaslow *et al.* 1998). Results of this study also indicated that the association between husband violence and suicide attempts was accounted for by feelings of distress and hopelessness and drug use, and abused women with less social support were more likely to have attempted suicide than abused women with more social support.

Other correlates of husband violence

Health problems

Although this chapter focuses on the psychological sequelae associated with husband violence, it should not be forgotten that for many women, husband violence also results in serious physical health problems and injuries (Berrios and Grady 1991; Council on Scientific Affairs 1992; Sullivan 1991). For example, in an emergency department sample 11.7 percent of women who had a current male partner were seeking emergency medical treatment for symptoms resulting from husband violence (Abbott *et al.* 1995). In a study of women receiving emergency medical services, about 25 percent had histories of physical abuse and escalating injury severity (Stark, Flitcraft and Frazier 1979). During pregnancy, wife abuse also appears to be a serious concern (Parker *et al.* 1993). Results from a national survey indicated that 15.4 percent of pregnant women were assaulted by their partners during the first four months of pregnancy, and 17 percent were physically abused during the last five months of pregnancy (Gelles 1988). The authors of another study of pregnant women found that eight percent reported being physically abused during their pregnancy. (Helton, McFarlane and Anderson 1987). The implications of these findings are far-reaching, given that women abused during pregnancy are at increased risk for delivering low-birthweight infants (Bullock and McFarlane 1989; Parker, McFarlane and Soeken 1994; Schei, Samuelsen and Bakketeig 1991) and using alcohol and drugs during pregnancy (Amaro *et al.* 1990).

Sexual assault

A substantial proportion of women in intimate relationships have been raped by their male partners (e.g., Browne 1993). For example, Russell (1982) found that among rape victims, twice as many women reported being raped by their male partners as by strangers. Among battered women, the prevalence of sexual assault appears to be even higher. For example, of the 193 women who responded to a newspaper advertisement for 'women with serious relationship problems' 43 out of 97 women (44%) who reported being battered also reported that they had been sexually abused by their partners (Campbell 1989b). Numerous other researchers have also found that sexual assault of women often occurs in the context of 'non-sexual' husband violence (Fagan *et al.* 1984; Russell 1982; Walker 1984), (e.g., Frieze 1983; Shields and Hanneke 1983; Sullivan and Bybee 1999; Walker 1984). In addition, the abuse perpetrated by men who are both physically and sexually violent is more severe than abuse committed by men who perpetrate only one type of violence (Shields and Hanneke 1983; Walker 1984).

Social isolation

Accompanying, and likely exacerbating, many of the difficulties just described, husband violence has been found to be associated with social
isolation in samples of women in battered women's shelters (e.g., Mills 1985;
Mitchell and Hodson 1983). Some studies, however, with community or
non-clinic samples have failed to find this relation (e.g., Eisikovits *et al.* 1993;
Zlotnick *et al.* 1998). This discrepancy is not surprising, however, given that
shelters are often considered a resource of 'last resort'. That is, many women
seek help, at least initially, from family members or friends before they
contact more 'formal' sources of support such as shelters or police (Dobash *et
al.* 1985). Thus, it may be the case that many women who turn to shelters for
safety and support are those who have exhausted all other possible sources of
support or have none to begin with and/or those who have been most
isolated by their batterer. In addition to social isolation, husband violence is
often associated with a lack of 'institutional' resources for women in battered
women's shelters (Mitchell and Hodson 1983). Indeed, Sullivan and Bybee
(1999) suggest that social isolation and lack of support from community
resources (e.g., social service agencies, assistance with housing, medical
treatment, legal and law enforcement assistance) often increase a woman's
risk of continued husband violence.

Homelessness and economic deprivation

In some cases, battered women are confronted with homelessness and severe
economic hardship when they separate from their abusive partners. In fact,
Mason (1992) estimated that between 25 percent and 50 percent of
homeless families who are headed by a woman became homeless as a result
of fleeing from domestic violence. Homelessness and poverty are no doubt
related to many of the difficulties described previously in complex and
reciprocal ways. For example, the social isolation, economic hardship and
lack of instrumental or agency support that some battered women experience
tend to make it more difficult for them to be able to obtain employment
quickly and set up housing independent of their batterers. Likewise, the
extreme stress that is related to a lack of housing and income, plus an
uncertain future, may result in anxiety, depression and demoralization. It is
also likely that the depression, low self-esteem, post-trauma symptomatology, physical health problems and injuries that many battered women
experience, in turn, complicate the task of obtaining the basic resources they
need to remain independent from their abusive partner.

Child maltreatment

Several investigators draw attention to the high prevalence of child maltreatment in families that are characterized by husband violence. Appel and Holden (1998) note that estimates of co-occurrence of spousal and child abuse range from 6 percent in community samples to 20–100 percent in clinical samples of abused children or physically abused women; however, they suggest that a conservative definition of child abuse results in a prevalence estimate of 40 percent. Consistent with these findings, Edleson (1999) found that in approximately 50 percent of the studies he reviewed, 30–60 percent of families had overlapping child maltreatment and adult domestic violence, with estimates ranging from a low of 6.5 percent (Dobash 1976–77) to 97 percent (Kolbo 1996). Similarly, in a national sample of more than 6000 families, Straus and Gelles (1990) found that 50 percent of men in families characterized by frequent husband violence were also physically abusive to one or more of their children.

We said before that the state of the existing research on husband violence does not allow for the definitive conclusion that the physical violence itself is responsible for the problems of battered women. Few would dispute, however, that husband violence is extremely distressing to those who are its victims; it is clear from this review of the literature on the correlates of husband violence that battered women are at risk for a number of serious mental health and social problems. We now turn to a discussion of how to identify and begin to address those problems.

Assessment considerations

This review of the psychological problems and difficulties of many battered women highlights the need to develop assessment strategies that allow for identification of a particular woman's needs so that appropriate services can be delivered. Accuracy and efficiency of such assessments are important, given that most agencies serving battered women have limited staff resources to devote to assessment. Several other issues complicate this type of endeavor as well.

First, at any one point in time, only a relatively small percentage of battered women ever seek refuge or services from domestic violence shelters, agencies or other 'formal institutions' (Fawcett et al. 1999). In fact, Straus (1990) reported that only 13 of the 622 women who indicated in a national survey that they had experienced husband violence had ever sought shelter-based services. Because in some areas avenues to mental health services for battered women (e.g., assessment of mental health needs, referral to local service providers) are available primarily through battered women's shelters, a large number of battered women may never have access to such services. An encouraging sign, however, is that many nurses, physicians and emergency center workers have become increasingly active in developing programs and procedures which help them identify and respond to the needs of battered women who present for medical treatment. Unfortunately, however, other professionals who have opportunities to assess and address the needs of battered women may remain relatively uninformed about these concerns. For example, some battered women first reach out to clergy or social workers for support and assistance (Dobash *et al.* 1985). At times, such professionals may focus on elements that are familiar to many troubled marriages (e.g., communication problems, unrealistic spousal expectations) without also recognizing or assessing whether husband violence is occurring. Consistent with findings that indicate that marital violence is often present among discordant couples, Cascardi *et al.* (1992) found that 50 percent or more women of presenting for marital counseling had experienced husband violence. As suggested by O'Leary, Vivian and Malone (1992), husband violence may go undetected in clinical settings because spouses may not spontaneously report physical abuse or may not identify it as a problem in their relationship. These researchers found that of 132 couples who sought marital counseling, 44 percent of the women acknowledged physical abuse in response to direct interview questions and 53 percent acknowledged one or more acts of physical abuse on a questionnaire which assessed for specific acts of abuse. However, only 6 percent of the women acknowledged that physical abuse was a problem in their relationship on an initial written intake questionnaire. Taken together, these findings suggest that the needs of many battered women go unrecognized and unaddressed because many women are not identified (i.e., as having been battered) by those who might offer help and because only a small percentage of battered women turn to domestic violence agencies or shelters for assistance.

A second concern is that some communities – especially those in rural areas – have limited resources available to assess and address the needs of battered women. Because many small communities do not have a shelter for battered women, women in these areas may lack the opportunity to receive services that could identify their needs and direct them to the appropriate resources. In addition, even those communities that have sheltered housing may not have sufficient funds for hiring staff to assess a woman's specific needs. While some types of screening measures may require a minimal level of training, other tools, such as those appropriate for a more thorough evaluation, may require advanced training and experience. It is important to note, however, that even if screening and assessment procedures are available to identify a battered woman's specific needs, many communities lack the resources, such as social service agencies, that could begin to address the woman's concerns and needs.

Furthermore, many women come to a shelter traumatized, frightened and exhausted, and the first few days at a shelter may be confusing and overwhelming. Thus, it is an important, though not easy, task to develop interviews and procedures that can help identify a woman's primary needs as efficiently and with as little additional stress as possible. Because many battered women who seek shelter-based services remain only a short time at a shelter, it is important to assess for their needs as soon as it is reasonable to do so. For a variety of reasons, not only are many shelter stays brief, but also shelter departures may be sudden and premature as well. These issues suggest that shelters should make arrangements to have staff on-call seven days a week, whenever possible, so that every resident can have an opportunity to participate in a needs assessment and screening interview.

There is also a need to develop screening and assessment procedures that are appropriate for non-English-speaking abused women. The validity and reliability of many standard questionnaires that are used to identify the psychological needs of non-English-speaking women have not yet been established, and many of these instruments do not have established norms that would allow for their meaningful interpretation when used with women who do not speak English. Additionally, in some areas, simply finding bilingual staff to conduct screenings and assessment interviews is a challenge. This area of concern points to the need for research and service communities to work together to develop effective methods and measures for assessing the needs of battered women with diverse ethnic and cultural backgrounds.

Assessment recommendations

First, current research findings on the psychological correlates of husband violence have important implications for the development of specific screening procedures and assessment tools. For example, we reviewed findings indicating that some battered women are at risk for suicidal behavior. These findings suggest the need to assess carefully for suicidality. In addition, because husband violence has been found to be associated with women's depression, substance abuse and PTSD symptoms, it is important to assess for these as well. Finally, given a growing awareness about the co-occurrence of wife abuse and child maltreatment in many families, systematic assessments are needed to identify such families so that the safety of the children can be assured.

Second, although many battered women appear to be coping well in spite of the abuse they have suffered, others are often experiencing one or more of the difficulties described above. In addition, the first day or two in a shelter is often stressful; it is a chaotic and confusing time in which women and their children must learn about shelter schedules, rules and policies. Most women also spend a major portion of their time during a shelter residence trying to arrange for employment and housing. The many competing demands that a shelter stay imposes on women's time and energy, and the wide range of mental health needs of battered women, suggest that relatively brief screening instruments should be utilized as a first step in identifying the needs and problems of battered women. Such screening instruments should help to determine whether or not a more comprehensive assessment is warranted and, if so, which behaviors or problems should be examined more thoroughly. In comparison to conducting a full-blown mental health evaluation, a brief initial screen would be more desirable from the women's perspective and certainly more feasible for shelter staff to administer.

Third, so that all shelter residents have an opportunity to participate in an assessment interview, it is recommended that shelters have staff who are trained in administering these interviews and who are available throughout the week and at least one weekend day. Given that a large proportion of women leave shelters within the first few days of their shelter stay, the interview should ideally take place either at shelter intake or within the first 24 hours of the stay. One shelter in our community has addressed this problem by having staff on-site or on-call to interview and screen the needs of every woman within the first 48 hours of her shelter stay. Although this may sound daunting, by committing its resources and staff to this objective, the shelter has been able to interview the majority of shelter residents within the first two days of their stay. An early assessment also provides an opportunity for the woman to 'tell her story' to a sympathetic and supportive person – a first for many battered women.

Fourth, mental health screening measures should ideally be presented as part of an intake interview that is conducted by shelter staff for purposes of assessing the woman's needs in general. That is, in addition to mental health needs, the intake would also cover the need for housing, transportation, legal assistance, employment, child care, and so on. In terms of the mental health screening component, examples of queries might include:

- Have you ever been treated for emotional or psychological problems?

- Have you ever sought treatment for alcohol or drug problems or have you ever had difficulties caused by your use of drugs or alcohol?

- Have you ever felt so distressed that you considered hurting yourself?

- Are you having any nerve problems or psychological problems that you would like help with?

For women with children, similar queries, which could help identify their children's needs, should also be included. In our work, these types of general questions have allowed us to identify a number of women whose immediate mental health needs had not otherwise been identified by typical shelter intake procedures. For example, in fleeing from their batterers, several women had left psychotropic medications behind, but when this became known as a result of our screening procedures, they received assistance in obtaining the necessary prescriptions. Following the screen, a rather brief self-report questionnaire that assesses for different types of psychological distress (e.g., anxiety, depression, psychotic processes) can be presented. Together, these procedures generally take 10–15 minutes to complete. If certain types of concerns are identified (e.g., suicidal behavior or ideation, a history of serious mental illness, problems with drugs or alcohol, anxiety), the shelter staff conducting the screening intake should consult with supervisors about the appropriateness of providing a referral to a mental health professional for a more comprehensive assessment.

Fifth, given that a woman's first contact with shelter staff creates a powerful first impression and may even influence her decision to remain in the shelter, staff should also be carefully trained not to miss opportunities for building rapport and offering support. To this end, we recommend that staff who will be responsible for administering screening interviews should be trained in using an approach which helps to establish and strengthen rapport (e.g., beginning the interview with a welcoming statement, making eye contact, calling the woman by her name, making statements that demonstrate concern and support). Although such suggestions may seem like common sense and 'second nature' for those who are dedicated to helping battered women, discussing these specific kinds of strategies and practicing them in role-plays can help staff fine-tune their interviewing skills.

Finally, regarding the construction of the screening interview protocol, as well as the selection of more comprehensive, follow-up assessment instruments, it is recommended that these tasks be informed by collaboration with mental health professionals, service providers and local agencies. For example, mental health researchers could collaborate with community clinicians and local shelters or agencies which serve battered women to design and administer screening or assessment 'packages' that are appropriate for the needs and resources of a particular shelter, agency or community. In such a collaboration, the designers of the screening interview or assessment procedures should work together to:

- identify *what* constructs are important to include in the screen or assessment (e.g., depression, suicidal ideation, PTSD)

- specify *why* the constructs are important; that is, stipulate the purpose(s) for assessing a particular construct (e.g., to identify and deliver appropriate services for a specific woman, to improve certain shelter services, to collect information about the needs of battered women so that programs can be developed to meet these needs)

- decide *how* the constructs will be measured; that is, identify and select the best strategies (e.g., interview, self-report questionnaires) and measures to identify designated constructs of concern

- *train* staff and *administer* the selected strategies and tools

- *evaluate* whether or not the strategies and tools were effective in obtaining the desired information.

Future considerations

Given the complex and difficult circumstances that many battered women experience, well-intentioned but piecemeal efforts to address their mental health needs may be benign at best and counter-productive at worst. For example, we have found that approximately 50 percent of women in battered women's shelters lack available transportation (e.g., no car, no available mass transit or public transport options). In such circumstances, identifying a battered woman's PTSD symptomatology and then referring her to a local mental health clinic for treatment may serve little purpose if she has no means of transportation to reach those services. In addition, providing a woman with services to address identified needs (e.g., parenting classes, psychotherapy) is likely to have limited benefit if the woman continues to be isolated, 'marginally' homeless (i.e., moving from place to place) and/or harassed or threatened by her batterer. Thus, future efforts should be directed to developing the necessary resources and systems to address both the social and psychological needs of battered women. Such systems would include clinical treatment among 'a broader set of health and safety goals designed to reduce the impact of violence and ultimately prevent its occurrence' (Chalk and King 1998, p.231).

As a means of beginning to address the need for an 'integrated frame-work', dedicated, good faith efforts need to be made to encourage the collaboration between researchers and service providers. Historically, there has often been not only a lack of cooperation and communication between these two groups, but even at times outright friction and disdain. The result of such divisiveness has been to narrow and entrench the perspectives of both groups and impede efforts to develop, deliver, evaluate and maintain effective, comprehensive programs to meet the needs of battered women. Finally, efforts to address the needs of battered women should be informed by input from the community at large and – most importantly – from the real 'experts' in the community, the abused women themselves.

References

Abbott, J., Johnson, R., Koziol-McLain, J. and Lowenstein, S.R. (1995) 'Domestic violence against women: incidence and prevalence in an emergency department population.' *Journal of the American Medical Association 273*, 1763–1767.

Aguilar, R.J. and Nightingale, N.N. (1994) 'The impact of specific battering experiences on the self-esteem of abused women.' *Journal of Family Violence 9*, 35–45.

Amaro, H., Fried, L., Cabral, H. and Zuckerman, B. (1990) 'Violence during pregnancy and substance use.' *American Journal of Public Health 80*, 575–579.

American Psychiatric Association (1994) *Diagnostic and Statistical Manual of Mental Disorders – Fourth Edition.* Washington DC: American Psychiatric Association.

Andrews, B. and Brown, G.W. (1988) 'Marital violence in the community: a biographical approach.' *British Journal of Psychiatry 153*, 303–312.

Appel, A.E. and Holden, G.W. (1998) 'The co-occurrence of spouse and physical child abuse: a review and appraisal.' *Journal of Family Psychology 12,* 4, 578–599.

Astin, M.C., Lawrence, K.J. and Foy, D.W. (1993) 'Posttraumatic stress disorder among battered women: risk and resilience factors.' *Violence and Victims 8,* 17–28.

Bergman, B. and Brismar, B. (1991a) 'Suicide attempts by battered wives.' *Acta Psychiatrica Scandinavia 83,* 380–384.

Bergman, B. and Brismar, B. (1991b) 'A Five-Year Follow-up study of 117 battered Women.' *American Journal of Public Health, 81,* 11, 1486–1489.

Berrios, D.C. and Grady, D. (1991) 'Domestic violence: risk factors and outcomes.' *Western Journal of Medicine 155,* 133–135.

Bland, R. and Orn, H. (1986) 'Family violence and psychiatric disorders.' *Canadian Journal of Psychiatry 31,* 2, 129–137.

Browne, A. (1993) 'Violence against women by male partners: prevalence, outcomes, and policy implications.' *American Psychologist 48,* 1077–1087.

Bullock, L. and McFarlane, J. (1989) 'The birth-weight/battering connection.' *American Journal of Nursing 89,* 1153–1155.

Campbell, J.C. (1989a) 'A test of two explanatory models of women's responses to battering.' *Nursing Research 38,* 18–24.

Campbell, J.C. (1989b) 'Women's responses to sexual abuse in intimate relationships.' *Heath Care for Women International 10,* 4, 335–346.

Campbell, J.C., Kub, J., Belknap, R.A. and Templin, T. (1997) 'Predictors of depression in battered women.' *Violence Against Women 3,* 3, 271–293.

Cantos, A.L., Neidig, P.H. and O'Leary, K.D. (1994) 'Injuries of women and men in a treatment program for domestic violence.' *Journal of Family Violence 9,* 113–124.

Cascardi, M., Langhinrichsen, J. and Vivian, D. (1992) 'Marital aggression: impact, injury, and health correlates for husbands and wives.' *Archives of Internal Medicine 152,* 1178–1184.

Cascardi, M. and O'Leary, K.D. (1992) 'Depressive symptomatology, self-esteem, and self-blame in battered women.' *Journal of Family Violence 7,* 249–259.

Cascardi, M. and Vivian, D. (1995) 'Context for specific episodes of marital violence: gender and severity of violence differences.' *Journal of Family Violence 10,* 265–293.

Chalk, R. and King, P.A. (eds) (1998) *Violence in Families: Assessing Prevention and Treatment Programs.* Washington DC: National Academy Press.

Christian, J.L., O'Leary, K.D. and Vivian, D. (1994) 'Depressive symptomatology in maritally discordant women and men: the role of individual and relationship variables.' *Journal of Family Psychology 8,* 32–42.

Council on Scientific Affairs, American Medical Association (1992) 'Violence against women: relevance for medical practitioners.' *Journal of the American Medical Association 267,* 23, 3184–3189.

Dobash, R.E. (1976–77) 'The relationship between violence directed at women and violence directed at children within the family setting.' Appendix 38, Parliamentary Select Committee on Violence in the Family. London: HMSO.

Dobash, R.E. and Dobash, R. (1979) *Violence Against Wives: A Case Against the Patriarchy.* New York: Free Press.

Dobash, R.E., Dobash, R. and Cavanagh, K. (1985) 'The contact between battered women and social and medical agencies.' In J. Pahl (ed) *Private Violence and Public Policy: The Needs of Battered Women and the Response of the Public Services.* London: Routledge & Kegan Paul.

Dobash, R.P., Dobash, R.E., Wilson, M. and Daly, M. (1992) 'The myth of sexual symmetry in marital violence.' *Social Problems 39,* 71–91.

Edleson, J.L. (1999) 'The overlap between child maltreatment and woman battering.' In J.L. Edleson (ed) *Violence Against Women.* Thousand Oaks, CA: Sage.

Eisikovits, Z.C., Guttman, E., Sela-Amit, M. and Edleson, J.L. (1993) 'Woman battering in Israel: the relative contributions of interpersonal factors.' *American Journal of Orthopsychiatry 63,* 313–317.

Fagan, J., Friedman, E., Wexler, S. and Lewis, V. (1984) *The National Family Violence Evaluation: Final Report, Volume I, Analytical Findings.* San Francisco, CA: URSA Institute.

Fawcett, G.M., Heise, L.L., Isita-Espejel, L. and Pick, S. (1999) 'Changing community responses to wife abuse: a research and demonstration project in Iztacalo, Mexico.' *American Psychologist 54,* 1, 41–49.

Flitcraft, A. (1990) 'Medical news and perspectives.' *Journal of the American Medical Association 264,* 8, 943.

Follingstad, D.R., Rutledge, L.L., Berg, B.J., Hause, E.S. and Polek, D.S. (1990) 'The role of emotional abuse in physically abusive relationships.' *Journal of Family Violence 5,* 107–120.

Frieze, I.H. (1983) 'Investigating the causes and consequences of marital rape.' *Signs 8,* 532–552.

Gelles, R.J. (1988) 'Violence and pregnancy: are pregnant women at greater risk of abuse?' *Journal of Marriage and the Family 50,* 841–847.

Gelles, R.J. and Straus, M.A. (1988) *Intimate Violence.* New York: Simon & Schuster.

Gleason, W.J. (1993) 'Mental disorders in battered women: an empirical study.' *Violence and Victims 8,* 53–68.

Helton, A., McFarlane, J. and Anderson, E. (1987) 'Battered and pregnant: a prevalence study.' *American Journal of Public Health 77,* 1337–1339.

Holtzworth-Munroe A., Smutzler, N. and Bates, L. (1997) 'A brief review of the research on husband violence. Part III: sociodemographic factors, relationship factors, and differing consequences of husband and wife violence.' *Aggression and Violent Behavior 2,* 285–307.

Holtzworth-Munroe, A., Smutzler, N., Jouriles, E.N. and Norwood, W.D. (2000) 'Victims of domestic violence.' In A.S. Bellack and M. Hersen (eds) *Comprehensive Clinical Psychology, Volume 9.* Oxford: Pergamon.

Houskamp, B.M. and Foy, D.W. (1991) 'The assessment of posttraumatic stress disorder in battered women.' *Journal of Interpersonal Violence 6*, 367–375.

Hudson, W.W. and McIntosh, S. (1981) 'The assessment of spouse abuse: two quantifiable dimensions.' *Journal of Marriage and the Family 43*, 873–885.

Jaffe, P., Wolfe, D.A., Wilson, S. and Zak, L. (1986) 'Emotional and physical health problems of battered women.' *Canadian Journal of Psychiatry 31*, 625–629.

Johnson, M.P. (1995) 'Patriarchal terrorism and common couple violence: two forms of violence against women.' *Journal of Marriage and the Family 57*, 283–294.

Jouriles, E.N., McDonald, R., Norwood, W.D., Ware, H.S., Spiller, L.C. and Swank, P.R.. (1998) 'Knives, guns, and interparent violence: relations with child behavior problems.' *Journal of Family Psychology 12*, 178–194.

Kaplan, M.L., Asnis, G.M., Lipschitz, D.S. and Chorney, P. (1995) 'Suicidal behavior and abuse in psychiatric outpatients.' *Comprehensive Psychiatry 36*, 229–235.

Kaslow, N.J., Thompson, M.P., Meadows, L.A., Jacobs, D., Chance, S., Gibb, B., Bornstein, H., Hollins, L., Rashid, A. and Phillips, K. (1998) 'Factors that mediate and moderate the link between partner abuse and suicidal behavior in African American women.' *Journal of Consulting and Clinical Psychology 66*, 3, 533–540.

Kemp, A., Green, B.L., Hovanitz, C. and Rawlings, E.I. (1995) 'Incidence and correlates of posttraumatic stress disorder in battered women: shelter and community samples.' *Journal of Interpersonal Violence 10*, 43–55.

Kolbo, J.R. (1996) 'Risk and resilience among children exposed to family violence.' *Violence and Victims 11*, 113–128.

Koss, M.P. (1990) 'The women's mental health research agenda: violence against women.' *American Psychologist 45*, 374–380.

Langhinrichsen-Rohling, J., Neidig, P. and Thorn, G. (1995) 'Violent marriages: gender differences in levels of current violence and past abuse.' *Journal of Family Violence 10*, 159–176.

Malamuth, N.M., Linz, D., Heavey, C.L., Barnes, G. and Acker, M. (1995) 'Using the confluence model of sexual aggression to predict men's conflict with women: a ten year follow-up study.' *Journal of Personality and Social Psychology 69*, 353–369.

Mason, J.O. (1992) 'The dimensions of an epidemic of violence.' *Public Health Reports 108*, 1–3.

Miller, B. (1990) 'The interrelationships between alcohol and drugs and family violence.' In M. De La Rosa, E. Lambert and B. Gropper (eds) *Drugs and Violence: Causes, Correlates and Consequences.* NIDA Research Monograph 103. Rockville, MD: National Institute of Drug Abuse.

Miller, B.A., Downs, W.R. and Gondoli, D.M. (1989) 'Spousal violence among alcoholic women as compared to a random household sample of women.' *Journal of Studies on Alcohol 50*, 6, 533–540.

Mills, T. (1985) 'The assault on the self: stages in coping with battering husbands.' *Qualitative Sociology 8*, 103–123.

Mitchell, R.E. and Hodson, C.A. (1983) 'Coping with domestic violence: social support and psychological health among battered women.' *American Journal of Community Psychology 11*, 629–654.

Murphy, C. and Cascardi, M. (1993) 'Psychological aggression and abuse in marriage.' In R.L. Hampton, T.P. Gollotta, G.R. Adams, E.H. Potter and R.P. Weissberg (eds) *Family Violence: Prevention and Treatment.* Newbury Park, CA: Sage.

Murphy, C.M. and O'Leary, K.D. (1989) 'Psychological aggression predicts physical aggression in early marriage.' *Journal of Consulting and Clinical Psychology 57*, 579–582.

Nicarthy, G. (1986) *Getting Free: A Handbook for Women in Abusive Relationships,* 2nd edn. Seattle, WA: Seal.

O'Leary, K.D. (1999) 'Psychological abuse: a variable deserving critical attention in domestic violence.' *Violence and Victims 14*, 1, 3–23.

O'Leary, K.D. and Murphy, C.M. (1999) 'Clinical issues in the assessment of partner abuse.' In R. Ammerman (ed) *Assessment of Family Violence,* 2nd edn. New York: Wiley.

O'Leary, K.D., Vivian, D. and Malone, J. (1992) 'Assessment of physical aggression against women in marriage: the need for multimodal assessment.' *Behavioral Assessment 14*, 5–14.

Parker, B., McFarlane, J., Soeken, K., Torres, S. and Campbell, D. (1993) 'Physical and emotional abuse in pregnancy: a comparison of adult and teenage women.' *Nursing Research 42*, 173–177.

Parker, B., McFarlane, J. and Soeken, K. (1994) 'Abuse during pregnancy: effects on maternal complications and birth weight in adult and teenage women.' *American Journal of Obstetrics and Gynecology 84*, 3, 323–328.

Perilla, J.L., Bakeman, R. and Norris, F.H. (1994) 'Culture and domestic violence: the ecology of abused Latinas.' *Violence and Victims 9*, 325–339.

Ratner, P.A. (1993) 'The incidence of wife abuse and mental health status in abused wives in Edmonton, Alberta.' *Revue Canadienne de Santé Publique 84*, 246–249.

Rhodes, N.R. (1992) 'Comparison of MMPI psychopathic deviate scores of battered and nonbattered women.' *Journal of Family Violence 7*, 297–307.

Roberts, G.L., Lawrence, J.M., O'Toole, B.I. and Raphael, B. (1997) 'Domestic violence in the Emergency Department. I: two case-control studies of victims.' *General Hospital Psychiatry 19*, 5–11.

Roberts, G.L., Lawrence, J.M., Williams, G.M. and Raphael, B. (1998) 'The impact of domestic violence on women's mental health.' *Australia and New Zealand Journal of Public Health 22,* 7, 796–801.

Rodenburg, F. and Fantuzzo, J. (1993) 'The measure of wife abuse: steps toward the development of a comprehensive assessment technique.' *Journal of Family Violence 8,* 203–228.

Russell, D.E.H. (1982) *Rape in Marriage.* New York: Macmillan.

Sackett, L.A. and Saunders, D.G. (1999) 'The impact of different forms of psychological abuse on battered women.' *Violence and Victims 14,* 1, 105–117.

Sato, R.A. and Heiby, E.M. (1992) 'Correlates of depressive symptoms among battered women.' *Journal of Family Violence 7,* 229–245.

Saunders, D.W. (1994) 'Posttraumatic stress symptom profiles of battered women: a comparison of survivors in two settings.' *Violence and Victims 9,* 31–43.

Schei, B., Samuelsen, S.O. and Bakketeig, L.S. (1991) 'Does spousal physical abuse affect the outcome of pregnancy?' *Scandinavian Journal of Sociology and Medicine 19,* 1, 26–31.

Shepard, M.F. and Campbell, J.A. (1992) 'The abusive behavior inventory: a measure of psychological and physical abuse.' *Journal of Interpersonal Violence 7,* 291–305.

Shields, N. and Hanneke, C.R. (1983) 'Battered wives' reactions to marital rape.' In D. Finkelhor, R.J. Gelles, G.T. Hotaling and M.A. Straus (eds) *The Dark Side of Families.* Beverly Hills, CA: Sage.

Stark, E. and Flitcraft, A. (1988) 'Violence among intimates: an epidemiologic review.' In V.B. van Hasselt, R.L. Morrison, A.S. Bellack and M. Herson (eds) *Handbook of Family Violence.* New York: Plenum.

Stark, E. and Flitcraft, A. (1991) 'Spouse abuse.' In M. Rosenberg and M.A. Fenley (eds) *Violence in America: A Public Health Approach.* New York: Oxford University Press.

Stark, E. and Flitcraft, A. (1996) *Women at Risk: Domestic Violence and Women's Health.* Thousand Oaks, CA: Sage.

Stark, E., Flitcraft, A. and Frazier, W. (1979) 'Medicine and patriarchal violence: the social construction of a "private" event.' *International Journal of Health Services 9,* 461–493.

Stark, E., Flitcraft, A., Zuckerman, D., Gray, A., Robinson, J. and Frazier, W. (1981) *Wife Abuse in the Medical Setting: An Introduction for Health Personnel.* Monograph 7. Washington DC: Office of Domestic Violence.

Stets, J.E. (1990) 'Verbal and physical aggression in marriage.' *Journal of Marriage and the Family 52,* 501–514.

Stets, J.E. and Straus, M.A. (1990) 'Gender differences in reporting marital violence and its medical and psychological consequences.' In M.A. Straus and R.J. Gelles (eds) *Physical Violence in American Families: Risk Factors and Adaptation to Violence in 8,145 Families.* New Brunswick, NJ: Transaction.

Straus, M.A. (1990) 'The national family violence surveys.' In M.A. Straus and R.J. Gelles (eds) *Physical Violence in American Families: Risk Factors and Adaptation to Violence in 8,145 Families.* New Brunswick, NJ: Transaction.

Straus, M.A. and Gelles, R.J. (1986) 'Societal change and change in family violence from 1975 to 1985 as revealed by two national surveys.' *Journal of Marriage and the Family 48,* 465–479.

Straus, M.A. and Gelles, R.J. (1988) 'How violent are American families? Estimates from the National Family Violence Resurvey and other studies.' In G.T. Hotaling, D. Finkelhor, J.T. Kirkpatrick and M.A. Straus (eds) *Family Abuse and its Consequences.* Newbury Park, CA: Sage.

Straus, M.A. and Gelles, R.J. (1990) *Physical Violence in American Families: Risk Factors and Adaptation to Violence in 8,145 Families.* New Brunswick, NJ: Transaction.

Straus, M.A., Gelles, R.J. and Steinmetz, S. (1980) *Behind Closed Doors: Violence in the American Family.* Garden City, NJ: Anchor/Doubleday.

Sullivan, C.M. (1991) 'The provision of advocacy services to women leaving abusive partners: an exploratory study.' *Journal of Interpersonal Violence 6,* 45–54.

Sullivan, C.M. and Bybee, D.I. (1999) 'Reducing violence using community-based advocacy for women with abusive partners.' *Journal of Consulting and Clinical Psychology 67,* 1, 43–53.

Tolman, R.M. (1989) 'The development of a measure of psychological maltreatment of women by their male partners.' *Violence and Victims 4,* 159–177.

Vivian, D. and Langhinrichsen-Rohling, J. (1994) 'Are bi-directionally violent couples mutually victimized? A gender-sensitive comparison.' *Violence and Victims 9,* 107–123.

Walker, L. (1979) *The Battered Woman.* New York: Harper & Row.

Walker, L. (1984) *The Battered Woman Syndrome.* New York: Springer.

Woods, S.J. and Campbell, J.C. (1993) 'Posttraumatic stress in battered women: does the diagnosis fit?' *Issues in Mental Health Nursing 14,* 2, 173–186.

Zlotnick, C., Kohn, R., Peterson, J. and Pearlstein, T. (1998) 'Partner physical victimization in a national sample of American families.' *Journal of Interpersonal Violence 13,* 1, 156–166.

CHAPTER 5

Children's Perspectives
of Family Violence

Implications for Research and Intervention

John H. Grych

Stress and coping theorists argue that how children perceive and interpret stressful events mediates their impact (Compas 1987; Garmezy 1983; Rutter 1983). Whether they are involved in them as victims or observers, family interactions involving aggression and violence are stressful experiences that may threaten children's physical well-being, their attachment figures and their sense of safety and security. At present, we know little about children's perceptions of domestic violence because most research in this area has relied on parents to provide information about children's exposure to interparental and parent–child aggression. However, it cannot be assumed that children's and parents' reports are interchangeable; in fact, empirical evidence indicates that their ratings of family aggression are not highly correlated (Jouriles *et al.* 1997; McCloskey, Figueredo and Koss 1995; Sternberg *et al.* 1993). The discrepancies between child and parent reports may be due to a number of factors, including differences in the interactions that children and parents have observed or participated in, the salience of particular events and the ways in which children and parents perceive, understand and remember these events. Children provide a unique perspective on family violence, and studying this perspective may provide insight into the effects of interparental and parent–child aggression on their functioning and suggest avenues for clinical intervention.

This chapter considers how investigating children's social cognitive processes – how they perceive, interpret and remember incidents of family aggression – may shed light on the short- and long-term effects of domestic violence on children. First, conceptual and empirical work on cognitive processing proposed to occur when children witness aggression will be reviewed. Second, the effects of violence on children's processing of later interpersonal interactions will be examined. In each section, implications of this work for clinical intervention will be discussed.

Children's perceptions of family aggression

There have been few attempts to provide a theoretical basis for studying children's subjective experience of interparental and parent–child aggression (see Cummings 1998; Rossman 1998). However, conceptual models have been developed to describe how children perceive and respond to interparental conflict (Crockenberg and Forgays 1996; Davies and Cummings 1994; Grych and Fincham 1990). Because these models concern interactions that are often angry, coercive and aggressive, they may also be helpful for understanding the impact of more violent interactions. In addition, since hostile but nonviolent interactions occur frequently in violent families, examining their impact may provide broader understanding of children's experiences in these families. The generalizability of these models to interactions in which violence occurs and in which the child is a victim rather than an observer will need to be examined empirically, but they provide a starting point for examining the kinds of processes that might be important for mediating the effects of aggressive interactions.

Conceptual models focusing on children's subjective responses to conflict propose that the meaning of conflict to children plays a significant role in determining its impact (Crockenberg and Forgays 1996; Davies and Cummings 1994; Grych and Fincham 1990). These models are similar in positing that meaning is shaped by cognition and emotion, but differ in their relative emphasis of these factors. Grych and Fincham's (1990) cognitive-contextual framework describes social cognitive processes in the most detail and so will be used to guide the discussion of children's perceptions of aggression. Although the framework was developed to explain children's responses to interparental conflict, the constructs and processes it describes may apply to other types of stressful interactions, including interparental and parent–child violence.

The cognitive-contextual framework

In the cognitive-contextual framework, the effect of a conflictual interaction is proposed to be mediated by children's *appraisals*, or their evaluation of its significance for their well-being (Grych and Fincham 1990; see also Lazarus 1991). This framework suggests that when conflict or aggression occurs in the family, children try to understand how it may affect them, why it is occurring and what, if anything, they should do in response. Their initial emotional response provides signals about the level of threat the event poses (e.g., Campos, Campos and Barrett 1989), and can influence or disrupt cognitive processing. Children's appraisals are proposed to guide their continuing emotional and behavioral response to the conflict and to influence its long-term effects on their functioning. The kinds of appraisals that children make in a given situation are hypothesized to be influenced by two factors: the properties or characteristics of the conflict (e.g., hostility, resolution) and contextual factors, such as children's prior experiences with conflict in the family and the nature of parent–child relationships.

The cognitive-contextual framework emphasizes the importance of three kinds of appraisals: perceptions of threat, attributions and coping efficacy. When children first become aware of an angry or conflictual interaction, they evaluate whether the interaction threatens important goals, such as their physical and emotional well-being or the stability and harmony of the family as a whole (see also Davies and Cummings 1994). Whereas children's perceptions of the threat posed by nonviolent conflict vary considerably, aggressive family interactions are likely to be perceived as highly threatening by most children. Parent–child aggression obviously poses a direct threat to the health and well-being of children, and interparental aggression is threatening because it may adversely affect one or both of the child's attachment figures. Moreover, since parent–child aggression is more likely to occur in families in which interparental aggression occurs (for a review see Appel and Holden 1998), children may fear that anger or conflict between their parents may spread to them.

If an interaction is viewed as threatening, children seek to understand why it is occurring and how they can respond. Understanding the cause of stressful or aversive events is adaptive because it enables individuals to better anticipate what might happen and determine what kind of response may be effective (Fabes *et al.* 1991; van den Broek 1997). Children's causal attributions are proposed to have important implications for their emotional and behavioral reactions. Children who blame themselves for making their parents angry or causing a conflict between them may feel guilty and sad; they may be motivated to try to do something to 'fix' or resolve whatever led to the conflict or anger. Children may also feel responsible for ending or preventing interparental conflicts even if they do not believe that they are to blame for starting them (O'Brien, Margolin and John 1995). The potential for interparental aggression to elicit child-blaming attributions is increased when the topic of a conflict is child related (Grych 1998; Grych and Fincham 1993), which may be quite common since parenting and child behavior are frequent sources of disagreement among couples. Moreover, parent–child aggression often arises in situations in which parents perceive their children as misbehaving, and so children may be especially likely to see themselves as the cause of parental anger (if not necessarily the abusive behavior) in these situations. Perceiving a parent as the cause of an aggressive interaction is also likely to have implications for the child and family. Blaming a parent for causing harm to other family members may adversely affect the child's relationship with that parent and make the child more likely to ally with the other parent.

The perceived stability and globality of the cause of conflict and aggression may also be important (see Doherty 1981). Inferring that the cause of a conflict is stable requires children to recognize that the same factor has occurred previously and is likely to recur in the future, whereas global attributions involve the inference that the cause has occurred in other contexts. These are sophisticated judgements, and so may be more common in older children. However, consistency in the content or nature of parental disagreements may promote these kinds of attributions. For example, if parents typically argue about money, even young children are likely to attribute conflict to a stable cause. Angry or aggressive interactions that reflect stable causes (e.g., parental incompatibility) are likely to be seen as more threatening to the family than those attributed to unstable causes (e.g., a parent's stressful day at work). Children who see conflict as arising from longstanding, pervasive problems in the marriage may be more likely to fear that conflicts may lead to the disruption of the relationship and family. Such attributions thus are also most likely to threaten children's emotional security (Davies and Cummings 1994).

Children's response to conflict and aggression is also proposed to depend on their coping efficacy, or beliefs that they can change the interaction or reduce their own distress (Grych and Fincham 1990). Children who feel helpless when aggression occurs are likely to experience it as even more stressful, whereas children who believe that they can do something to cope with the situation may experience less stress. However, if children's choice of coping strategy involves intervening directly into a conflict that does not initially involve them, they may put themselves in harm's way or be triangulated in the conflict. Although children have little ability to solve marital problems, there is evidence that they are successful in temporarily stopping parental disagreements (Covell and Miles 1992; Jenkins, Smith and Graham 1989) and thus may believe that they have some control over these interactions. Similarly, children may have the belief that they can exert control over parents who are directing aggression at them, perhaps by avoiding them when they are angry or trying to be particularly 'good' so that parents will not become angry with them. Ultimately, however, children's control pales to that of their parents in these situations, and they are faced with the need to confront stressful situations in which their coping efforts have little effect on reducing the stressor.

Research on the cognitive-contextual framework

The hypotheses outlined in the cognitive-contextual framework have been tested in several studies, some involving children from violent homes. The results of these studies are summarized in the next section.

CONFLICT PROPERTIES AND CHILDREN'S APPRAISALS

The first studies of the cognitive-contextual framework examined the hypothesis that appraisals are shaped by the degree of hostility expressed during the conflict and the content of the conflict. Using an analog procedure in which children listened to audiotaped conflicts between two adults described as parents of a similarly aged child, Grych and Fincham (1993) varied the degree of anger expressed and whether the conflict concerned a child-related issue. The results showed that both conflict properties systematically affected children's reports of their cognitions and emotions. Specifically, greater interparental hostility led to greater negative affect, fears that the disagreement would escalate and that the child would be drawn into the conflict, and self-blame, and child-related conflict led to greater reported shame, self-blame and greater coping efficacy. These findings suggest that verbally aggressive conflict elicits a number of fears from children about how the conflict will progress and that child-related conflicts may be especially upsetting because children feel responsible for them and thus motivated to intervene.

The role of children's attributions was underscored in a study (Grych and Fincham 1993, Study 2) in which the 'parents' on the taped vignettes provided an explanation for the conflict. Given the impact of child-related topics identified in the prior study, this study included only arguments in which the child was the topic of discussion. The explanations were designed either to absolve the child of responsibility or to reinforce the perception that the conflict was his or her fault. When children were told explicitly that the conflict was *not* their fault, their feelings of shame and self-blame decreased significantly and they were less inclined to try to intervene in the conflict. Children who heard explicit confirmation of their role in the conflicts evidenced even more negative affect and threat than children who did not hear an explanation. Thus, children's understanding of the cause of a conflict – in particular, whether they are at fault – appears to be a powerful predictor of how children feel and cope with discordant interactions. Unfortunately, it is not uncommon for parents in discordant homes to make statements that implicitly or explicitly blame the child for causing anger or conflict.

These studies provide empirical support for hypotheses derived from the cognitive-contextual framework, but because they were conducted with fairly well-functioning families reporting low levels of marital discord, their generalizability to families in which aggression has occurred is open to question. To address this limitation, Grych (1998) assessed a sample of children exposed to a wide range of interparental conflict, including children who had witnessed physical aggression between their parents. These 7–12-year-olds listened to the same audiotaped conflicts used in the Grych and Fincham (1993) study and responded to questions regarding their appraisals. Similar results were found for the effects of conflict dimensions on children's appraisals, though the girls in the sample showed stronger relations between conflict intensity and their perceptions of threat than did the boys.

CONTEXTUAL FACTORS AND CHILDREN'S APPRAISALS

Grych (1998) also examined whether a number of variables viewed as contextual factors in the cognitive-contextual framework predicted children's appraisals of the conflict vignettes. Children's exposure to interparental aggression proved to be the most powerful of the predictors: children who had witnessed higher levels of verbal and physical aggression between their parents reported feeling more threatened by the nonaggressive conflict vignettes and described more pessimistic expectations regarding the efficacy of their coping responses. These findings support the 'sensitization effect' described in prior research (see Cummings and Davies 1994) in which children exposed to higher levels of interparental conflict are more reactive to and more distressed by later instances of conflict than children exposed to lower levels of conflict. The basis for the sensitization effect is not well understood, but it may reflect expectations that children develop for the course and consequences of angry or conflictual interactions (Grych and Cardoza-Fernandes forthcoming). Children exposed to high levels of interparental conflict and aggression may come to expect that parental disagreements will escalate, and so respond with higher levels of fear and low levels of coping efficacy. This idea will be discussed further in the section on 'Effects of violence on children's beliefs about relationships' (pp.115–120).

Children's age also consistently predicted their appraisals, with younger children (7–9 years) reporting more threat, negative affect, self-blame and negative coping expectations than older children (10–12 years). As children get older they appear to be less distressed by interparental conflict, better able to anticipate the outcome of such disagreements and more able to cope effectively with stress. In addition, decreasing egocentricity, more sophisticated causal reasoning and greater understanding of parental and marital roles makes them less likely to view parental conflicts as caused by children's behavior (see Grych and Cardoza-Fernandes forthcoming).

Finally, links between children's experiences with aggression in parent–child relationships and their perceptions of interparental conflict were explored. Although parental warmth and parent–child aggression showed few significant correlations with children's appraisals, parent–child aggression interacted with interparental aggression such that children who had experienced both types of family aggression reported the greatest levels of threat and lowest coping efficacy in response to the marital conflict vignettes. Similarly, Hennessy et al. (1994) found that both parent–child and interparental aggression predicted abused children's emotional responses to conflict; in fact, in this sample of maltreated children, parent–child aggression was a stronger predictor than interparental aggression. Thus, the occurrence of aggression in one type of relationship (e.g., parent–child) appears to affect how children perceive interactions in other family relationships. Perhaps children who have been both victims and observers of aggression come to expect that hostility or violence may spread from one relationship to another, and so the occurrence of parental conflict leads them to anticipate that aggression will be directed at them as well.

O'Brien et al. (1991) also provided evidence that children's prior exposure to interparental aggression predicted their responses to taped conflicts. Boys aged 8–11 years of age listened to audiotaped conflicts portraying either interparental or parent–child conflicts and were asked to report what they were thinking or feeling during the conflicts. Boys exposed to physical aggression between their parents reported more physiological arousal than those exposed to verbal aggression, and made more self-distracting comments and comments that reflected involvement in the conflict than children from verbally aggressive or low conflict homes. Children from low conflict homes made more positive evaluations of the conflict and expressed more positive expectations for the outcome of the conflict. These findings suggest that boys exposed to domestic violence not only find conflict more anxiety provoking and threatening but also feel a responsibility to resolve the conflict or protect a parent, which, if unsuccessful, may lead to feelings of guilt or powerlessness.

LINKS BETWEEN APPRAISALS, AFFECT AND COPING

The cognitive-contextual framework hypothesizes that children's appraisals should be linked to their affective and coping responses. Grych and Fincham (1993) examined the associations between these factors and found that children's appraisals of threat and self-blame were associated with greater negative affect, and that children reporting higher self-blame indicated they would be more likely to intervene in the conflict. Grych's (1998) study provided evidence for linkages between particular appraisals. Attributing blame for conflict to fathers was associated with greater perceived threat, whereas attributing blame to mothers was associated with lower threat. Given that fathers in this sample were reported to behave more aggressively toward their spouses and children than were mothers, children's attributions may reflect the perception that conflicts are more likely to escalate because of fathers' behavior. In contrast, children perceived conflicts attributed more to their mothers as less likely to escalate and more amenable to change through children's behavior. This is an intriguing finding that may reflect differences in the course of conflicts initiated by mothers and fathers. An observational study of marital interaction reported that conflicts initiated by wives to address their concerns were more often met with 'stonewalling' or avoidance by husbands than conflicts initiated by men (Heavey, Layne and Christensen

1993). In contrast, when men initiated the conflict, they tended to be more expressive and demanding. If fathers have a tendency to become angry and coercive when disagreements arise, the conflicts that they initiate may become more hostile and aggressive. In contrast, mother-initiated conflicts may be short-lived and less hostile because fathers avoid engaging in them. Further research is needed to clarify how children's perceptions of each parent's behavior relates to their appraisals and behavior.

In sum, studies investigating children's appraisals of conflictual inter-parental interactions support the hypotheses that children's perceptions are influenced both by properties of the conflictual interaction and contextual factors, and that their perceptions in turn are linked to their emotional and coping responses. Perhaps more important for understanding the process by which domestic violence affects children, the cognitive-contextual framework also predicts that children's appraisals have implications for their broader adjustment.

LINKS BETWEEN APPRAISALS AND ADJUSTMENT

Grych and Fincham (1990) proposed that children may develop consistent ways of appraising parental conflicts, and that, over time, repeatedly making certain kinds of appraisals may adversely affect children's adjustment. Specifically, children who repeatedly feel threatened, unable to cope and responsible for causing or failing to stop interparental conflict may develop persistent feelings of anxiety, sadness and diminished self-esteem. In order to test linkages between these more generalized appraisals and child func-tioning, Grych, Seid and Fincham (1992) developed a questionnaire, the Children's Perception of Interparental Conflict (CPIC) scale, to assess children's perceptions of specific dimensions of marital conflict as well as subjective appraisals of conflict.

Psychometric properties of the scale were investigated with a sample of 222 9–12-year-old children and cross-validated on a sample of 144 children of the same age. Factor analyses indicated that the items on the scale could be represented by 3 dimensions, labeled 'Conflict Properties' (consisting of items reflecting the frequency, intensity and resolution of conflict), 'Per-ceived Threat' (threat and coping efficacy) and 'Self-Blame' (attributions and content), each of which demonstrated satisfactory internal consistency (average alpha = 0.85) and test–retest (average r = 0.71) reliability. The validity of the CPIC was demonstrated through significant correlations between the Conflict Properties subscale and parental reports of marital conflict and aggression, and between the Self-Blame and Perceived Threat scales and children's appraisals of specific conflict episodes. More importantly, children's perceptions of the frequency, intensity and resolution of conflict were shown to be better predictors of their adjustment (as assessed by parents, teachers, peers and the children themselves) than were parental reports of conflict (Grych *et al.* 1992).

Several additional studies have found that children's appraisals significantly predict their adjustment, both in samples reporting relatively low levels of interparental aggression (e.g., Cummings, Davies and Simpson 1994) and in violent families (e.g., Grych *et al.* forthcoming). However, correlations between these constructs do not indicate *how* appraisals may be related to adjustment problems. In order for the construct of appraisal to be useful for understanding how exposure to domestic violence affects children's development and informing clinical intervention, the processes linking appraisals and adjustment must be described and tested. Grych *et al.* (forthcoming) elaborated on the cognitive-contextual framework by proposing that appraisals of threat and self-blame mediate the effects of interparental conflict and aggression on children's internalizing problems. That is, that problems with anxiety and depression occur when children perceive these interactions as highly threatening and/or feel responsible for causing or failing to stop them.

This mediational hypothesis was tested in two large samples of 10–14-year-old children, one drawn from the community (n = 317) and the other from battered women's shelters (n = 145). Results were largely consistent across the samples. For boys in both groups and girls in the shelter sample, perceived threat and self-blame each independently mediated the association between their exposure to destructive conflict and internalizing problems. For girls in the community sample, only perceived threat was a significant mediator. Although appraisals were correlated with externalizing problems as well, they did not mediate their association with conflict. Research conducted with Australian samples (Dadds *et al.* 1999) and Canadian samples (Kerig 1998a) similarly have found that threat and self-blame mediate the association between conflict and internalizing, but not externalizing problems. However, in another study Kerig (1998b) failed to find support for mediation in a sample of Canadian children drawn from the community.

These findings indicate that the effect of conflict on internalizing problems may depend on how children perceive and interpret the conflict, whereas externalizing problems appear to be attributable to other processes, such as modeling or disruptions in parent–child relationships. However, three limitations of these studies for understanding the effects of domestic violence must be noted. First, all of these studies were cross-sectional and consequently do not show that appraisals are *causally* related to internalizing problems. Longitudinal research is needed to explore how the relations between conflict, appraisals and adjustment may develop over time. Second, even though some of the studies included children from violent families, the appraisals assessed were of interparental conflict, not aggressive or violent interactions. It is possible that children's appraisals of violent conflict may differ, and their appraisals of interactions in which they are directly involved may differ from those in which they are observers. Studies directly comparing children's responses to interparental and parent–child interactions are needed to address this question. Finally, research on appraisals has focused primarily on 8–14-year-old children, and whether these processes apply to older and younger children is not known. There is some evidence that cognitive variables become stronger predictors of child adjustment as children get older (Jouriles *et al.* 1999; Nolen-Hoeksema, Girgus and Seligman 1992; Turner and Cole 1994), suggesting that there may be developmental changes in the role that appraisals play in relation to children's adjustment.

Clinical implications

Research on appraisals of interparental conflict supports the view that children's perceptions of stressful events may mediate the impact of those events. Consequently, attention to how children perceive and interpret conflict and aggression in the family may be useful for working clinically with children from violent homes. Of course, the most important intervention when aggression occurs in a family is to try to stop it so that children are no longer exposed to this distressing and sometimes traumatic experience. However, if it is not possible to reduce children's exposure to stress, helping them to cope more effectively is an important alternative approach. The links described above between children's appraisals, emotions, coping responses and adjustment suggest a number of ways that the impact of aggressive interactions may be reduced.

As a first step, assessing children's perceptions of aggressive and conflictual family interactions will provide a sense of whether children's appraisals are exacerbating or reducing the stressfulness of these interactions.

Strategies used in research to elicit children's thoughts and feelings about conflict can be applied to clinical settings. For example, O'Brien *et al.* (1997) used a semistructured interview to assess 8–13-year-old children's responses to verbally and physically aggressive arguments between their parents, adding probes as needed to obtain a thorough description of what children thought, felt and did during the arguments. For younger children with less well-developed verbal abilities, narrative techniques may provide insight into children's thought processes. Story-telling tasks using dolls and other props have proven to be effective for eliciting reliable information about children's experiences in the family in empirical studies, and may be similarly useful here (see Bretherton, Ridgeway and Cassidy 1990). In a clinical setting, they provide a way for children to talk about their experiences and for clinicians to develop hypotheses about how they may be perceiving and understanding events in their own families.

The cognitive-contextual framework suggests that the impact of conflict and aggression can be reduced by decreasing children's perceptions of the threat posed by an interaction, enhancing their coping efficacy, or changing their attributions. Children living in violent families would not be well served by ignoring or minimizing signs of danger, but it may be possible to decrease children's perception of threat when conflictual but nonviolent interactions occur. Helping children to focus on situational cues rather than their fears and expectations may help them to discriminate between 'garden variety' and genuinely threatening interactions, and consequently may reduce their sensitivity to anger and conflict. At times, this may involve making automatic processes conscious. Cognitive processing of events can become so well learned that individuals are not aware that it is occurring (see Bargh and Chartrand 1999; Lazarus 1991). Consequently, they operate off assumptions and beliefs, ignoring situational information that is inconsistent with these beliefs. Helping children to detect cues that indicate whether an interaction is likely to escalate into aggression will fine-tune their ability to perceive threat in the family accurately.

Another way to reduce the threat posed by conflictual interactions is to increase children's coping efficacy. Children who feel helpless and unable to cope are likely to experience these events as more threatening than children who believe that they can do something to reduce the stress they experience. In general, increasing children's coping repertoire is likely to improve their belief that they can cope effectively. Interparental conflict presents a difficult situation for children to cope with. Although children appear motivated to intervene directly in interparental conflicts in order to stop them and at times may be successful in doing so, ultimately their involvement in marital problems is likely to be maladaptive both for them and their family (Emery 1982). In addition to placing the children at risk for becoming a victim of verbal or physical aggression, such problem-focused strategies cross the boundary of the marital relationship and may promote the development of cross-generational alliances and triangulation of the child (see Minuchin 1974). It may be safer and more effective to help children develop emotion-focused coping strategies (Compas 1987), or ways to regulate their emotional distress without becoming involved in the conflict directly. Seeking support from another family member, distraction by focusing on another activity and thinking positive thoughts may all help children feel better when conflict occurs, although there is evidence that children do not regularly use emotion-focused coping strategies until they near adolescence (Compas, Malcarne and Fondacaro 1988). Younger children still may be able to learn concrete behaviors that could reduce their distress without intervening in the conflict. Developing a plan for keeping themselves safe when aggression occurs in the family may reduce feelings of helplessness as well as improve the likelihood that they will avoid becoming the victim of violence themselves.

Finally, children's efforts to understand the cause of aggressive inter-actions presents a potential target for intervention. Helping children to recognize that they are not responsible for causing parental aggression or for preventing it from occurring is likely to reduce the guilt, anxiety and sadness that children experience when they blame themselves for conflict. Since self-blame is linked to the motivation to intervene (Grych and Fincham 1993), changing children's attributions may also affect their coping behav-ior. Understanding why aggression occurs may also help children to avoid inappropriately blaming one parent and thereby affect the nature of their relationships with their parents.

Perhaps the most important effect that clinicians can have on children's understanding of the causes of family aggression is to help parents discuss the meaning of these interactions with their children. Although the emphasis in this section has been on children's immediate appraisals, children may also think about conflict or aggression after it ends, and this later processing also shapes its meaning for them. Explanations given for the cause of conflicts alter children's emotional and cognitive responses (Grych and Fincham 1993) and may have a similar effect on their long-term understanding of how conflicts are managed in relationships. Teaching parents how to talk with their children after an aggressive interaction may help them understand their role in it and its potential consequences for the child and family. It may be difficult to change the tendency of some parents to perceive their children as the cause of marital problems, or, especially, parent–child aggression, but because parents are present when the interactions occur they have the best opportunity to help children make sense of these upsetting interactions.

As noted above, children's age influences how they perceive and respond to hostility and aggression; consequently clinicians need to be sensitive to their level of cognitive development. Children aged from 7 to 9 years appear to be more likely to blame themselves for conflict and to feel threatened and unable to cope effectively than older children, but little is known about how children younger than the age of 7 or 8 perceive these kinds of interactions. Although even infants and toddlers are sensitive to displays of anger and appear to be distressed when interparental conflict occurs, young children's thinking is likely to be fairly concrete and egocentric, focusing more on the immediate consequences of the interaction for their well-being and less on more long-term implications for the marriage or family (see Grych and Cardoza- Fernandes forthcoming). It is still useful to assess whether cognitive distortions, such as self-blame, may be exacerbating the stress caused by aggressive interactions, but since their ability to reflect on their own thinking processes is limited, intervention is likely to focus primarily on helping them to develop effective ways for coping with conflict.

Effects of violence on children's beliefs about relationships

In addition to providing a mechanism for understanding how family aggression may lead to adjustment problems, social cognitive processes also may shed light on long-term implications of domestic violence for children's functioning in interpersonal relationships. Several writers have proposed that interparental and parent–child aggression affect the development of children's mental representations of relationships (Crittendon and Ainsworth 1989; Davies and Cummings 1994; Graham-Berman 1998; Grych 1998; O'Brien and Chin 1998; Rossman 1998). These representations, in turn, are proposed to shape children's perceptions and behavior in later interpersonal interactions. Although little empirical research has been conducted to investigate these hypotheses, they represent a promising approach to understanding how experiences with family aggression may have subtle but pervasive effects on children's development.

The idea that children form mental representations of interpersonal interactions that guide later behavior has its roots in attachment and object relations theories (see Bretherton *et al.* 1990; Graham-Berman 1998). For example, Bowlby (1973) proposed that interactions between children and their caregivers are stored in memory as 'working models', which consist of beliefs and expectations about the self, others and relationships. Working models lead individuals to perceive and respond to events in ways that are consistent with these beliefs. For example, children who believe that caregivers neglect their signs of distress are unlikely to seek nurturance if they are sick or injured. Empirical research indicates that children who have suffered abuse at the hands of their parents tend to develop insecure or disorganized attachment relationships (Carlson *et al.* 1989), which in turn are associated with negative long-term consequences for children's social and emotional development, such as increased aggressiveness and poor peer relationships (e.g., Lyons-Ruth, Alpern and Repacholi 1993).

Social and cognitive research on schemas and scripts similarly proposes that individuals develop an organized set of beliefs, expectations and emotions about people, situations and events based on their experiences with them (for reviews see Baldwin 1992; Brewer and Nakamura 1984). These knowledge structures function to guide how children perceive, interpret and respond when they encounter new instances of the subject. Information consistent with the working model or schema tends to be attended to and remembered, and ambiguous or incomplete information interpreted in light of preexisting knowledge and beliefs. Given that social information often is incomplete, ambiguous or vague, schemas provide a way to understand quickly and efficiently and to respond in complex circumstances. However, they can be maladaptive when they lead to misinterpretation or discounting of situational information or to a rigid way of perceiving or responding in particular situations.

Constructs like working models and schemas are useful for understanding the effects of family violence because they suggest that these experiences influence what children come to expect in relationships and how they interact with others. When caregivers are hostile, coercive or physically aggressive toward each other or their children, it may lead children to develop general beliefs about people or relationships, such as that relationships can be dangerous (Rossman 1998) or that attempts to dominate and control others are effective and justifiable (Graham-Berman 1998). Children's beliefs about gender roles may also be influenced by observation of how their mother and father treat each other (Graham-Berman 1998). Because aggression often arises in situations where conflict or anger occurs, schemas may be formed that include more specific expectations about what happens when parents disagree or the child misbehaves. Schemas might also include emotions associated with these situations (see Fiske and Pavelchak 1987b) and ideas about how the individual can respond (Rossman 1998). For example, Rossman (1998) notes that children who are ineffective in getting their needs met by their parents in these situations

> may learn coping strategies of avoidance or aggression and strategies that do not depend on other people. If the cues to caretaker aggressive interactions or the child's ability to avoid or stop them are variable, children may also learn that their safety is unpredictable, that contingencies do not exist between their behavior and its outcome, and that one needs to be continually prepared to take action. (Rossman 1998, p.225)

Children's representations of anger and conflict are likely to be accessed when children encounter discord in later interactions, both in and outside of the family. These representations, in conjunction with situational information, would then be expected to guide children's attention, interpretation and behavior in the situation. The most direct effects of schemas are expected to be seen in children's responses to interparental and parent–child aggression, but may generalize to other relationships as well.

Schemas and children's responses to family aggression

Theorizing about the effects of interparental and parent–child aggression on children's representations of relationships is just beginning, and to date there have been few empirical investigations of the content or function of the proposed schema. However, a number of studies provide evidence suggesting that children may develop schemas for interparental conflict. Research on the sensitization effect showing that children's prior exposure to interparental aggression predicts their cognitive and emotional responses to new episodes of conflict is consistent with the prediction that children's prior experiences shape their perceptions of new instances of conflict (Grych 1998; O'Brien et al. 1991). These studies also provide evidence that experiences in the parent–child relationship can affect how children respond to conflict between parents (Grych 1998; Hennessy et al. 1994). Similarly, Graham-Berman (1996) found that children exposed to family violence (aged 6–12) reported more worries about the safety of their mothers and sisters, and about their father causing harm, than children living in less violent families. However, these studies did not attempt to assess children's schemas directly, and therefore do not provide clear evidence that it is children's beliefs and expectations that predict their responses to new conflict. Although children exposed to more conflict and aggression would be expected to develop schemas that reflect greater threat and fear, assessing children's exposure to conflict is not equivalent to assessing their schema.

Two studies have assessed children's beliefs about conflict separate from their experiences with family aggression. First, O'Brien and Chin (1998) assessed the content of children's schema with an incidental recall task. They had children fill out questionnaires about conflict and listen to audiotaped disagreements between two adults in an effort to 'activate' children's schema for interparental conflict. They then presented the children with a list of words that were either aggressive (e.g., 'hit') or nonaggressive (e.g., 'discuss') and asked them to recall which of the words they had either read on the questionnaires or heard on the tape. The number of previously heard aggressive words that were correctly recalled and the number of 'new' aggressive words that were incorrectly recognized served as an index of the content of their schema. O'Brien and Chin (1998) found that children exposed to higher levels of interparental conflict reported more aggressive words than children exposed to low levels of conflict, lending support for the notion that children's experiences guide their encoding and recall of new information and lead to schema-consistent cognitive processing (see also Burks et al. 1999; Rudolph, Hammen and Burge 1995).

Second, Davies and Cummings (1998) took a different approach to assessing children's representations of interparental conflict. They played children an audiotaped conflict between two adults and asked them a set of questions designed to assess children's thoughts about the conflict and its implications for family relationships. Specifically, they assessed children's expectancies for the course of conflict, its long-term consequences for the marriage and its impact on how parents treat the child. Children's responses were coded and combined to form an overall index of the emotional security of their representations. Davies and Cummings (1998) found that children exposed to higher levels of marital conflict had more negative or less secure representations, and that these representations mediated the association between their exposure to conflict and the expression of internalizing problems.

Thus, the limited empirical evidence that exists suggests that children develop schemas for conflictual or aggressive interparental interactions and that these schemas are correlated with their exposure to conflict as well as their adjustment. A second prediction that flows from the conflict schema hypothesis is that experiences with interparental conflict may generalize to other interpersonal contexts.

Schemas and children's behavior in other relationships

Experiences in the family may lead to the development of beliefs about relationships that influence children's functioning in relationships outside of the family. For example, these schemas may affect how children respond to anger or conflict in peer relationships. Perhaps the most salient extra-familial context, because of its similarity to marriage, is a dating relationship. Children who develop beliefs about how to manage discord and disagreements by watching their parents may apply these ideas to relationships with their own romantic partners. Those who have witnessed or directly experienced aggression in the family may come to expect aggression to occur in their own relationships, and perhaps view aggression as effective in gaining compliance from or controlling others. Children's exposure to interparental aggression has been linked to violence in courtship and marital relationships (e.g., Riggs and O'Leary 1996) and schematic functioning would provide one explanation for this association. Alternatively, these children may become hypervigilant to signs of anger and discord, and try to avoid conflict in their relationships.

However, a number of other factors will affect how influential these schemas may be in other contexts. Individuals' perceptions and behavior in a situation is a function of both past experiences and current circumstances, and situational factors are likely to play an important role in determining whether violence occurs in a particular context. Children's beliefs about relationships will also be shaped by other kinds of experiences, including their own relationships with friends and dating partners, knowledge of friends' relationships and images garnered from popular media (Anderson 1993). To the extent that these other experiences are inconsistent with family experiences, exposure to family aggression is likely to have less influence over children's later behavior.

Clinical implications

The potential impact of domestic violence on children's schemas or working models has important implications for the treatment of children from violent homes and the prevention of the intergenerational transmission of violence. Clinically, it may not be enough to help children learn to cope more effectively when conflict and aggression occur; it may be as important to address their fundamental beliefs about relationships. When working with children exposed to family violence, clinicians may need to address directly the content of children's schemas about aggression and violence in order to prevent maladaptive beliefs and expectations from continuing to affect their relationships. Providing alternative models of how to manage anger and conflict and directly challenging beliefs about aggression may help children become aware of, and change their ideas about, the place of aggression in close relationships.

Many of the same approaches discussed earlier may be effective for eliciting children's general beliefs about violence and relationships. In fact, since children's appraisals are guided in part by these knowledge structures, they provide an avenue for assessing and discussing how exposure to domestic violence has shaped children's view of what is normal or acceptable in relationships. If children do express problematic beliefs about inter-personal conflict and aggression, clinicians can directly address these cog-nitions in order to change how children perceive and respond to anger and conflict both in and outside of the family. For young children, this may involve the use of stories or play in which characters treat each other with respect and care when discord arises. Older children will be able to think more abstractly and hypothetically about their values and beliefs regarding interpersonal relationships and to discuss their experiences more directly.

The difficulty in changing schemas is that inconsistent information tends to be filtered out and not remembered. For new and different ideas to take root, it is important to expose children repeatedly to different models and alternative ways of handling the disagreements and frustrations that inevi-tably occur in relationships. With older children and adolescents, who are likely to have more ingrained ways of thinking about relationships, it may also be necessary to help them recognize what their beliefs are and how they came about, and to examine how they affect their present relationships, whether they are with the clinician or (especially) other people. These kinds of interventions may not immediately impact children's adjustment, but may well have a longer-term, preventive effect on the use of coercion, control and violence in dating and marital relationships.

Future directions

This chapter has focused on two social cognitive constructs – appraisals and schema – that may prove useful for understanding children's subjective experience of domestic violence. Most of the work on these constructs has focused on conflictual but nonviolent marital interactions, and there is a clear need to examine empirically how well they explain children's responses to violent family interactions, particularly those in which they are a victim rather than observer. In addition, it is important to consider other processes that may be important for understanding the effects of domestic violence. For example, exposure to family aggression may lead to chronic fear and vigilance, and this heightened state of arousal may have adverse consequences for children's emotional, cognitive and behavioral development (McCloskey *et al.* 1995). Rossman (1998) also argued that repeated exposure to traumatic events such as family violence could affect children's perceptual and cognitive processing in several ways, including reducing the flexibility of schematic functioning, leading to distortions in relationship schema, and producing a 'leveling' (vs 'sharpening') cognitive style in which new information is assimilated into preexisting schema slowly and inaccurately. Investigation of these ideas will provide a more complete picture of the ways in which social cognitive processes affect and are affected by aggression in the family.

Moreover, it is important to place these processes in the larger context of family functioning to try to understand how other aspects of family life (e.g., supportive parent–child relationships) may influence children's experiences of aggression and violence. Although acts of violence are highly salient and aversive, they are relatively rare compared to nonviolent interactions that involve controlling or conflictual interactions. The cognitive-contextual framework suggests that experiencing violence will affect how children interpret and respond to nonviolent interactions, and nonviolent interactions in turn will affect children's responses to violence. Integrating these ideas with other models positing direct and indirect effects of conflict and aggression on child development will provide a more comprehensive understanding of how domestic violence affects children.

References

Anderson, P.A. (1993) 'Cognitive schemata in personal relationships.' In S. Duck (ed) *Individuals in Relationships.* Newbury Park, CA: Sage.

Appel, A.E. and Holden, G.W. (1998) 'The co-occurrence of spouse and physical child abuse: a review and reappraisal.' *Journal of Family Psychology 12,* 578–599.

Baldwin, M.W. (1992) 'Relational schemas and the processing of social information.' *Psychological Bulletin 112,* 461–484.

Bargh, J.A. and Chartrand, T.L. (1999) 'The unbearable automaticity of being.' *American Psychologist 54,* 462–479.

Bowlby, J. (1973) *Attachment and Loss. Volume 2: Separation.* New York: Basic Books.

Bretherton, I., Ridgeway, D. and Cassidy, J. (1990) 'Assessing internal working models of the attachment relationship.' In M.T. Greenberg, D. Cicchetti and E.M. Cummings (eds) *Attachment in the Preschool Years.* Chicago: University of Chicago Press.

Brewer, W.F. and Nakamura, G.V. (1984) 'The nature and function of schemas.' In R.S. Wyer and T.K. Srull (eds) *Handbook of Social Cognition.* Hillsdale, NJ: Erlbaum.

Burks, V.S., Dodge, K.A., Price, J.M. and Laird, R.D. (1999) 'Internal representational models of peers implications for the development of problematic behavior.' *Developmental Psychology 35,* 802–810.

Campos, J.J., Campos, R.G. and Barrett, K.C. (1989) 'Emergent themes in the study of emotional development and emotion regulation.' *Developmental Psychology 25,* 394–402.

Carlson, V., Cicchetti, D., Barnett, D. and Braunwald, K. (1989) 'Finding order in disorganization: lessons from research on maltreated infants' attachment to their caregivers.' In D. Cicchetti and V. Carlson (eds) *Child Maltreatment: Theory and Research on the Causes and Consequences of Child Abuse and Neglect.* Cambridge: Cambridge University Press.

Compas, B.E. (1987) 'Coping with stress during childhood and adolescence.' *Psychological Bulletin 101,* 393–403.

Compas, B.E., Malcarne, V.L. and Fondacaro, K.M. (1988) 'Coping with stressful events in older children and adolescents.' *Journal of Consulting and Clinical Psychology 56,* 405–411.

Corell, K. and Miles, B. (1992) 'Children's beliefs about strategies to reduce parental anger.' *Child Development 63,* 381–390.

Crittendon, P.M. and Ainsworth, M.D.S. (1989) 'Child maltreatment and attachment theory.' In D. Cicchetti and V. Carlson (eds) *Child Maltreatment: Theory and Research on the Causes and Consequences of Child Abuse and Neglect.* Cambridge: Cambridge University Press.

Crockenberg, S. and Forgays, D.K. (1996) 'The role of emotion in children's understanding and emotional reactions to marital conflict.' *Merrill-Palmer Quarterly 42,* 22–48.

Cummings, E.M. (1998) 'Children exposed to marital conflict and violence: conceptual and theoretical directions.' In G.W. Holden, R. Geffner and E.N. Jouriles (eds) *Children Exposed to Marital Violence: Theory, Research, and Applied Issues*. Washington DC: American Psychological Association.

Cummings, E.M. and Davies, P.T. (1994) *Children and Marital Conflict*. New York: Guilford.

Cummings, E.M., Davies, P.T. and Simpson, K.S. (1994) 'Marital conflict, gender, and children's appraisals and coping efficacy as mediators of child adjustment.' *Journal of Family Psychology 8*, 141–149.

Dadds, M.R., Atkinson, E., Turner, C., Blums, G.J. and Lendich, B. (1999) 'Family conflict and child adjustment: evidence for a cognitive-contextual model of intergenerational transmission.' *Journal of Family Psychology 13*, 194–208.

Davies, P.T. and Cummings, E.M. (1994) 'Marital conflict and child adjustment: an emotional security hypothesis.' *Psychological Bulletin 116*, 387–411.

Davies, P.T. and Cummings, E.M. (1998) 'Exploring children's emotional security as a mediator of the link between marital relations and child adjustment.' *Child Development 69*, 124–139.

Doherty, W.J. (1981) 'Cognitive processes in intimate conflict: I. Extending attribution theory.' *American Journal of Family Therapy 9*, 3–13.

Emery, R.E. (1982) 'Interparental conflict and the children of discord and divorce.' *Psychological Bulletin 92*, 310–330.

Fabes, R.A., Eisenberg, N., Nyman, M. and Michealieu, Q. (1991) 'Young children's appraisals of others' spontaneous emotional reactions.' *Developmental Psychology 27*, 858–866.

Fiske, S.T. and Pavelchak, M.A. (1986) 'Category-based vs. piecemeal-based affective responses: Developments in schema-triggered affect.' In R.M. Sorrentino and E.T. Higgins (eds) *Handbook of Motivation and Cognition*. New York: Guilford Press.

Garmezy, N. (1983) 'Stressors of childhood.' In N. Garmezy and M. Rutter (eds) *Stress, Coping, and Development in Children*. New York: McGraw-Hill.

Graham-Berman, S.A. (1996) 'Family worries: The assessment of interpersonal anxiety in children from violent and nonviolent families.' *Journal of Clinical Psychology 25*, 280–287.

Graham-Berman, S.A. (1998) 'The impact of woman abuse on children's social development: research and theoretical perspectives.' In G.W. Holden, R. Geffner and E.N. Jouriles (eds) *Children Exposed to Marital Violence*. Washington DC: American Psychological Association.

Grych, J.H. (1998) 'Children's appraisals of interparental conflict: situational and contextual influences.' *Journal of Family Psychology 12*, 437–453.

Grych, J.H. and Cardoza-Fernandes, S. (in press) 'Understanding the impact of interparental conflict on children: the role of social cognitive processes.' In J. Grych and F. Fincham (eds) *Interparental Conflict and Child Development: Theory, Research and Applications*. Cambridge: Cambridge University Press.

Grych, J.H. and Fincham, F.D. (1990) 'Marital conflict and children's adjustment: a cognitive-contextual framework.' *Psychological Bulletin 108*, 267–290.

Grych, J.H. and Fincham, F.D. (1993) 'Children's appraisals of marital conflict: initial investigations of the cognitive-contextual framework.' *Child Development 64*, 215–230.

Grych, J.H., Seid, M. and Fincham, F.D. (1992) 'Assessing marital conflict from the child's perspective.' *Child Development 63*, 558–572.

Grych, J.H., Fincham, F.D., Jouriles, E.N. and McDonald, R. (in press) 'Interparental conflict and child adjustment: testing the mediational role of appraisals in the cognitive-contextual framework.' *Child Development.*

Grych, J.H., Jouriles, E.N., Swank, P.R., McDonald, R. and Norwood, W.D. (2000) 'Patterns of adjustment among children of battered women.' *Journal of Consulting and Clinical Psychology, 68*, 84–94.

Heavey, C.L., Layne, C. and Christensen, A. (1993) 'Gender and conflict structure: a replication and extension.' *Journal of Consulting and Clinical Psychology 61*, 16–27.

Hennessy, K.D., Rabideau, G.J., Cicchetti, D. and Cummings, E.M. (1994) 'Responses of physically abused and nonabused children to different forms of interadult anger.' *Child Development 65*, 815–828.

Jenkins, J.M., Smith, M.A. and Graham, P.J. (1989) 'Coping with parental quarrels.' *Journal of the American Academy of Child and Adolescent Psychiatry 28*, 182–189.

Jouriles, E.N., Mehta, P., McDonald, R. and Francis, D.J. (1997) 'Psychometric properties of family members' reports of parental physical aggression toward clinic-referred children.' *Journal of Consulting and Clinical Psychology 65*, 309–318.

Jouriles, E.N., Spiller, L.C., Stephens, N., McDonald, R. and Swank, P. (1999) 'Variability in adjustment of children of battered women: the role of child appraisals of interparent conflict.' *Cognitive Therapy and Research.*

Kerig, P.K. (1998a) 'Moderators and mediators of the effects of interparental conflict on children's adjustment.' *Journal of Abnormal Child Psychology 26*, 199–212.

Kerig, P.K. (1998b) 'Gender and appraisals as mediators of adjustment in children exposed to interparental violence.' *Journal of Family Violence 15*, 345–363.

Lazarus, R.S. (1991) 'Cognition and motivation in emotion.' *American Psychologist 46*, 352–367.

Lyons-Ruth, K., Alpern, L. and Repacholi, B. (1993) 'Disorganized infant attachment classification and maternal psychosocial problems as predictors of hostile-aggressive behavior in the preschool classroom.' *Child Development 64*, 572–585.

McCloskey, L.A., Figueredo, A.J. and Koss, M.P. (1995) 'The effects of systemic family violence on children's mental health.' *Child Development 66*, 1239–1261.

Minuchin, S. (1974) *Families and Family Therapy.* Cambridge, MA: Harvard University Press.

Nolen-hoeksema, S., Girgus, J.A. and Seligman, M.E.P. (1992) 'Predictors and consequences of childhood depressive symptoms: A 5-year longitudinal study.' *Journal of Abnormal Psychology 101,* 405–422.

O'Brien, M. and Chin, C. (1998) 'The relationship between children's reported exposure to interparental conflict and memory biases in the recognition of aggressive and constructive conflict words.' *Personality and Social Psychology Bulletin 6,* 647–656.

O'Brien, M., Margolin, G., John, R.S. and Krueger, L. (1991) 'Mothers' and sons' cognitive and emotional reactions to simulated marital and family conflict.' *Journal of Consulting and Clinical Psychology 59,* 692–703.

O'Brien, M., Margolin, G. and John, R.S. (1995) 'Relations among marital conflict, child coping, and child adjustment.' *Journal of Clinical Child Psychology 24,* 346–361.

O'Brien, M., Bahadur, M.A., Gee, C., Balto, K. and Erber, S. (1997) 'Child exposure to marital conflict and child coping responses as predictors of child adjustment.' *Cognitive Therapy and Research 21,* 39–59.

Riggs, D.S. and O'Leary, K.D. (1996) 'Aggression between heterosexual dating partners: An examination of a causal model of courtship aggression.' *Journal of Interpersonal Violence 11,* 519–540.

Rossman, B.B.R. (1998) 'Descartes' error and posttraumatic stress disorder: cognition and emotion in children who are exposed to parental violence.' In G.W. Holden, R. Geffner and E.N. Jouriles (eds) *Children Exposed to Marital Violence.* Washington DC: American Psychological Association.

Rudolph, K.D., Hammen, C. and Burge, D. (1995) 'Cognitive representations of self-family and peers in school-aged children: links with social competence and sociometric status.' *Child Development 66,* 1385–1402.

Rutter, M. (1983) 'Stress, coping, and development: some issues and some questions.' In N. Garmezy and M. Rutter (eds) *Stress, Coping, and Development in Children.* New York: McGraw-Hill.

Sternberg, K.J., Lamb, M.E., Greenbaum, C., Cicchetti, D., Dawud, S., Cortes, R.M., Krispin, O. and Lorey, F. (1993) 'Effects of domestic violence on children's behavior problems and depression.' *Developmental Psychology 29,* 44–52.

Turner, D.S. and Cole, D.A. (1994) 'Developmental differences in cognitive diatheses for child depression.' *Journal of Abnormal Child Psychiatry 22,* 15–32.

van den Broek, P. (1997) 'Discovering the cement of the universe: the development of event comprehension from childhood to adulthood.' In P. van den Broek, P.J. Bauer and T. Bourg (eds) *Developmental Spans in Event Comprehension and Representation.* Mahweh, NJ: Erlbaum.

CHAPTER 6

The Community Advocacy Project
A Model for Effectively Advocating for Women with Abusive Partners

Cris M. Sullivan

Interventions designed to alleviate pressing social problems are predicated on beliefs and theoretical positions regarding the root of the social problem in question. For example, whether one believes unemployment is due to social conditions or individual shortcomings guides whether one argues for additional and better jobs or for job training programs. Similarly, in the area of intimate male violence against women,[1] interventions have included psychological counseling for victims (Gauthier and Levendosky 1996; Whipple 1985), group therapy or behavioral treatment for batterers (Edleson and Syers 1991; Edleson and Tolman 1994), domestic violence shelter programs (Bowker and Maurer 1985; Schechter 1982) and the creation of legal protections for survivors (Ferraro 1993; Lewis *et al.* 1997), to name just a few. Each intervention is based on theoretical suppositions regarding the causes and repercussions of intimate male violence against women.

Not unlike other interventions, the Community Advocacy Project, developed at Michigan State University,[2] was grounded in a number of assumptions. An exhaustive review of the scholarly literature coupled with numerous conversations with survivors of intimate male violence had led me to the following conclusions:

- Intimate male violence against women is too widespread to be attributed to intrapsychic dysfunction.

- Intimate male violence against women is tolerated, if not condoned, by many segments of the community, including the criminal justice system.

- Women with abusive partners are by-and-large active helpseekers who go to great lengths to protect themselves and their children.

- The community response to domestic violence is a critical factor in whether a woman will be victimized (and revictimized) by an intimate partner or ex-partner.

A brief review of the literature

Intimate male violence against women is severe and widespread (Browne and Williams 1993; Straus and Gelles 1986), often resulting in injuries (Berrios and Grady 1991; Sullivan 1991b), long-term health problems (Alpert 1995; Eby *et al.* 1995; Sutherland, Bybee and Sullivan 1998), psychological distress (Campbell, Sullivan and Davidson 1995; Kemp *et al.* 1995; Koss 1990) and sometimes even death (Browne 1987; Browne and Williams 1993; Jurik and Winn 1990).

Battering cuts across lines of ethnicity, class, religion and age, and occurs in between 2 million and 4 million relationships each year in the USA alone (Browne and Williams 1993; Straus and Gelles 1986). In spite of the pervasiveness of this social problem, common perception persists that domestic violence must be a result of 'dysfunctional relationships'. Abusers must be abusive alcoholics and/or criminally insane, and victims must be masochistic and/or suffer from such low self-esteem that they cannot protect themselves or their children. Empirical evidence, however, suggests that batterers come from all walks of life and use violence as a means of maintaining power and control within their relationships (Edleson, Eisikovits and Guttman 1985). Likewise, women who are battered have not been found to have predisposing characteristics suggesting they would tolerate abuse; rather, most women are surprised when abuse occurs in their relationships, and they go to great lengths to protect themselves and their children (Henderson 1990; Hilton 1992; Hoff 1990). Unfortunately, numerous structural barriers exist that impede women's abilities to end the violence once it starts.

Many women with abusive partners turn to the criminal justice system for protection from their assailants. Although system response continues to improve arrest for domestic violence is still unlikely to occur (Hirschel *et al.* 1992), and those arrested are unlikely to be prosecuted or to receive sanctions greater than probation (Buzawa and Buzawa 1990). Other systems that have historically failed to detect domestic abuse and to protect survivors include the health care system (Dobash, Dobash and Cavanagh 1985;

McFarlane, Parker and Soeken 1995), the social service system (Dobash *et al.* 1985) and religious institutions (Alsdurf 1985; Thompson 1989).

In spite of numerous community obstacles and fear of worse violence, many women employ a variety of strategies to protect themselves and their children. They turn to family and friends (Donato and Bowker 1984; Mitchell and Hodson 1983) as well as to formal sources of support (Gondolf 1988; Sullivan 1991a; Wauchope 1988). These efforts are often in vain, as many communities lack a collaborative, effective response to domestic violence (Sullivan 1997).

Development of the current intervention

The Community Advocacy Project was predicated on the belief that battered women should not be expected to shoulder the burden of protecting themselves and their children alone. A review of the literature suggested that access to community resources might help women escape intimate violence and improve their overall quality of life. Community-based domestic violence programs have used paraprofessional advocates to assist women in obtaining resources for years. Based in large part on these earlier efforts, and in collaboration with survivors and advocates, I created the Community Advocacy Project.

The intervention was designed as a 'family-centered model', focusing on the strengths and unmet needs of clients as opposed to client 'deficits' (Dunst, Johanson and Trivette 1991; Sullivan and Bybee 1999). The family-centered model requires that families guide the services they receive, and that clients' natural support networks are involved in the advocacy process. The efficacy of the family-centered model and the positive implications for consumers served from a family-centered paradigm have been established across different service domains (Marcenko and Smith 1992; Scannapieco 1994; Trivette, Dunst and Hamby 1996; Weiss and Jacobs 1988; Weissbourd and Kagan 1989).

Although some family-centered interventions employ professionals to work with families, paraprofessional volunteers have been found to be highly successful change agents for numerous populations (Davidson *et al.* 1987; Durlak 1981). The use of paraprofessionals increases the generalizability of the intervention, as it is often easier and less costly for communities to locate, train and supervise them. Therefore, the decision was made to train undergraduate college students to serve as the paraprofessional advocates.

The intervention

Training of advocates

Training and supervision of advocates was provided through a two-semester undergraduate university course. Small groups of students (average eleven per semester) received ten weeks of manualized training from two instructors. Each week students mastered new material, including

- theories of domestic violence
- barriers faced by women with abusive partners
- assessing unmet needs
- implementing the advocacy intervention
- monitoring and adjusting the intervention
- terminating the intervention.

Additional topics covered during training were empathy and active listening, developing safety plans, understanding diversity and oppression and maintaining confidentiality. A training manual was created specifically for this course and describes each unit in more detail (Sullivan, Sutherland and Allen 1998).

Supervision of advocates

After students successfully completed training, they were assigned to work one-on-one with a woman who had recently left a domestic violence shelter program. Each advocate worked with only one woman, spending four to six hours per week over a period of ten weeks together. During this time, advocates continued to meet once a week in groups of five or six students and two supervisors. During weekly supervision, advocates reported on their goals for the week, the activities they engaged in to meet those goals and their planned goals for the coming week. Supervisors were on-call twenty-four hours a day in case of emergency, and advocates had each other's telephone numbers in case they needed to discuss their cases and obtain advice or information outside of class. Having each other's telephone numbers also provided a needed emotional outlet for advocates, as they were not permitted to discuss their cases with anyone outside of the project.

Components of the intervention

The two primary components of the advocacy intervention were first, to help women protect themselves and their children from further violence, and second, to generate and mobilize community resources women reported needing. Safety plans were discussed and individualized based on each woman's unique circumstances. For women living with their abusive partners, advocates discussed the pros and cons of hiding money and keys, removing weapons from the home and having appropriate documents ready in case women needed to leave the home quickly. Regardless of whether women were living with their assailants or not, advocates discussed what to do in case of emergencies and they established plans in case they were ever surprised by the assailants. Some assailants knew about the advocates and the intervention, others received some degree of information, while others had no idea the advocate was working with the survivor. These decisions were made by survivors based on their history with the assailant, and all decisions were respected by program staff. Although each woman was told at the beginning of the advocacy intervention that the advocate would be rescinded if there was any indication that she might be in danger, such action was never necessary. This is probably due to the degree to which safety was prioritized and discussed throughout training and the intervention. Through role-plays and extensive discussion, safety plans for both the women and the advocates were created and modified as needed.

The type of advocacy provided through this intervention consists of five distinct phases: assessment, implementation, monitoring, secondary implementation and termination.

ASSESSMENT

Assessment consists of two components: gathering important information regarding the client's needs and goals, and determining which community resources might appropriately meet those needs. Assessing the client's needs occurs through direct conversation, observation and discussion with important people in the woman's life (with her permission). For example, a woman might live with her sister, and the sister might mention the client's pressing need for child care. In response to each unmet need that was identified, advocates and their clients assess what resources exist that might meet the need. During this phase it is important to distinguish between unmet needs and community resources. If a woman reports needing a job, for example, she has just mentioned a community resource, not an unmet need. The advocate's role is to help the client determine the need behind the resource. While most people want a job in order to make money, others are looking for a way to 'contribute to society'. Wanting a job might also be a response to boredom or lack of interaction with other adults. It is always important, therefore, to step back and determine the true unmet need, in order to brainstorm various appropriate resources to meet that need. Staying with this example, if a woman mentions wanting to get a job because she wants to feel as though she is contributing to society, the advocate might assist her in finding volunteer work as well as looking for a job. If the underlying unmet need is actually money, obtaining a job is only one potential resource for meeting this need. The advocate would also discuss other strategies with the client that involve either obtaining funds or reducing expenses (e.g., getting a roommate to share expenses or having a garage sale).

IMPLEMENTATION

After the unmet need has been determined and various community resources have been brainstormed, the advocate and woman move into the implementation phase of generating or mobilizing the community resources. It is not enough to determine *what* resource is needed; the advocate and woman must also determine *who* controls the resource and *how* to best approach obtaining the resource. Sometimes this is very straightforward, but other situations require persistence and determination in 'not taking no for an answer'.

The implementation stage involves actively working in the community to obtain resources and to make the community more responsive to women's needs. If, for example, the woman decides to obtain a personal protection order, the advocate's role is not simply to hand her the address and telephone number of the appropriate agency. Rather, the advocate would accompany the client through the entire process. This active participation has a number of beneficial outcomes: the client feels emotionally supported through difficult processes, the woman is sometimes treated more respectfully or expeditiously because she is accompanied by an advocate, and the advocate becomes a witness to events in case there is a later dispute between the woman and the agency. Another benefit of this type of teamwork is that the advocate gains firsthand knowledge about the hassles and difficulties involved in obtaining many community resources, which often increases her respect for her client's diligence and determination.

MONITORING AND SECONDARY IMPLEMENTATION

Monitoring the effectiveness of the implemented intervention is accomplished by assessing whether the resource has been successfully obtained, and whether it is satisfactory to meeting the unmet need. If it is not, the advocate initiates a secondary implementation to meet the client's needs more effectively. For example, the advocate and client might obtain convenient and affordable child care for the preschool children. The advocate's role would be to continue to ask how the child care is working out: do the children enjoy it? Is the mother satisfied? Is there a backup plan in case of emergency? If the resource is not as adequate as originally hoped, a secondary implementation – generating or mobilizing a different community resource – is necessary.

TERMINATION

Termination begins approximately seven to eight weeks into the ten-week intervention. With the ultimate goal of 'putting themselves out of a job', advocates give women termination packets containing lists of resources and strategies for obtaining those resources. These termination packets should include information not only about resources the woman currently needs, but also about resources that might be needed in the future. For example, a woman with preschool-aged children would not have been working on school issues. Thinking ahead, the advocate would also include information about neighborhood schools, counselors and recreational activities that the children would become eligible for as they grew older.

During the termination phase, advocates work more intensively on transferring all of the skills they learned throughout training and supervision. Through role-plays, coaching and/or discussions, the advocate ensures that the woman can effectively advocate on her own behalf with resistant or hostile community providers.

MULTIPLE INTERVENTIONS

While the five phases of advocacy intervention were described here as distinct stages for clarification purposes, in reality advocates engage in various phases simultaneously. Multiple interventions may occur throughout the ten weeks, such that, for example, the advocate may be monitoring one intervention while initiating another.

Importance of the program's underlying philosophy

Although each advocacy intervention must be individualized to meet the unique needs of each participant, all interventions should be guided by three theoretical tenets which contribute to project effectiveness. First, the participant, not the advocate, should guide the direction and activities of the intervention. Second, the role of the advocate is to make the community more responsive to women's needs. This relates to the third supposition, which is the belief that survivors are competent adults capable of making sound decisions for themselves. This is in direct contrast to some advocacy interventions — especially some legal advocacy programs — designed to convince women to behave in a certain manner (e.g., file police reports, testify in court, end the relationship).

Application of the model

Case illustration 1[3]

Bindhu, an Indian woman married to an Indian man with US citizenship, was dependent on her husband to sponsor her to become an American citizen as well. Bindhu had no knowledge of her rights in the USA and her husband had told her that if he were to divorce her she would be left on the street with nothing. Shortly after Bindhu became pregnant, her husband brutally beat her. Although he had struck her in the past, the abuse had never been this severe, and Bindhu ran to the next door neighbor for help. The neighbor took Bindhu to the domestic violence shelter, where she then learned about our program.

Bindhu returned to her husband after leaving the shelter, and agreed to work with an advocate as long as her husband believed the advocate was with a 'pregnancy program' and not a 'domestic violence program'. Bindhu's husband worked from 8 a.m. to 5 p.m., giving Bindhu and her advocate ample time to work together privately.

Bindhu and her advocate first assessed her unmet needs. Initial discussions revealed that Bindhu had no citizenship papers, could not legally work in the USA, was pregnant, did not feel she could return to India in disgrace, had no driver's license and was not sure if she wanted her marriage to work. Bindhu and her advocate prioritized the unmet needs and began implementing strategies. They first went to a divorce workshop through a local community college, where Bindhu discovered her rights should her husband divorce her. There she learned that she would not end up on the streets if they divorced, and that he would have to pay her alimony and child support. The two also contacted a female community police officer, who agreed to sit down with Bindhu and tell her exactly what would happen if the police were called out to the house. She answered all of Bindhu's questions and explained her rights in the USA to her. The advocate also helped Bindhu learn to drive and study for her driving test. They went to the community college and learned how Bindhu's skills from her homeland could be translated into skills in the USA should she decide to try to get a job. Throughout this time they also worked on getting Bindhu permanent status in the USA, with or without her husband's sponsorship.

Bindhu's husband was a member in good standing in the community. He had a well-paid, high-status job and would have been ashamed to have the neighbors know he was abusive. Bindhu knew this and used it to her advantage. When the advocate discussed a safety plan with Bindhu, it involved going to the next door neighbor – the one who first took her to the shelter – and telling her that it was acceptable for her to call the police if she heard screams coming from Bindhu's house. She also left a bag of clothes and some important bank and personal information at the neighbor's home in case she should have to leave quickly. The more Bindhu learned of her rights, the more power she felt within her relationship. She informed her husband that if he ever struck her again she would call the police, tell the neighbors and go back to the shelter.

Case illustration 2

Kathy and her four young children moved in temporarily with Kathy's mother after leaving the shelter. The primary goal that Kathy wanted her advocate to focus on was permanent housing, although they also immediately obtained a personal protection order against Kathy's ex-boyfriend. Four weeks into the intervention they had still not found affordable housing for a family of five, and after a serious argument with her mother, Kathy and the children were living in her car in freezing weather. Kathy could not return to the domestic violence shelter program because she was not being abused, and she feared for her children's safety in the local shelters for homeless people. The only person offering Kathy a warm place to stay was her ex-boyfriend.

For two weeks the advocate lost all contact with Kathy and her children. While searching for her at shelters, her mother's home and on the streets, the advocate continued looking for permanent housing. Finally the advocate was successful in collaborating with a local organization that provides transitional housing to homeless families. The advocate convinced the organization staff to move Kathy's family up on the two-year waiting list, and in week nine of the ten-week intervention, a home was reserved for her. Kathy also called the advocate in response to one of the many notes left for her throughout the community, and they were able to move Kathy into her new home during their last meeting together.

Individualized interventions

These two cases illustrate how individualized advocacy interventions must be. Some women need assistance to terminate their relationships successfully while other women want to maintain their relationships if the abuse ends. Some women need more information about resources while others have the necessary information but need tangible assistance in obtaining such resources. Interventions should be flexible enough to meet each woman's needs but must also remain true to the underlying strengths-based philosophy of the project.

Effectiveness of the intervention

The effectiveness of the advocacy intervention was determined by randomly assigning 278 battered women to the advocacy (experimental) or services-as-usual (control) condition. Participants were interviewed 6 times over 2 years, with interviews occurring pre-intervention, post-intervention and at 6, 12, 18 and 24 month follow-up. An elaborate protocol was implemented to maximize retention of the sample over time. Strategies included making multiple contacts in the community, obtaining written Release of Information forms from participants and paying women for participating in the research interviews. This protocol resulted in retention rates at any given time point being 94 percent or higher, and rates were not significantly different between the advocacy and control conditions (x^2 (1, $n = 278$) = 0.56, ns). The specific components of the retention plan can be found in Sullivan et $al.$ (1996).

The immediate impact of the advocacy intervention in helping women access resources was assessed post-intervention by a simple between-conditions comparison of women's ratings of their effectiveness. Women in the advocacy condition reported being more effective in reaching their goals than women in the control condition (t (263) = 5.91, p <0.001; $n^2 = 0.14$). Means were 2.7 ($SD = 0.73$) for the control condition and 3.2 ($SD = 0.62$) for the experimental group.

Multivariate analysis of variance (MANOVA) examined the persistence of condition differences through the 2 year follow-up period. Both the time (multivariate $F (3, 261) = 10.85$, $p < 0.01$) and the condition $\times$ time (multivariate $F (3, 261) = 2.73$, $p < 0.05$) effects were significant. Although difficulty obtaining resources decreased steadily for both groups, the slope for the advocacy condition was significantly steeper. Within-time condition differences were significant only at 24 month follow-up.

The short-term impact of the advocacy intervention on the major outcome variables – experience of further physical violence, psychological abuse, depression, social support and quality of life – was tested through multivariate analysis of covariance (MANCOVA). This strategy allowed a between-group comparison on all outcome measures at the same point in time (post-intervention), controlling for individuals' pre-intervention levels. A significant effect for condition was found (multivariate $F (5, 254) = 5.18$, $p < 0.001$; $n^2 = 0.09$), which led to conducting follow-up univariate ANCOVAs for each outcome variable. Physical violence, psychological abuse and depression were lower in the advocacy condition, while quality of life and social support were higher. For all individual outcome variables except psychological abuse, the comparison between the conditions was statistically significant.

Doubly multivariate repeated measures MANOVAs were then used to test for the persistence of experimental–control group differences on the major outcomes across the next two years. The analysis indicated a significant time $\times$ condition interaction (multivariate $F (20, 244) = 1.91$, $p < 0.01$) accounting for 14 percent of the multivariance, a significant time effect (multivariate $F (20, 244) = 2.45$, $p < 0.001$) accounting for 16 percent, and a condition effect (multivariate $F (5, 259) = 1.56$, $p = 0.17$) that, while not significant, was suggestive, considering the directional nature of the experimental–control group comparison.

To identify group differences between individual outcome variables, follow-up repeated measures MANOVAs were conducted. Women who worked with advocates reported higher quality of life and social support over time, as well as decreased difficulty obtaining community resources. Perhaps most importantly, they also experienced less violence over time than did the women who did not work with advocates. A more detailed description of the multivariate analyses and findings can be found in Sullivan and Bybee (1999). These promising findings can now be used by domestic violence service programs and others to justify developing or expanding similar advocacy programs across other communities.

Adopting/adapting the model to other communities

The Community Advocacy Project can be adapted to meet a variety of community needs. Although it originated in a mid-sized city close to a university campus, it could be modified to larger cities as well as more rural communities. As more and more individuals consider replicating or modifying this program, questions arise regarding implementation issues. The most common concerns are discussed below.

How do you keep women from becoming too dependent on the advocate?

For those individuals who are prone to becoming overly dependent on others, such dependency is minimized by the short time frame (ten weeks) of the intervention and the clearly delineated termination date. It is important to note, however, that this question typically arises from individuals who view women with abusive partners as 'not like me'. We all depend on informal or formal advocacy-type assistance at various times in our lives (whether in the form of family helping us gain employment, friends accompanying us to the doctor, colleagues sharing information about opportunities or commodities, etc.). The more disenfranchised that individuals are from society, the fewer networks they have to rely on for such assistance. This advocacy model is predicated on the belief that we could all use more information about resources and how to obtain them, and that we can all use a supportive person in our lives through difficult times.

We don't have a university in our area. Would this type of advocacy project still work using volunteers instead of students?

An important next step in exploring the usefulness and generalizability of this intervention is to investigate whether volunteers would advocate for women as effectively as university students. One reason why college students are preferable to volunteers is that they are paying for the experience (through tuition) and earning a grade and potential letter of recommendation for their efforts. This maximizes the likelihood of their working the required hours each week and making this intervention a priority in their lives. It is only natural that when busy individuals have to prioritize their time, it is their volunteer work that usually gets the short shrift. A major concern in using volunteers as advocates is that they may be more likely to quit mid-way through the intervention or to put in fewer hours or less effort than is necessary to be effective.

On the other hand, volunteers are quite capable of becoming excellent advocates, and with appropriate training and supervision (ideally from a paid staff member) could do as well as, if not better than, university students. Another advantage of using volunteers is that they may come from more diverse backgrounds than typical university students. The majority of our students were white, under 24 years of age, and had never been mothers. While they clearly did an excellent job and generally bonded well with the women with whom they worked, one could imagine that older advocates with more life experiences could potentially do even better. Domestic violence service programs might consider aligning with church groups, community organizations or other volunteer programs to obtain a paraprofessional advocacy workforce conducive to their individual needs.

Shouldn't an intended goal of the project be to help women leave the relationship?

It cannot be overemphasized that an integral component of this model is to follow the woman's lead in determining goals. Encouraging a client to make certain choices over others not only is disrespectful, but also is likely to fail in creating lasting change. Individuals have multiple and complex reasons for making life choices, including relationship decisions. Ending the relationship does not necessarily end the violence; it sometimes escalates the violence (Jones 1994; Mahoney 1991). The advocate's role must be to help women do what they can to protect themselves and their children, regardless of whether women are in or out of the relationship. Advocates can offer information to help women make decisions, but they should never push a woman toward one path over another. Working from a strengths perspective involves viewing individuals as naturally competent and capable, possessing valuable skills and abilities to make decisions and create positive change in their own lives.

Had we assumed in our research that leaving the relationship should be a desired outcome for all women, we would have analyzed whether women who worked with advocates were more effective in leaving the relationship than were women in the control group. This analysis would have indicated no differences between the two groups. However, when we looked at group differences only for women reporting that they *wanted* to end the relationship, the significant difference emerged. Women who worked with advocates were more effective in ending the relationship *when they wanted to* than were women in the control condition (96% vs 87%; x^2 (1, $n = 193$) = 4.64, p <0.03).

If a major goal of the advocacy intervention is to help women become safe, why not just focus on legal advocacy?

Interestingly, only 72 percent of the women worked on legal advocacy issues during their intervention, and not all of those issues pertained to the assailant. Some women, for example, were fighting their landlords in court or had been charged with other crimes themselves. Although the individual interventions have not yet been examined in sufficient detail to state confidently what worked to help women become more safe over time, it appears there were multiple pathways through which this occurred. One woman, for example, knew that if she could end the relationship and move to another US state it would be extremely difficult for her assailant to follow her. Her main obstacle? Divorcing the assailant would result in her losing her medical benefits, and she suffered severe epileptic attacks. Without letting her husband know she was even working with the Community Advocacy Project, she and her advocate checked into her options and not only obtained affordable health insurance but also convinced a local church to pay her bus fare to a new location. Was this easy? No. But with determination and hard work it was accomplished within the ten weeks. This particular woman was not abused again across the follow-up time periods, yet she never involved the criminal justice system.

Legal advocacy programs are important and necessary resources for women choosing to use the court system. However, many women choose alternatives to the criminal justice system to keep themselves and their children safe. The more generalized our advocacy efforts can be, the more lives we can effectively touch.

Conclusion

No one solution exists to end intimate violence against women. The advocacy intervention described in this chapter is one response that has effectively helped a number of women. It will not always be successful and it is not necessarily needed by all women with abusive partners and ex-partners. Community-based advocacy interventions should be one component of a larger, coordinated community response to holding perpetrators accountable and assuring continued safety for survivors and their children.

Notes

1. Intimate violence refers to psychological, physical and/or sexual abuse perpetrated against an intimate partner or ex-partner.

2. The Community Advocacy Project was originally funded by the George Gund Foundation, and was then funded for eight years by the National Institute of Mental Health (R01 MH 44849).

3. Names and identifying information have been changed to protect the women's privacy.

References

Alpert, E.J. (1995) 'Violence in intimate relationships and the practicing internist: new "disease" or new agenda?' *Annals of Internal Medicine 123*, 774–781.

Alsdurf, J.M. (1985) 'Wife abuse and the church: the response of pastors.' *Response to the Victimization of Women and Children 8*, 1, 9–11.

Berrios, D.C. and Grady, D. (1991) 'Domestic violence: risk factors and outcomes.' *Western Journal of Medicine 155*, 2, 133–135.

Bowker, L.H. and Maurer, L. (1985) 'The importance of sheltering in the lives of battered women.' *Response to the Victimization of Women and Children 8*, 2–8.

Browne, A. (1987) *When Battered Women Kill.* New York: Macmillan/Free Press.

Browne, A. and Williams, K.R. (1993) 'Gender, intimacy, and lethal violence: trends from 1976–1987.' *Gender and Society 7*, 78–98.

Buzawa, E.S. and Buzawa, C.G. (1990) *Domestic Violence: The Criminal Justice Response.* Newbury Park, CA: Sage.

Campbell, R., Sullivan, C.M. and Davidson, W.S. II (1995) 'Women who use domestic violence shelters: changes in depression over time.' *Psychology of Women Quarterly 19*, 237–255.

Davidson, W.S., Redner, R., Blakely, C.H., Mitchell, C.M. and Emshoff, J.G. (1987) 'Diversion of juvenile offenders: an experimental comparison.' *Journal of Consulting and Clinical Psychology 55*, 1, 68–75.

Dobash, R.E., Dobash, R.P. and Cavanagh, K. (1985) 'The contact between battered women and social and medical agencies.' In J. Pahl (ed) *Private Violence and Public Policy: The Needs of Battered Women and the Response of the Public Services.* London: Routledge & Kegan Paul.

Donato, K. and Bowker, L. (1984) 'Understanding the helpseeking behavior of battered women: a comparison of traditional service agencies and women's groups.' *International Journal of Women's Studies 7*, 2, 99–109.

Dunst, C.J., Johanson, C. and Trivette, C. (1991) 'Family-oriented early intervention policies and practices: family-centered or not.' *Exceptional Children 58*, 2, 115–126.

Durlak, J.A. (1981) 'Evaluating comparative studies of paraprofessional and professional helpers: a reply to Nietzel and Fisher.' *Psychological Bulletin 89*, 3, 566–569.

Eby, K.K., Campbell, J.C., Sullivan, C.M. and Davidson, W.S. II. (1995) 'Health effects of experiences of sexual violence for women with abusive partners.' *Health Care for Women International 16*, 563–567.

Edleson, J.L. and Syers, M. (1991) 'The effects of group treatment for men who batter: an 18-month follow-up study.' *Research on Social Work Practice 1*, 3, 227–243.

Edleson, J.L. and Tolman, R.M. (1994) 'Group intervention strategies for men who batter.' *Directions in Mental Health Counseling 4*, 7, 1–16.

Edleson, J.L., Eisikovits, Z. and Guttman, E. (1985) 'Men who batter women: a critical review of the evidence.' *Journal of Family Issues 6*, 2, 229–247.

Ferraro, K.J. (1993) 'Cops, courts, and woman battering.' In P.B. Bart and E.G. Moran (eds) *Violence Against Women: The Bloody Footprints*. Beverly Hills, CA: Sage.

Gauthier, L.M. and Levendosky, A.A. (1996) 'Assessment and treatment of couples with abusive male partners: guidelines for therapists.' *Psychotherapy 33*, 3, 403–417.

Gondolf, E. (1988) *Battered Women as Survivors: An Alternative to Learned Helplessness*. Lexington, MA: Lexington Books.

Henderson, A. (1990) 'Children of abused wives: their influence on their mothers' decisions.' *Canada's Mental Health 38*, 10–13.

Hilton, N.Z. (1992) 'Battered women's concerns about their children witnessing wife assault.' *Journal of Interpersonal Violence 7*, 1, 77–86.

Hirschel, J.D., Hutchison, I.W., Dean, C.W. and Mills, A.M. (1992) 'Review essay on the law enforcement response to spouse abuse: past, present, and future.' *Justice Quarterly 9*, 247–283.

Hoff, L.A. (1990) *Battered Women as Survivors*. London: Routledge.

Jones, A. (1994) *Next Time She'll Be Dead: Battering and How to Stop It*. Boston, MA: Beacon.

Jurik, N. and Winn, R. (1990) 'Gender and homicide: a comparison of men and women who kill.' *Violence and Victims 5*, 4, 227–242.

Kemp, A., Green, B.L., Hovanitz, C. and Rawlings, E.I. (1995) 'Incidence and correlates of posttraumatic stress disorder in battered women: shelter and community sample.' *Journal of Interpersonal Violence 10*, 1, 43–55.

Koss, M.P. (1990) 'The women's health research agenda: violence against women.' *Violence and Victims 5*, 4, 227–242.

Lewis, R., Dobash, R.P., Dobash, R.E. and Cavanagh, K. (1997) 'Protection, prevention, rehabilitation or justice? Women using the law to challenge domestic violence.' Paper presented at American Society of Criminology meeting, San Diego, CA, November.

McFarlane, J., Parker, B. and Soeken, K. (1995) 'Abuse during pregnancy: frequency, severity, perpetrator and risk factors of homicide.' *Nursing Research* 45, 1, 38–44.

Mahoney, M.R. (1991) 'Legal images of battered women: redefining the issue of separation.' *Michigan Law Review 90*, 1–94.

Marcenko, M.O. and Smith, L.K. (1992) 'The impact of a family-centered case management approach.' *Social Work in Health Care 17*, 4, 87–100.

Mitchell, R. and Hodson, C. (1983) 'Coping with domestic violence: social support and psychological health among battered women.' *American Journal of Community Psychology 11*, 629–654.

Scannapieco, M. (1994) 'Home-based service program: effectiveness with at risk families.' *Children and Youth Services 16*, 5–6, 363–377.

Schechter, S. (1982) *Women and Male Violence.* Boston, MA: South End Press.

Straus, M.A. and Gelles, R. (1986) 'Societal change and change in family violence from 1975 to 1985 as revealed by two national surveys.' *Journal of Marriage and the Family 48*, 465–479.

Sullivan, C.M. (1991a) 'Battered women as active helpseekers.' *Violence Update 1*, 12, 1, 8, 10.

Sullivan, C.M. (1991b) 'The provision of advocacy services to women leaving abusive partners: an exploratory study.' *Journal of Interpersonal Violence 6*, 1, 41–54.

Sullivan, C.M. (1997) 'Societal collusion and culpability in intimate male violence: the impact of community response toward women with abusive partners.' In A.P. Cardarelli (ed) *Violence between Intimate Partners: Patterns, Causes, and Effects.* Boston, MA: Allyn & Bacon.

Sullivan, C.M. and Bybee, D.I. (1999) 'Reducing violence using community based advocacy for women with abusive partners.' *Journal of Consulting and Clinical Psychology 67*, 1, 43–53.

Sullivan, C.M., Rumptz, M.H., Campbell, R., Eby, K.K. and Davidson, W.S. (1996) 'Retaining participants in longitudinal community research: a comprehensive protocol.' *Journal of Applied Behavioral Science 32*, 3, 262–276.

Sullivan, C.M., Sutherland, C. and Allen, N. (1998) *Training Paraprofessionals to Successfully Advocate for Women with Abusive Partners.* East Lansing, MI: Michigan State University.

Sutherland, C., Bybee, D. and Sullivan, C. (1998) 'The long-term effects of battering on women's health.' *Women's Health: Research on Gender, Behavior, and Policy 4*, 1, 41–70.

Thompson, C. (1989) 'Breaking through walls of isolation: a model for churches in helping victims of violence.' *Pastoral Psychology 38*, 35–38.

Trivette, C., Dunst, C. and Hamby, D. (1996) 'Characteristics and consequences of help-giving practices in contrasting human service programs.' *American Journal of Community Psychology 24*, 2, 273–293.

Wauchope, B. (1988) 'Help-seeking decisions of battered women: a test of learned helplessness and two stress theories.' Paper presented at Eastern Sociological Society meeting, Durham, NH, March.

Weiss, H. and Jacobs, F. (eds) (1988) *Evaluating Family Support Programs.* Hawthorne, NJ: Aldine de Gruyter.

Weissbourd, B. and Kagan, S.L. (1989) 'Family support programs: catalysts for change.' *American Journal of Orthopsychiatry 59*, 20–31.

Whipple, V. (1985) 'The use of reality therapy with battered women in domestic violence shelters.' *Journal of Reality Therapy 5*, 1, 22–27.

CHAPTER 7

Helping Children of Battered Women

A Review of Research, Sampling of Programs and Presentation of Project SUPPORT

Elizabeth Ezell, Renee McDonald and Ernest N. Jouriles

Violence toward women by their male intimate partners is a serious problem for our society. As detailed in several other chapters in this volume, such violence is prevalent and appears to precipitate a number of mental health problems for women, including low self-esteem, anxiety, depressive symptoms, Posttraumatic Stress Disorder and suicidal behavior (see Chapter 4 in this volume). Although women are the most obvious victims, it is also important for service providers to recognize that the deleterious effects of domestic violence do not stop with women; rather, many children of battered women are affected as well.

The problem of children's exposure to domestic violence is beginning to gain recognition as an important health and social concern (Holden, Geffner and Jouriles 1998a). In fact, a number of well-designed studies now show that the children of battered women are at heightened risk for emotional and behavioral problems. Furthermore, there is growing evidence that certain problems are not likely to dissipate with time and/or distance from the violent event. That is, the problems do not simply go away without some sort of assistance or intervention. In short, children of battered women appear to be at risk for a variety of problems, and they comprise an important target for effective interventions.

There are several extensive reviews of the research linking domestic violence and child adjustment (e.g., Holtzworth-Munroe *et al.* 1998; Jouriles *et al.* 2000b; Margolin 1998). Complementing this literature are several detailed reviews of treatment programs and services designed to help children of battered women (e.g., Graham-Berman 2000; Peled 1997). In this chapter, we briefly summarize the research literature on children exposed to domestic violence, drawing attention to the current status of our knowledge about the varied psychological outcomes of children of battered women and highlighting points that are pertinent to practitioners delivering services to this population. We also present a sampling of different approaches to intervening with this population of children, and we provide a detailed presentation of one program and the initial results of its evaluation.

The link between domestic violence and child adjustment problems

Many early studies in the mid-1980s on children of battered women focused on providing descriptive information on the types of problems experienced by these children. Families were typically recruited from agencies serving victims of domestic violence, such as shelters for battered women, and the investigators gathered information on the child problems that were evident in these families. According to these early studies, the children of battered women appear to experience a very wide range of adjustment difficulties, including fear, anxiety, trauma symptoms, and aggressive and defiant behavior (e.g., Carlson 1984; Layzer, Goodson and DeLange 1986). Unfortunately, most of these early studies suffered from serious methodological flaws, making it impossible to conclude with confidence that domestic violence leads to child problems. For example, very few of these early studies included a group of children from nonviolent families for comparison; thus, comparisons could not be made between violent and nonviolent families. Also, very few of these studies used psychometrically sound instruments for data collection or collected data from participants systematically. However, in spite of such methodological flaws, these early studies called attention to the plight of children of battered women and provided descriptive data regarding the types of problems they experience.

These initial investigations were followed by a series of more carefully controlled studies in which the children of battered women, usually living with their mothers at women's shelters, were compared to children living at home with nonviolent parents. Most of these studies examined child adjustment on the two broadband indices of child behavior – externalizing problems (aggressive, delinquent behavior) and internalizing problems (withdrawn, somatic complaints, anxious/depressed) – using standard, frequently used measures of child problems. These studies, as a group, clearly showed that children of battered women exhibit higher levels of externalizing and internalizing problems than children in community comparison samples (for recent reviews, see Holtzworth-Munroe *et al*. 1998; Jouriles *et al*. 2000b; Margolin 1998). Indeed, a consistent finding among these studies is that many children in domestically violent families score at or above clinical levels on standard measures of child problems (i.e., their scores are similar to those of children who are brought to clinics because of behavioral/emotional problems). For example, McDonald and Jouriles (1991) reported that between 25 percent and 70 percent of children from families characterized by violence exhibit clinical levels of behavior problems compared to 10–20 percent of children in community comparison groups.

Several of these controlled studies provided additional noteworthy results. Specifically, domestic violence appears to be a more potent risk factor for child problems than does verbal conflict or general marital discord (Fantuzzo *et al*. 1991; Jouriles, Murphy and O'Leary 1989; McDonald, Jouriles and Ware 1999; Rossman and Rosenberg 1992). However, studies have not been uniform in their support of this conclusion (e.g., Hershorn and Rosenbaum 1985; Rosenbaum and O'Leary 1981). Given that domestic violence often occurs in the context of significant marital discord and verbal conflict, and that such discord and conflict is associated with child adjustment problems, it is important to know whether domestic violence increases the risk for child problems beyond the risk attributable to nonviolent marital discord and conflict. That is, if we are to conclude that domestic violence is a unique risk factor for child adjustment problems, we must first consider the independent contribution to child problems of factors correlated with domestic violence, such as marital discord and nonviolent conflict. The failure to consider such factors makes it impossible to determine the extent to which domestic violence itself increases risk for child behavior problems.

It should also be noted that several of the more recent controlled studies have recruited domestically violent families who were *not* seeking services because of domestic violence. In these studies of violent community families, domestic violence continues to be associated with child adjustment problems (e.g., Fantuzzo *et al*. 1991). However, this relation has not emerged as dramatically or as consistently as it has with agency samples. In fact, this research has indicated that the children of mothers who seek shelter from domestic violence tend to experience significantly more adjustment problems than children in violent community families (Fantuzzo *et al*. 1991; Rossman and Rosenberg 1992).

Studies that recruit violent community samples are extremely important if we are to understand more clearly the link between domestic violence and child adjustment problems. Domestically violent families in which the women are seeking services from an agency, such as a shelter, appear to differ dramatically from domestically violent families in which the mothers do not seek services. For example, families seeking help from women's shelters are typically experiencing very frequent and severe levels of domestic violence (Johnson 1995; Jouriles *et al.* 2000b). Our own research indicates that most children at women's shelters come from homes characterized by over 60 acts of violence per year, with over half of these children exposed to domestic violence involving the threat or use of knives or guns (Jouriles *et al.* 1998). Such extreme violence appears to be rare among violent community families, at least according to community survey research (Straus and Gelles 1990). Furthermore, families residing in shelters face a number of stressors that could contribute to child maladjustment and that are often not shared by families in the community (e.g., frequent changes in residence, living with many other families). Controlled studies with violent community samples are thus needed to inform our understanding of how domestic violence, as it most often occurs within our society, is associated with child problems.

Several additional points should be highlighted from the empirical literature. For example, it is clear that many children exposed to domestic violence show maladaptive emotional and/or behavioral symptoms. However, it is also clear that there is great variability in children's responses to domestic violence (Grych *et al.* 2000; Hughes and Luke 1998). Exposure to domestic violence has been associated with a variety of child problems, such as aggression (Jaffe *et al.* 1986b), anxiety (Christopoulos *et al.* 1987), depression (Sternberg *et al.* 1993) and low self-esteem (Hughes and Barad 1983). However, studies linking domestic violence to clinical levels of child problems have revealed no clear pattern of maladjustment. Some studies report higher levels of both internalizing and externalizing problems among children of battered women (e.g., Jouriles *et al.* 1989), whereas other studies report only higher internalizing (e.g., Hughes and Barad 1983) or externalizing problems (e.g., Jaffe *et al.* 1986b; Wolfe *et al.* 1985). Still other studies have reported no differences in children's adjustment between domestically violent and nonviolent families (Hershorn and Rosenbaum 1985; Rosenbaum and O'Leary 1981).

Recognition that there is great variability in children's responses to domestic violence has very important implications for the design and implementation of clinical services for such children and their families. Many children of battered women with maladaptive emotional and/or behavioral symptoms could benefit from services. However, our knowledge about the variability in children's responses to domestic violence suggests that we cannot assume that *all*, or even *most*, children of battered women are in need of services. Nor can we assume that any given child needs services for a particular kind of problem. For this reason, children of battered women, as a group, should not simply be targeted to receive services for a specific type of problem, such as depression, low self-esteem or Posttraumatic Stress Disorder, without first assessing whether each child displays the specific problem. The practice of providing programs for specific problems to all children of battered women (e.g., all those who enter a particular battered women's shelter) makes poor use of scarce resources, at best. At worst, such programs could have unanticipated negative effects for certain children.

The variability in children's responses to domestic violence also suggests that the relation between children's exposure to violence and their adjustment difficulties is complex. Various processes have been hypothesized to link domestic violence with child adjustment problems, with different processes likely to figure more prominently in different types of child problems. For example, children's appraisals of their parents' marital interactions appear to be very important for understanding the link between interparent conflict and child internalizing problems such as depression and anxiety (Grych *et al.* forthcoming). However, these appraisals do not appear to be as important for understanding the link between interparent conflict and child externalizing problems (Grych *et al.* forthcoming). The evident variability in child outcomes, combined with knowledge that different processes are likely to be important for certain outcomes and not others, raises questions about global intervention programs designed to help *all* children of battered women. In short, given the diversity of child outcomes in response to domestic violence, we believe that it is impossible for any one program to be able to address the needs of all children of battered women.

Practitioners should also recognize that most of the research on domestic violence and child adjustment focuses on short-term child outcomes (i.e., how the children are functioning shortly after the violence occurs). Although these studies, together, suggest that children of battered women are at risk for experiencing adjustment difficulties (particularly during the time their mothers are in shelter or are receiving services from some other type of agency), it is unclear whether these difficulties persist over time. In fact, there is some evidence that many of the problems experienced by children who are residing at women's shelters with their mothers (perhaps with the exception of clinical levels of externalizing child problems) diminish several months following departure from the shelter (Holden *et al.* 1998b; Ware *et al.* 1999). These findings, however, should *not* be interpreted to suggest that children of battered women are not affected by the violence. Again, certain problems, such as severe conduct problems, have been found to persist for several months following a family's exit from a battered women's shelter, and there are data suggesting that children's exposure to wife abuse is associated with aggressive, criminal behavior in adulthood (e.g., McCord 1979; McNeal and Amato 1998). Also, a growing body of retrospective data suggests that children's exposure to wife abuse relates to internalizing symptoms in adulthood, such as depression, trauma and low self-esteem (Forsstrom-Cohen and Rosenbaum 1985; Henning *et al.* 1996; Silvern *et al.* 1995). Thus, it appears that children of battered women may be affected in such a way that puts them at risk for experiencing difficulties later in life.

Evaluations of interventions for children of battered women

As one might expect from the growing recognition of children's exposure to domestic violence as a health and social concern, a large number of interventions have been developed and implemented with the intention of helping the children of battered women. These intervention programs differ greatly as to their purpose and the specific problems they target. For example, some focus specifically on reducing existing adjustment problems, with certain programs intended to reduce specific types of problems (e.g., anxiety, aggression) and others to reduce problems in general. Other intervention programs, however, do not have the reduction of existing child problems as their main focus. For example, some attempt to teach safety skills intended to keep children of battered women out of harm's way (e.g., how to protect themselves when dad hits mom), while others provide children with infor-mation about the dynamics of domestic violence and focus on changing attitudes and/or beliefs about violence as an appropriate method for resolv-ing conflict. Programs also vary greatly on certain structural components, such as the setting in which the interventions are delivered (e.g., shelters, homes, community centers), the format in which they are offered (e.g., individual, family, group), the length of the programs, and the participants included (e.g., children of different ages, mothers, siblings, peers).

A number of shelter-based interventions have been developed for children of battered women. Unfortunately, most of these programs have not been evaluated empirically or even documented sufficiently for others to be able to provide and/or evaluate these services. Without evaluation, it is impossible to know whether an intervention or service program accomplishes its goals or uses resources efficiently. Also, unless the results of evaluations are disseminated, other service providers do not have access to information about the range of programs available and their effectiveness. We limit our presentation to those programs that have been evaluated and for which evaluations have been published.

Honore Hughes was one of the first to implement, evaluate and publicize a program for children of battered women. Hughes' (1982) program provided treatment to children throughout their stay in a shelter, in both individual and group formats. Individual approaches ranged from recreational contact with a mentor to more intensive contacts designed to be more like psychotherapy. Group approaches included small, weekly process groups for children of similar ages to discuss their feelings, fears, attitudes towards violence and ways of coping with the upheaval in their lives. Family meetings were also conducted, with the goal of improving communication within the family. Mothers met in weekly group parenting meetings designed to help mothers improve the quality of their relationships with their children, learn basic principles of child development and acquire effective, nonviolent discipline techniques. Furthermore, shelter staff were trained to use the same parenting skills so that they could model them for mothers. The evaluation of this program included twelve children, who were assessed after an average of twenty-one days of shelter residence. The evaluation did not employ a control group or follow-up assessments. Hughes and Barad (1982, 1983) reported lower levels of child anxiety upon completion of the program; however, no differences were found in overt child behavior or parenting skills. Thus, children who went through the program exhibited lower levels of anxiety but did not exhibit lower levels of externalizing behavior problems. Despite the limited empirical support for the effectiveness of this program, this effort is notable in that it was one of the first models for intervening with children of battered women.

Jaffe and colleagues (Jaffe, Wilson and Wolfe 1986a, 1988; Wilson et al. 1989) developed a group-based psychoeducational program for children whose mothers were residing in shelters. This ten-week program employed weekly, ninety-minute sessions in a small group format with children aged 8 to 13 years. The intervention sought to increase children's knowledge about domestic violence, alter their attitudes about domestic violence, address their feelings of responsibility for the violence and teach safety skills and positive conflict resolution skills. Initial evaluation of the program did not include a comparison group or follow-up assessments, but the authors reported changes in children's attitudes about violence (Jaffe et al. 1986a, 1988; Wilson et al. 1989). Wagar and Rodway (1995) subsequently transported this intervention to a community setting, with a small sample of children referred from clinical and social service agencies and randomly assigned to treatment and control groups. Pre- and post-treatment assessments were conducted with the children and their mothers. Results of the study were limited by the small sample and lack of follow-up assessments; however, there were several intriguing findings. Although no group differences were observed post-treatment in children's knowledge of safety skills or use of social support, Wagar and Rodway (1995) reported that the intervention significantly reduced children's self-blame for domestic violence and that participation had significant positive effects on children's attitudes and on their responses to anger.

Peled and Edleson (1992) conducted a qualitative evaluation of a similar group-based program for children of battered women. The Domestic Abuse Project's (Minneapolis) Children's Program was a ten-week, manualized program for 4–12-year-old children who had witnessed domestic violence and whose custodial parent was participating in a structured domestic violence program. The children's program was provided to thirty children in eight groups, with concurrent voluntary parenting groups available and an optional family meeting upon completion of the program. Goals of the intervention included creating a safe and positive atmosphere for discussion of domestic violence, teaching means of self-protection, and promoting children's self-esteem. The evaluation did not include a comparison group or follow-up assessments; however, Peled and Edleson (1992) concluded from interviews with children, parents and group leaders that the intervention facilitated children's discussion of domestic violence, increased their knowledge of domestic violence, and changed their attitudes about violence.

Graham-Berman (1992) developed the Kids' Club, a group-based intervention for 6–12-year-old children and their mothers who had experienced domestic violence. Participants in the Kids' Club were recruited from the community and were randomly assigned to one of three conditions: child-only intervention, child-plus-mother intervention, and wait list. The child intervention consisted of ten weekly group sessions focused on children's knowledge, attitudes and beliefs regarding domestic violence, as well as their emotional adjustment and social skills. The mother intervention consisted of a ten-week empowerment group, with the goals of improving mothers' parenting skills and enhancing their social and emotional adjustment via discussion of their parenting fears and worries in a supportive atmosphere. Group leaders received considerable training and supervision, and both interventions were manualized.

In their evaluation of this program, assessments were conducted with 181 children and their mothers at pre-treatment, post-treatment and at an eight month follow-up. Data were gathered on multiple measures and from multiple sources (children, mothers, teachers and group leaders). Results of the evaluation indicated that children in all three conditions improved with regard to internalizing symptoms, aggression and conduct problems. However, children in the treatment groups also evidenced reduced self-blame for domestic violence, increased coping skills and greater knowledge about the prevention of domestic violence. Notably, the greatest changes occurred in the child-plus-mother group with regard to knowledge and attitudes about domestic violence and reduction of externalizing behaviors.

The Family Follow-up Study (Sullivan and Davidson 1998) evaluated advocacy services for battered women and their children, ages 7 to 11 years. Eighty-five families were randomly assigned to one of two groups: a sixteen-week advocacy group or a group that received no specific services. Children in the advocacy group participated in a ten-week support and education group, and had regular contact with a college student who served as a mentor. The student mentors were trained to provide advocacy services to mothers in the treatment group with regard to legal issues, housing, transportation, employment, education, child care, social support and obtaining goods and services. Assessments were conducted before and after the intervention and at eight months post-treatment. Mothers in the advocacy group experienced lowered levels of depression at post-treatment as well as enhanced self-esteem. Although there were no group differences in child functioning, the eight month follow-up revealed fewer incidents of child abuse in the advocacy group as well as increased social support for the mothers in that group.

The programs outlined above are admirable attempts to intervene on behalf of children of battered women. These programs illustrate a number of ways providers can try to enhance the quality of these children's lives, ameliorate the effects of domestic violence and curtail its transmission from one generation to the next. Despite clear progress in the number of programs developed for children of battered women since the early 1980s, this field as a whole is still quite young, especially with regard to the evaluation of existing interventions. In fact, the programs described above are among the few that have been evaluated. Unfortunately, methodological weaknesses such as the lack of control groups, non-random assignment to groups and the lack of follow-up assessments to evaluate the maintenance of treatment effects greatly limit our knowledge about the effectiveness of most of these interventions.

It is important to reiterate that many additional programs have been implemented with children of battered women without being evaluated or publicized. It will be crucial in coming years for clinicians and researchers to conduct and disseminate evaluations of their interventions so that we may more effectively allocate the scarce resources available to meet the needs of children who witness domestic violence. It should also be noted that many of the programs described above were originally developed and implemented at a time when we had much less knowledge about the relation between domestic violence and child adjustment. That is, it is likely that many of these programs would have been designed differently if we had had the knowledge we now have about children of battered women.

An intervention in detail: Project SUPPORT

Project SUPPORT is a multi-component intervention designed to reduce conduct problems exhibited by children of battered women and, we hope, to end the cycle of violence that too often perpetuates itself in these families. In the rest of this chapter we highlight how the empirical literature (on children of battered women as well as on other topics) guided the design and implementation of Project SUPPORT. We provide a description of the families for whom Project SUPPORT services are intended; we consider the theoretical and empirical underpinnings of the intervention; and we present the intervention and its evaluation in detail.

Target population

Project SUPPORT was designed specifically for domestically violent families (mothers and children) in which the mother is trying to move away from the batterer and at least one child is exhibiting clinical levels of conduct problems. Childhood conduct problems are characterized by aggressive, oppositional and antisocial behaviors, such as getting into frequent physical fights, refusing to obey adults and destroying others' property. Conduct problems have repeatedly been found to differentiate groups of children from violent versus nonviolent homes, with children from violent homes showing higher rates of conduct problems than children from homes without spousal violence (e.g., McDonald and Jouriles 1991). Furthermore, it has been our experience that mothers in shelters often express great concern and frustration over their children's conduct problems.

Children of battered women who are exhibiting conduct problems at clinical levels comprise an important group for intervention. As indicated earlier, there is evidence that this particular type of child problem persists following a family's departure from a shelter (Ware et al. forthcoming). Evidence from additional sources indicates that child conduct problems, in general, show great persistence over time and often entail destructive consequences for the children, their families and society at large (Dishion, French and Patterson 1995; Huesmann et al. 1984; Sholevar and Sholevar 1995; Stattin and Magnusson 1996). For example, conduct problems in childhood are often associated with adolescent drinking and drug use, impaired family and social relations, school dropout and adult criminality (Coie and Dodge 1998; Loeber and Hay 1997; Moffit 1993; Stattin and Magnusson 1996). Furthermore, children with conduct problems are frequently alienated by their peers, have few friends, experience academic difficulties and receive much negative attention from adults as a result of their behaviors (see Kazdin 1995 for a review). Addressing the conduct problems exhibited by children of battered women is thus an important and worthwhile endeavor.

Our intervention is designed primarily for families with young children (we are evaluating the intervention with families of children between 4 and 8 years of age). We selected this age group because research demonstrates that without early intervention, conduct problems are relatively unresponsive to treatment efforts and much more difficult to address (Dishion and Patterson 1992; Reid 1993). We expect that our intervention will also benefit other children in these families who have not yet developed conduct problems. In other words, mothers who learn the child behavior management and nurturing skills may also apply them to their other children, perhaps preventing or alleviating conduct problems among siblings outside our targeted age range.

Theory and research supporting the intervention

The intervention, designed to reduce severe conduct problems among young children of battered women, draws heavily on Patterson's model of the development of antisocial behavior (Patterson 1982; Patterson, DeBarsyshe and Ramsey 1989; Patterson, Reid and Dishion 1992). It should be noted from the start that Patterson's model applies to childhood conduct problems broadly, not specifically to the development of these problems in the context of domestic violence. Furthermore, Patterson's theory highlights the role of parenting in the development of child conduct problems, with equal emphasis on the parenting of mothers and fathers. We believe that in domestically violent families, fathers' behavior plays a significant role in the chain of events hypothesized to contribute to child conduct problems. Fathers' violence not only models antisocial behavior to children but also may have direct and indirect consequences on mothers' parenting. For example, fathers' violence may create multiple and serious stressors for mothers that interfere with their ability to respond sensitively to their children, and some violent fathers directly instruct mothers to engage in poor parenting practices (e.g., 'If you don't hit him, I will'). In short, although Patterson's model emphasizes the importance of both mothers' and fathers' parenting in the development of childhood conduct problems, in a family characterized by wife abuse, conduct problems may emerge from the father's behavior toward the mother as well as toward the child. We shall return to these issues following our discussion of Patterson's theory and research pertaining to the development of Project SUPPORT.

According to Patterson, 'basic training for patterns of antisocial behavior prior to adolescence takes place in the home' (Patterson et al. 1992, p.11). This process begins with a breakdown in parental effectiveness in disciplinary confrontations (e.g., difficulties in setting limits; harsh or inconsistent discipline) accompanied by a lack of parental encouragement for the development of prosocial behavior such as social skills and academics. Specific parent behaviors are thus hypothesized to reinforce children's antisocial behavior.

Patterson's theory would suggest that domestic violence and concomitant stressors may disrupt parenting by contributing to breakdowns in parental discipline and failures to encourage prosocial child behavior. For example, violent marital interactions may cause parents to be irritable, distracted and emotionally drained, reducing their ability to be attentive and sensitive to their children's needs (Easterbrooks and Emde 1988; Holden and Ritchie

1991). Consistent with such thinking, experimental research indicates that marital conflict alters parent–child interaction (Jouriles and Farris 1992; Mahoney, Boggio and Jouriles 1996). There is also a great deal of research linking violence toward women with parental physical aggression toward children (Appel and Holden 1998), particularly toward boys (Jouriles and LeCompte 1991; Jouriles and Norwood 1995). Furthermore, research on the co-occurrence of wife abuse and child abuse suggests that children of battered women are at very high risk for physical child abuse, most often perpetrated by their mother's batterer (Spiller et al. 1999).

Inconsistent or ineffective discipline techniques may arise in a number of ways. It is likely that in many families who experience domestic violence, the number of daily stressors far exceeds the resources and supports available to parents, thus limiting the emotional wherewithal required for firm, consistent and responsive parenting. Couple this strained environment with one in which at least one parent (e.g., the batterer) may serve as a highly aggressive model for the child, and plentiful opportunities result for the child to learn and practice aggressive and defiant behaviors. Moreover, such environments often lack adequate prosocial models and provide children insufficient encouragement of prosocial behaviors.

Patterson maintains that early development of conduct problems leads to academic and social difficulties in early to middle childhood, contributing to an alienation from prosocial peers and alignment with other rejected, aggressive children (Patterson et al. 1992). Children of battered women who follow a similar developmental path may be further separated from their prosocial peers by the common social isolation of these families, the possible reluctance to have children in their home or to share their 'family secret', and the frequent moves and school changes that these children endure (Christopoulos et al. 1987; Wolfe et al. 1985). According to Patterson's model, then, children of battered women should be at risk for developing conduct problems, which in turn increases their risk for later antisocial behavior. The predictions of this model are consistent with the research reviewed earlier on wife abuse and child conduct problems.

The effectiveness of child management skills training

Patterson's model implies that teaching parents to change the way they interact with their children might be an effective means of helping such children and their families. This notion is consistent with the results of a number of outcome studies which indicate that training parents in child management skills is one of the most effective means of reducing conduct problems in young children (Kazdin 1997; Kazdin and Weisz 1998). These interventions typically focus on teaching parents how to enhance parent–child communication; promote desirable, prosocial child behavior; and decrease deviant, antisocial child behavior. Child management skills training has been shown to produce clinically significant effects, often reducing clinical levels of conduct problems to normative levels during the course of treatment. Sustained improvements have also been demonstrated, with children often maintaining gains one year after treatment, and in at least one case, for ten to fourteen years post-treatment (Long *et al.* 1994). Furthermore, the effects of these treatments have been shown to generalize to siblings and to improve mothers' psychological functioning (Kazdin 1998).

Are battered women to blame for their children's conduct problems?

It might be reasoned that an effort to provide such services to battered women implies that these women have caused their children's behavior problems. Although we do believe that mothers' disrupted parenting may contribute to child conduct problems (as we said earlier), a primary cause of this disrupted parenting is the experience of violence and abuse. That is, the battering partner may be the first link in this chain of events. Furthermore, evidence indicates that fathers' parenting may be extremely important in the development of child conduct problems in families characterized by wife abuse (Holden and Ritchie 1991). As we have already noted, men who abuse their partners are also likely to abuse their children. These fathers also model antisocial behavior and often fail to provide appropriate encouragement for prosocial behavior. Thus, one might argue that child management skills training gives mothers the tools to correct problematic child behavior which may have been caused by the battering partners.

We strongly suspect that given the time and resources necessary to establish themselves independently of their battering partner, many women will demonstrate healthy and appropriate parenting patterns. However, we are not certain that such parenting practices will be enough to *correct* the behavior of children who are already exhibiting frequent and severe conduct problems (i.e., to teach the child more appropriate behavior). Rather, it is likely that these children require more focused techniques to curb their conduct problems, and child management skills training provides these techniques (Kazdin 1997; Kazdin and Weisz 1998). Thus, we provide this training to mothers because we believe that they can play a key role in reversing their child's conduct problems, whatever their original cause, and there is an empirical literature supporting the efficacy of this approach in alleviating serious child behavior problems.

Mothers' psychological distress

It is easily understandable that women departing from shelters and establishing homes independent of their former partners experience considerable stress, leaving these mothers less available to their children. Research suggests that child management skills training interventions are less effective when parents are distressed (Webster-Stratton and Hammond 1990); however, responses to treatment can be greatly enhanced by addressing family stressors throughout the course of treatment (Miller and Prinz 1990). Our intervention aims to address the special needs of battered women leaving shelters, easing their transition so that they can allocate more attention and energy for their children. To this end, our program helps mothers procure goods and services available in the community, offers instrumental and social support and teaches stress-reducing decision-making skills and problem-solving skills.

Description of the intervention

Our intervention begins in local area shelters where our staff interview mothers who have children between the ages of 4 and 8 years. Initial interviews allow the staff to establish rapport and give mothers an opportunity to relate their experiences and express their feelings in a supportive environment, while providing us with information about their families and family members' functioning. This information is used to determine eligibility for our program and/or to provide mothers referrals when appropriate. Shelter staffs are often overburdened and are sometimes not as available to talk informally with individual mothers as they would like. The shelter staff and mothers, therefore, generally welcome our role as people to whom the mothers can turn for support, guidance and a listening ear.

During the initial interviews, which are conducted by advanced graduate students in clinical psychology and trained post-baccalaureate research assistants, we obtain information about family demographics, child behavior, mothers' emotional distress and prior experiences of family violence. Mothers whose children evidence clinical levels of conduct problems or oppositional behavior are asked to participate in our program. Women are offered referrals for alternative forms of treatment if they show evidence of drug or alcohol abuse or dependence, or if they return directly to the batterer upon leaving the shelter. We believe these families are not likely to benefit from Project SUPPORT because their circumstances would require additional treatment with a very different focus from what we provide. For example, it has been our experience that women currently abusing drugs or alcohol are unable to focus on the skills taught in our intervention and are inconsistent in their attendance throughout treatment. These women would instead benefit first from treatment that focuses on problems associated with their substance use.

Over 95 percent of families who are eligible for our program choose to participate, which illustrates the desirability of our services and the needs that these mothers perceive their children to have. Women and children who participate are diverse with regard to ethnicity (i.e., about one-third Hispanic, one-third African American and one-third Caucasian) but not with regard to income: most live in poverty. Once families elect to join our program, we maintain regular (i.e., at least weekly) contact with the mothers throughout their stay in the shelter, offering support and assessing their needs and plans regularly. Upon a family's departure from the shelter, we arrange for a visit to their new residence as soon as it is convenient for the family. At this time, we again assess the family's needs and safety arrangements, helping them to develop a plan of action in the event of an unwelcome return by the batterer. In addition, we provide the mothers with basic home supplies such as toiletries, clothing and kitchen utensils whenever possible.

During this initial home visit, we conduct the first of six comprehensive assessments (pre-treatment, mid-treatment, post-treatment and three follow-up assessments). These assessments involve the mothers completing question- naires that assess family functioning and resources across a number of domains (e.g., child behavior, mother's social support and psychological functioning, utilization of child management skills, family violence). Mothers are also videotaped with their children; these videotapes are later coded. In addition, we acquire data from children's teachers with regard to their school behavior and academic progress. Mothers are paid for their time and effort in completing each assessment, and the data we collect are used to measure the effects of our intervention.

Families are randomly assigned to one of two conditions upon com- pletion of the first comprehensive assessment: our intervention services or a comparison condition. Families in the comparison condition are contacted each month by telephone or in person. We offer the families information and referrals, and facilitate access to goods (food banks, donated clothing) as needed. These monthly contacts are designed to maintain rapport with the families and to increase our ability to follow our participants over the full duration of the project. For many reasons, families may move several times after leaving the shelter. Monthly contacts allow us to stay in touch with the families' plans for moving and provide a 'warmer trail' to follow in the event that we discover families have already moved and left no information about their new whereabouts. There are no restrictions on the families' use of services from other agencies or service providers in the community. They thus serve as a 'usual care' control group against which we can compare the effects of our intervention.

Families who receive our intervention are assigned a therapist and a child mentor, who together make weekly, hour-long visits to the family's home for up to eight months. At the conclusion of the intervention period, we maintain monthly contacts with the families throughout the duration of their participation in the project. The therapists in our program are drawn primarily from the local professional community; they are a diverse group, with roots in social work and psychology. Therapists are required to have at least two years of clinical experience and a minimum of a master's degree. All therapists in our program are familiar with learning theory principles and have experience working with multiple-problem families and teaching parents child management skills. The therapists receive intensive training for our program: they receive the equivalent of two full-day seminars focusing on parent training, family violence, safety, community resources and child abuse and neglect; they accompany an experienced therapist to observe therapy sessions with ongoing clients; they must pass a test of proficiency with required skills.

The treatment that the therapists provide is detailed in a manual, and the audiotaped sessions are checked regularly for fidelity to the treatment protocol. In addition, therapists receive weekly supervision from a licensed psychologist. Mentors are advanced undergraduate college students who have received training in child management and nurturing skills and who have experience working with children in shelters for battered women. Mentors create fun activities for the children to enjoy while the therapist is working with the mother, and they serve as role models both to the children and the mothers as they enact the very skills we teach.

Our program is designed to meet the unique needs of women departing from shelters, who often have few financial resources and lack transportation and telephones. Hence, our services are provided free of charge in the family's home, and our staff are very sensitive to each family's circumstances and specific needs. While our treatment is manualized, it allows considerable flexibility to address individual needs and cultural differences. For example, some women move in with their parents when they leave the shelter, and in some cases we may incorporate the grandparents into portions of the treatment, when appropriate. We view the therapist's relationship with the mother as crucial to the success of our intervention, and therapists make every effort to create a warm, reliable, accepting and supportive atmosphere for each participant.

The intervention is comprised of two major components, the first of which includes social and instrumental support, decision-making skills and problem-solving skills. These are often helpful to women as they make the transition from the shelter to independent living and single parenthood. In addition to providing women with emotional support, physical resources and referrals for services, we often help our participants learn how to go about obtaining goods and services on their own. Not only do we provide mothers with phone numbers for potential resource providers, but also we model for the mothers how to make these phone calls and later provide them with encouragement and feedback regarding their attempts to make similar calls.

The decision-making and problem-solving skills portion of our treatment is based on the work of D'Zurilla and Goldfried (1971). Women are taught through direct instruction how to identify problems, generate lists of possible solutions, evaluate the likely outcome of each solution and choose the strategy that is likely to be most helpful. With additional practice and feedback, we help women refine these skills and apply them to everyday problems as they arise during the course of treatment.

The second major component consists of child management skills training, which is used to reduce children's conduct problems. We recognize that mothers beginning our program vary with regard to the skills they already possess and use with their children. For example, some mothers may already be proficient in the skills we teach but do not use some or all of them effectively or consistently; other mothers have stopped using some of these skills in the midst of great upheaval in their lives; still others have limited knowledge of the skills we teach and could benefit from learning additional skills. Before teaching each set of skills, we assess informally (i.e. through observation and discussion) each mother's knowledge and competence in the use of these skills and identify problem areas before proceeding. In this way, we tailor our intervention to meet each family's particular needs most effectively, considering the specific strengths and needs of each mother and her child's particular behavior problems.

In the child management skills training part of the intervention (based on programs by Dangel and Polster 1988; Forehand and McMahon 1981; Wolfe 1991), mothers are taught to apply specific skills in particular situations to achieve the goal of reducing their children's severe behavior problems. These skills are designed to improve mothers' communication with their children, increase prosocial and desirable child behaviors, and decrease aversive and undesirable child behaviors. Examples of skills include providing praise and positive attention, listening to children, giving rewards, removing privileges and using time out. Mothers receive direct instruction in the skills and are provided with opportunities to practice the skills during and between sessions, with encouraging and constructive feedback from the therapist. In addition, mothers are instructed in ways to create a safe and enriching home environment for their children.

It should be noted that in teaching these parenting skills to mothers, we make it clear to them that they are not to blame for their children's behavior problems. Rather, we emphasize that they can help their children by using particular ways of responding to and interacting with their children. We explain that consistently using the skills we teach helps reduce children's behavior problems, regardless of how the problems originally developed. Most mothers in our program express great concern about their children's conduct problems, and many are highly motivated to find ways of helping them.

Nurturing skills (based on work by Eyberg 1988; Forehand and Long 1996; Hembree-Kigin and McNeil 1995; Wolfe 1991) complement the child management skills and promote warm and positive mother–child relations. These skills include effective ways of listening and responding to children, as well as comforting and playing with them. An important component is the use of 'Together Time', which involves a mother spending at least a few minutes every day playing individually with each child. During this time, the mother engages in activities of the child's choice, makes positive, reflective statements and avoids admonitions and commands. 'Together Time' provides the child with daily opportunities for warm and fun interactions with his or her mother. Some mothers routinely engage in this kind of activity with their children; however, others are less likely to do so and we endeavor to help them find ways to spend more positive time with their children. For most of the mothers, managing to keep 'Together Time' fun and positive can be quite a challenge given the difficult behavior of their children.

There are two additional important aspects of the intervention. First, we work diligently with the mothers to help them identify when to use each particular skill. Inappropriate use of the skills can be benign at best, or it may further exacerbate problems. It is for this reason that we observe mothers implementing the skills and provide corrective feedback, as necessary. Second, we emphasize to the mothers the importance of consistent use of the skills if their efforts are to be successful.

The work involved in changing family interaction patterns, that is, being vigilant in observing and diligent in utilizing alternative responses to children's behaviors, requires substantial effort – effort beyond the already considerable demands of ordinary parenting. The mothers who undertake such extra efforts are to be commended; they do so during a time of great distress and uncertainty in their lives. However, after new patterns have stabilized and children's behavior problems are improved, family life becomes easier and more rewarding to both the mothers and their children, and the mothers have the satisfaction of knowing they were instrumental in helping their children overcome the effects of the earlier violence and upheaval in their lives.

Preliminary results of the intervention

In an initial attempt to evaluate the effectiveness of our program in reducing conduct problems among children of battered women, we have analyzed the data for thirty-six participating families in a preliminary outcome study of our intervention. The target children in these families included ten girls and twenty-six boys, with twenty-six children meeting criteria for a DSM-IV diagnosis of Oppositional Defiant Disorder and ten children qualifying for a DSM-IV diagnosis of Conduct Disorder (American Psychiatric Association 1994). Specific diagnoses were equally distributed across treatment and comparison conditions, and the two groups did not differ with regard to sociodemographic variables.

Standardized questionnaires and direct observational coding of parent and child behaviors were used to measure child and mother outcomes. The externalizing scale of the Child Behavior Checklist (CBCL: Achenbach 1991) provided a measure of children's conduct problems, such as non-compliance and aggression. The General Severity Index of the Symptom

Checklist-90-Revised (SCL-90-R: Derogatis, Rickels and Rock 1976) gave an index of mothers' psychological distress. Reviews of the videotaped interactions described above allowed for direct observational ratings of mothers' use of child management and nurturing skills and children's conduct problems.

To evaluate the effectiveness of our intervention, we examined changes in child and parent behavior and adjustment over the twenty months in which families were followed. Consistent with our expectations, conduct problems of children in families receiving our intervention improved to a greater extent and at a faster rate than did the problems of children in the comparison families. Similarly, mothers' psychological distress decreased more quickly for mothers in the intervention condition than for mothers in the comparison condition, although the reduction in distress was equal across the groups by the end of the follow-up period. Finally, mothers in the intervention group experienced greater and faster improvements in parenting skills than mothers in the comparison group. The results of our preliminary study thus appear quite promising and suggest that our treatment is effective in reducing child conduct problems, decreasing mothers' psychological distress, and enhancing mothers' parenting skills.

Directions for future interventions and evaluations

Children's exposure to domestic violence has gained recognition as a social problem in need of attention. Research on the effects of domestic violence on children has clearly grown in sophistication from its early roots of un-controlled, descriptive studies. However, controlled studies employing community samples of domestically violent families and longitudinal studies of children of battered women are still in short supply. Such controlled and longitudinal research is badly needed, not only to shed light on the nature of these children's problems and the processes involved, but also to inform our intervention efforts.

Existing research on children whose mothers have sought shelter from domestic violence suggests that although many of these children do not exhibit chronic or severe problems, a large subset is less fortunate. Thus, there is a great need for effective services for these children. We described a sampling of the broad range of interventions developed to help children of battered women. The developers of these programs are to be commended for their efforts not only to help these children and their mothers, but also to document the effectiveness of their services. Unfortunately, such evaluations of interventions are scarce. Without evaluation, we have no way of knowing whether our well-intended efforts bear fruit, nor can we effectively guard against unintended or harmful effects. It is therefore crucial for future developers to evaluate their services and publish their results.

Finally, we encourage program developers to use available research when designing interventions for children of battered women. Research and theory can inform the design of effective services and facilitate the efficient use of resources by directing our efforts where they are most needed and suggesting potential mechanisms for change. While no one intervention can correct or prevent the varied problems of children of battered women, research-informed programs can improve these children's lives.

References

Achenbach, T.M. (1991) *Manual for the Child Behavior Checklist/4–18 and 1991 Profile.* Burlington, VT: Department of Psychology, University of Vermont.

American Psychiatric Association (1994) *Diagnostic and Statistical Manual of Mental Disorders – Fourth Edition.* Washington DC: American Psychiatric Association.

Appel, A.E. and Holden, G.W. (1998) 'The co-occurrence of spouse and physical child abuse: a review and appraisal.' *Journal of Family Psychology 12,* 578–599.

Carlson, B.E. (1984) 'Children's observations of interpersonal violence.' In A. Roberts (ed) *Battered Women and their Families.* New York: Springer.

Christopoulos, C., Cohn, D.A., Shaw, D.S., Joyce, S., Sullivan-Hanson, J., Kraft, S.P. and Emery, R.E. (1987) 'Children of abused women. I: adjustment at time of shelter residence.' *Journal of Marriage and the Family 49,* 611–619.

Coie, J. and Dodge, K. (1998) 'Aggression and antisocial behavior.' In W. Damon (ed) *Handbook of Child Psychology, Volume 3.* New York: Wiley.

Dangel, R.F. and Polster, R.A. (1988) *Teaching Child Management Skills.* New York: Pergamon.

Derogatis, L., Rickels, K. and Rock, A. (1976) 'The SCL-90 and the MMPI: a step in the validation of a new self-report scale.' *British Journal of Psychiatry 128,* 280–289.

Dishion, T.J. and Patterson, G.R. (1992) 'Age effects in parent training outcome.' *Behavior Therapy 23,* 719–729.

Dishion, T.J., French, D.C. and Patterson, G.R. (1995) 'The development and etiology of antisocial behavior.' In D. Cicchetti and D.J. Cohen (eds) *Developmental Psychopathology. Volume 2: Risk, Disorder, and Adaptation.* New York: Wiley.

D'Zurilla, T.J. and Goldfried, M.R. (1971) 'Problem solving and behavior modification.' *Journal of Abnormal Psychology 78,* 107–126.

Easterbrooks, M.A. and Emde, R.N. (1988) 'Marital and parent–child relationships: the role of affect in the family system.' In R.A. Hinde and J.

Stevenson-Hinde (eds) *Relationships within Families: Mutual Influences.* New York: Oxford University Press.

Eyberg, S.M. (1988) 'Parent–child interaction therapy: integration of traditional and behavioral concerns.' *Child and Family Behavior Therapy 10,* 33–46.

Fantuzzo, J.W., DePaola, L.M., Lambert, L., Martino, T., Anderson, G. and Sutton, S. (1991) 'Effects of interparental violence on the psychological adjustment and competencies of young children.' *Journal of Consulting and Clinical Psychology 59,* 258–265.

Forehand, R.L. and Long, N. (1996) *Parenting the Strong-Willed Child.* Chicago: Contemporary Books.

Forehand, R.L. and McMahon, R.J. (1981) *Helping the Noncompliant Child: A Clinician's Guide to Parent Training.* New York: Guilford.

Forsstrom-Cohen, B. and Rosenbaum, A. (1985) 'The effects of parental marital violence on young adults: an exploratory investigation.' *Journal of Marriage and the Family 47,* 467–472.

Graham-Berman, S.A. (1992) *Kids' Club Manual.* Published by author.

Graham-Berman, S.A. (2000) 'Designing interventions for children exposed to family violence: applications of research and theory.' In S. Graham-Berman and J. Edleson (eds) *Intimate Violence in the Lives of Children: The Future of Research, Intervention, and Social Policy.* Washington DC: American Psychological Association.

Grych, J.H., Fincham, F.D., Jouriles, E.N. and McDonald, R. (in press) 'Interparental conflict and child adjustment: testing the mediational role of appraisals in the cognitive-contextual framework.' *Child Development.*

Grych, J.H., Jouriles, E.N., Swank, P.R., McDonald, R. and Norwood, W.D. (2000) 'Patterns of adjustment among children of battered women.' *Journal of Consulting and Clinical Psychology, 68,* 84–94.

Hembree-Kigin, T.L. and McNeil, C.B. (1995) *Parent–Child Interaction Therapy.* New York: Plenum.

Henning, K., Leitenberg, H., Coffey, P., Turner, T. and Bennett, T. (1996) 'Long-term psychological and social impact of witnessing physical conflict between parents.' *Journal of Interpersonal Violence 11,* 35–51.

Hershorn, M. and Rosenbaum, A. (1985) 'Children of marital violence: a closer look at the unintended victims.' *American Journal of Orthopsychiatry 55,* 260–266.

Holden, G.W. and Ritchie, K.L. (1991) 'Linking extreme marital discord, child rearing, and child behavior problems: evidence from battered women.' *Child Development 6,* 311–327.

Holden, G.W., Geffner, R.E. and Jouriles, E.N. (1998a) 'Appraisal and outlook.' In G.W. Holden, R. Geffner and E.N. Jouriles (eds) *Children Exposed to Marital Violence: Theory, Research, and Applied Issues.* Washington DC: American Psychological Association.

Holden, G.W., Stein, J.D., Ritchie, K.L., Harris, S.D. and Jouriles, E.N. (1998b) 'Parenting behaviors and beliefs of battered women.' In G.W. Holden, R.

Geffner and E.N. Jouriles (eds) *Children Exposed to Marital Violence: Theory, Research, and Applied Issues.* Washington DC: American Psychological Association.

Holtzworth-Munroe, A., Jouriles, E.N., Smutzler, N. and Norwood, W.D. (1998) 'Victims of domestic violence.' In A.S. Bellack and M. Hersen (eds) *Comprehensive Clinical Psychology, Volume 9.* Oxford: Pergamon.

Huesmann, L.R., Eron, L.D., Lefkowitz, M.M. and Walder, O. (1984) 'Stability of aggression over time and generations.' *Developmental Psychology 20,* 1120–1134.

Hughes, H.M. (1982) 'Brief interventions with children in a battered women's shelter: a model preventive program.' *Family Relations 31,* 495–502.

Hughes, H. and Barad, S. (1982) 'Changes in the psychological functioning of children in a battered women's shelter: a pilot study.' *Victimology 7,* 60–68.

Hughes, H. and Barad, S. (1983) 'Psychological functioning of children in a battered women's shelter: a preliminary investigation.' *American Journal of Orthopsychiatry 53,* 525–531.

Hughes, H.M. and Luke, D.A. (1998) 'Heterogeneity in adjustment among children of battered women.' In G.W. Holden, R. Geffner and E.N. Jouriles (eds) *Children Exposed to Marital Violence: Theory, Research, and Applied Issues.* Washington DC: American Psychological Association.

Jaffe, P.G., Wilson, S.K. and Wolfe, D.A. (1986a) 'Promoting changes in attitudes and understanding of conflict resolution among child witnesses of family violence.' *Canadian Journal of Behavioural Sciences 18,* 356–366.

Jaffe, P., Wolfe, D., Wilson, S.K. and Zak, L. (1986b) 'Family violence and child adjustment: a comparative analysis of girls' and boys' behavioral symptoms.' *American Journal of Psychiatry 143,* 74–76.

Jaffe, P., Wilson, S. and Wolfe, D. (1988) 'Specific assessment and intervention strategies for children exposed to wife battering: preliminary empirical investigations.' *Canadian Journal of Community Mental Health 7,* 157–163.

Johnson, M.P. (1995) 'Patriarchal terrorism and common couple violence: Two forms of violence against women.' *Journal of Marriage and the Family 57,* 283–294.

Jouriles, E.N. and Farris, A.M. (1992) 'Effects of marital conflict on subsequent parent–son interactions.' *Behavior Therapy 23,* 355–374.

Jouriles, E.N. and LeCompte, S.H. (1991) 'Husbands' aggression toward wives and mothers' and fathers' aggression toward children: moderating effects of child gender.' *Journal of Consulting and Clinical Psychology 59,* 190–192.

Jouriles, E.N. and Norwood, W.D. (1995) 'Physical aggression toward boys and girls in families characterized by the battering of women.' *Journal of Family Psychology 9,* 69–78.

Jouriles, E.N., Murphy, C.M. and O'Leary, K.D. (1989) 'Interspousal aggression, marital discord, and child problems.' *Journal of Consulting and Clinical Psychology 57,* 453–455.

Jouriles, E.N., McDonald, R., Norwood, W.D., Ware, H.S., Spiller, L.C. and Swank, P.R. (1998) 'Knives, guns, and interparent violence: relations with child behavior problems.' *Journal of Family Psychology 12*, 178–194.

Jouriles, E.N., McDonald, R., Norwood, W.D. and Ezell, E. (2000a) 'Documenting the prevalence of children's exposure to domestic violence: issues and controversies.' In S. Graham-Berman and J. Edleson (eds) *Intimate Violence in the Lives of Children: The Future of Research, Intervention, and Social Policy.* Washington DC: American Psychological Association.

Jouriles, E.N., Norwood, W.D., McDonald, R. and Peters, B. (2000b) 'Domestic violence and child adjustment.' In J. Grych and F. Fincham (eds) *Child Development and Interparental Conflict.* Cambridge: Cambridge University Press.

Kazdin, A.E. (1995) *Conduct Disorder in Childhood and Adolescence,* 2nd edn. Thousand Oaks, CA: Sage.

Kazdin, A.E. (1997) 'Parent management training: evidence, outcomes, and issues.' *Journal of the American Academy of Child and Adolescent Psychiatry 36*, 1349–1356.

Kazdin, A.E. (1998) 'Psychosocial treatments for conduct disorder in children.' In P. Nathan and J. Gorman (eds) *A Guide to Treatments that Work.* New York: Oxford.

Kazdin, A.E. and Weisz, J.R. (1998) 'Identifying and developing empirically supported child and adolescent treatments.' *Journal of Consulting and Clinical Psychology 66*, 19–36.

Layzer, J.I., Goodson, B.D. and DeLange, C. (1986) 'Children in shelters.' In M. Hansen and M. Haraway (eds) *Battering and Family Therapy: A Feminist Perspective.* Newbury Park, CA: Sage.

Loeber, R. and Hay, D. (1997) 'Key issues in the development of aggression and violence from childhood to early adulthood.' *Annual Review of Psychology 48*, 371–410.

Long, P., Forehand, R., Wierson, M. and Morgan, A. (1994) 'Does parent training with young noncompliant children have long-term effects?' *Behaviour Research and Therapy 32*, 101–107.

McCord, J. (1979) 'Some child rearing antecedents to criminal behavior in adult men.' *Journal of Personality and Social Psychology 37*, 1477–1486.

McDonald, R. and Jouriles, E.N. (1991) 'Marital aggression and child behavior problems: research findings, mechanisms, and intervention strategies.' *Behavior Therapist 14*, 189–192.

McDonald, R., Jouriles, E.N. and Ware, H.S. (1999) 'Husbands' marital violence, general marital discord, and the behavior problems of clinic-referred children.' Manuscript submitted for publication.

McNeal, C. and Amato, P.R. (1998) 'Parents' marital violence: long-term consequences for children.' *Journal of Family Issues 19*, 123–139.

Mahoney, A., Boggio, R. and Jouriles, E.N. (1996) 'Effects of verbal marital disagreements on subsequent mother–son interactions in a child clinical sample.' *Journal of Clinical Child Psychology 25*, 262–271.

Margolin, G. (1998) 'Effects of domestic violence on children.' In P.K. Trickett and C.J. Schellenbach (eds) *Violence against Children in the Family and the Community*. Washington DC: American Psychological Association.

Miller, G.E. and Prinz, R.J. (1990) 'Enhancement of social learning family interventions for childhood conduct disorder.' *Psychological Bulletin 108*, 291–307.

Moffit, T.E. (1993) 'Adolescence-limited and life-course-persistent antisocial behavior: a developmental taxonomy.' *Psychological Review 100*, 674–701.

Patterson, G.R. (1982) *Coercive Family Processes*. Eugene, OR: Castalia.

Patterson, G.R., DeBarsyshe, B.D. and Ramsey, E. (1989) 'A developmental perspective on antisocial behavior.' *American Psychologist 44*, 329–335.

Patterson, G.R., Reid, J.B. and Dishion, T.J. (1992) *Antisocial Boys*. Eugene, OR: Castalia.

Peled, E. (1997) 'Intervention with children of battered women: a review of current literature.' *Children and Youth Services Review 19*, 277–299.

Peled, E. and Edleson, J. (1992) 'Multiple perspectives on group work with children of battered women.' *Violence and Victims 7*, 327–346.

Reid, J.B. (1993) 'Prevention of conduct disorder before and after school entry: relating interventions to developmental findings.' *Development and Psychopathology 5*, 243–262.

Rosenbaum, A. and O'Leary, K.D. (1981) 'Children: the unintended victims of marital violence.' *American Journal of Orthopsychiatry 51*, 692–699.

Rossman, B.B.R. and Rosenberg, M. (1992) 'Family stress and functioning in children: moderating effects of children's beliefs about their control over parental conflict.' *Journal of Child Psychology and Psychiatry 33*, 699–715.

Sholevar, G.P. and Sholevar, E.H. (1995) 'Overview.' In G.P. Sholevar (ed) *Conduct Disorders in Children and Adolescents*. Washington DC: American Psychiatric Press.

Silvern, L., Karyl, J., Waeld, L., Hodges, W.F., Starek, J. and Heidt, E. (1995) 'Retrospective reports of parental partner abuse: relationships to depression, trauma symptoms, and self-esteem among college students.' *Journal of Family Violence 10*, 177–202.

Spiller, L.C., Marsh, W., Peters, B., Miller, P. and Jouriles, E.N. (1999) 'Multiple types of wife abuse and child behavior problems.' Paper presented to the Society for Research on Child Development, Albuquerque, NM, April.

Stattin, H. and Magnusson, D. (1996) 'Antisocial development: a holistic approach.' *Development and Psychopathology 8*, 617–645.

Sternberg, K.J., Lamb, M.E., Greenbaum, C., Cicchetti, D., Dawud, S., Coretes, R.M., Kripsin, O. and Lorey, F. (1993) 'Effects of domestic violence on children's behavior problems and depression.' *Developmental Psychology 29*, 44–52.

Straus, M.A. and Gelles, R.J. (1990) *Physical Violence in American Families: Risk Factors and Adaptations to Violence in 8,145 Families.* New Brunswick, NJ: Transaction.

Sullivan, C. and Davidson, W. (1998) *Preliminary Findings from the Family Follow-up Study.* Funded by the National Center for Injury Prevention and Control, Centers for Disease Control and Prevention (R49/CCR510531), Michigan State University, Lansing, MI.

Wagar, J.M. and Rodway, M.R. (1995) 'An evaluation of a group treatment approach for children who have witnessed wife abuse.' *Journal of Family Violence 10,* 295–306.

Ware, H.S., Jouriles, E.N., Spiller, L.C., McDonald, R., Swank, P.R. and Norwood, W.D. (in press) 'Conduct problems among children at battered women's shelters: prevalence and stability of maternal reports.' *Journal of Family Violence.*

Webster-Stratton, C. and Hammond, M. (1990) 'Predictors of treatment outcome in parent training for families with conduct problem children.' *Behavior Therapy 21,* 319–337.

Wilson, S., Cameron, S., Jaffe, P. and Wolfe, D. (1989) 'Children exposed to wife abuse: an intervention model.' *Social Casework: Journal of Contemporary Social Work 70,* 180–184.

Wolfe, D.A. (1991) *Preventing Physical and Emotional Abuse of Children.* New York: Guilford.

Wolfe, D.A., Jaffe, P., Wilson, S. and Zak, L. (1985) 'Children of battered women: the relation of child behavior to family violence and maternal stress.' *Journal of Consulting and Clinical Psychology 53,* 657–665.

CHAPTER 8

Juvenile Crime Victims

Psychological Impact and Treatment

John P. Vincent, Gerald E. Harris, Cynthia N. Vincent, Jannette Cross and Anu Palapattu

This chapter summarizes what is known about the psychological impact of violent crime on juveniles as well as promising new trends in treatment. Violence occurs with alarming frequency in our society, and a great number of children and adolescents have experienced some form of victimization. Most conceptions of family violence emphasize intra-familial perpetrators. Often, however, families are affected by violence inflicted by nonfamily members or strangers. The psychological impact of extra-familial violence on children and families has received comparatively little attention, and few investigators have initiated programs to systematically develop and evaluate effective treatments. This chapter examines how violence perpetrated by nonfamily members impacts the psychological well-being of children and their families. First, we summarize what is known from the children's victimization literature and from our own clinical research program concerning the psychological reactions of children to violence. Factors that may affect the variability in type and frequency of trauma-related psychological reactions are outlined. Second, we describe the various treatment approaches that have been developed for this population as well as the theoretical rationale and components of our individualized cognitive-behavioral and supportive treatment programs. Third, we present treatment outcome findings from our ongoing research program as well as some of the challenges confronted by practitioners who work with victimized youth. Consistent with the desire to generate guidelines for research-informed practice, we present our own research program as an example of effective partnership between science and practice. We believe that the integration of empirical methods in a clinical setting is especially relevant for work with children and their families affected by crime. In light of the high rates of juvenile victimization and the absence of empirically supported treatments, an integrative clinical-research approach is ideally suited to efficient development, evaluation and dissemination of interventions that can help address this problem.

Although the issue of youth victimization received increased attention during the 1990s, work in the area is still fragmented and far from complete (Finkelhor and Dziuba-Leatherman 1994). There are few methodologically sound studies that address this topic and most of what is known is derived from studies of specific types of child victimization, such as intra-familial child abuse, natural disasters and adult studies of criminal victimization. Extrapolation from these studies should be done cautiously since it is not yet clear whether the type of victimization is important to understanding the specific manifestations of psychological distress and response to treatment. Generalizing from adult studies to children is particularly questionable, since, unlike adults, developmental and family factors figure much more prominently in children's response to victimization and treatment. Advances in clinically relevant knowledge with child victims of crime are best achieved by research initiatives that specifically target those children.

One such research initiative is the Victims' Resource Institute (VRI) at the University of Houston. Our clinical-research project has sought to study systematically the impact of victimization on juveniles and to develop and evaluate effective treatment protocols. Since 1992, VRI has evaluated and treated over 150 children and adolescents, ranging in age from 5 to 17 years, who have been victimized by violent crime perpetrated by nonfamily members. In addition to interventions designed to facilitate the emotional recovery process, specific attention has also been directed to the challenges faced by children who must testify in court. Preparing the client for court, presenting expert testimony on the impact of victimization and helping prevent revictimization associated with children's participation in the legal process are all parts of our role. Through this work we have learned a great deal about youth victimization, including the variety of manifestations of psychological impact, treatment strategies that appear to be effective, and challenges in conducting programmatic research with this population.

Prevalence of youth victimization

Stemming from the steep rise in violent crime during the 1980s, there has been growing attention to the impact of crime on juveniles. Reports indicate that youth are now at greatest risk for victimization compared to any other age group. According to the 1998 National Crime Victimization Survey (Bureau of Justice Statistics 1998), young people between the ages of 12 and 19 experience violent victimization rates four to five times higher than adults over 50. It has been estimated that about one-third of the female population has experienced sexual abuse by the age of 18 (Russell 1986). In a telephone survey of children between the ages of 10 and 16, over one-third reported having been the victim of a physical or sexual assault (Boney-McCoy and Finkelhor 1995a). Children in the USA below the age of 12 were victimized in roughly 600,000 violent incidents in 1992 (US Department of Justice 1994). While the rates of youth victimization are disturbing, they probably underestimate the enormity of the problem. In fact, it was estimated that in 1991, only 20 percent of juvenile victimizations were brought to the attention of law enforcement agencies (US Department of Justice 1994).

Depending on their age, differences emerge in the types of victimization that children experience. Younger children are more likely to be victimized by a family member, while older children tend to be victimized more often by an acquaintance or stranger. Children are more vulnerable to victimization than adults for a variety of reasons, including small physical stature, dependency on others and inability to escape or avoid abusive environments (Finkelhor and Dziuba-Leatherman 1994).

Children and adolescents are also victimized indirectly through their exposure to crimes against others (Morgan and Zedner 1992). Preliminary results of the National Survey of Adolescents estimate that almost 9 million young people witnessed serious violence (National Institute of Justice 1997). For example, approximately 10–20 percent of all homicides in California were witnessed by children (Pynoos and Eth 1986) while 90 percent of children in New Orleans had been exposed to violence and 40 percent had seen a dead body (Osofsky 1997).

Children's psychological reactions to victimization

In a review of the literature on children's stress reactions, Bendek (1985) and Fletcher (1996) noted that, prior to and during World War II, documentation of children's trauma reactions was unsystematic and infrequent. Accounts from this time period appear to minimize the psychological distress of children in response to trauma (Bendek 1985). It was presumed that children were resilient to trauma and that any reaction to experiencing a stressful event was temporary (Garmezy and Rutter 1985; Rigamer 1986).

More recently, it has become clear that children exhibit a host of adverse psychological reactions to victimization, the exact nature of which varies according to a number of factors. The first detailed accounts of children's psychological distress in response to trauma appeared in the 1970s and 1980s and were primarily anecdotal in nature (Bendek 1985; Eth and Pynoos 1985; Pynoos *et al.* 1987; Terr 1981, 1983, 1985, 1991). Systematic research on child victimization began to appear in the 1980s and 1990s (Boney-McCoy and Finkelhor 1995a; Browne and Finkelhor 1986; Finkelhor and Dziuba-Leatherman 1994; McFarlane 1987; Pynoos and Nader 1988), when investigators began to assess specific symptomatology, use standardized measures, gather larger sample sizes and employ comparative research designs to study the psychological reactions of traumatized and nontraumatized children (Fletcher 1996). Despite these advances, a number of unanswered questions remain, and most of what is known about juvenile crime victims has been extrapolated from adult studies of criminal victimization and studies of child victimization in other areas.

While many questions can be raised about the applicability of adult studies to furthering our understanding of children's reactions to trauma, research with adults has been more extensive than with children and it provides a beginning point in identifying children's reactions to criminal victimization. In their classic book, Bard and Sangrey (1979) observed that psychological reactions to victimization among adults appear to unfold over time in three stages. The *impact* stage begins immediately following the victimization and can last up to several days. During this stage, the victim experiences shock, disorientation, disbelief and denial. The victim may also feel numb, vulnerable, helpless, lonely and depressed. Physiological disturbances such as the inability to eat or sleep may also occur. The *recoil* stage lasts approximately three to eight months. Mood swings, nightmares, lack of trust and fantasies of retribution are common during this phase. The final or *reorganization* stage typically involves decreases in the intensity of feelings of anger and fear and an altered world-view incorporating the victimization. While Bard and Sangrey's (1979) three-stage model has not been subjected to empirical study, it provides a useful heuristic for describing the temporal factors that appear to affect the psychological reactions to adult victimization.

Researchers have also used psychiatric diagnoses, specifically Posttraumatic Stress Disorder (PTSD), to describe the symptoms exhibited by adult crime victims. In order to be diagnosed with PTSD using the *Diagnostic and Statistical Manual of Mental Disorders – Fourth Edition* (DSM-IV: American Psychiatric Association 1994), a person must have been exposed to a traumatic event in which 'the person experienced, witnessed, or was confronted with an event or events that involved actual or threatened death or serious injury, or a threat to the physical integrity of self or others, [and] the person's response involved intense fear, helplessness, or horror' (pp.427–428). Responses to a traumatic event must be exhibited in three different categories: *re-experiencing* (e.g., recurrent, distressing thoughts or dreams of the event, intense psychological distress when confronted with cues of the event), *avoidance* (e.g., efforts to avoid thoughts, feelings or reminders of the events, restricted range of affect) and *increased arousal* (e.g., angry outbursts, difficulty sleeping or concentrating). PTSD symptoms have been found in adult rape victims and in adults following a shooting at their children's school (Bownes, O'Gorman and Sayers 1991; Schwarz and Kowalski 1991). For most individuals, PTSD symptoms appeared to decline within three months, though fear and anxiety were reported to persist for a longer time period following a rape (Stekettee and Foa 1987). While we acknowledge the limited generalizability of these results to child victims, this research provides evidence that PTSD symptoms are common following exposure to crime.

Because of the scarcity of research with juvenile crime victims, it is also important to examine studies involving children's reactions to other traumas, such as natural disasters and war. Researchers in these areas have reported PTSD symptoms in children and adolescents following exposure to non-criminal trauma (Earls *et al.* 1988; McFarlane 1987; Pynoos *et al.* 1993; Stallard and Law 1994; Yule and Udwin 1991). Fletcher (1996) reported that, on average, 36 percent of children exposed to traumatic events were diagnosed with PTSD based on his meta-analysis of 2697 children from 47 samples. In general, the literature indicates that many of the symptoms, but not the full syndrome of PTSD, often emerge as a result of traumatization (Miller 1998). Most children and adolescents appear to be especially troubled by the *re-experiencing* symptoms (Fletcher 1996; Miller 1998). According to Fletcher (1996), seven of the eleven highest ranked DSM-IV symptoms were re-experiencing symptoms and included feeling or showing distress at reminders of the trauma; re-enactment of significant parts of the event through gestures, actions (drawing, play) or sounds; feeling as if the event were being relived; intrusive memories; bad dreams or nightmares; trauma-specific fears; and talking excessively about the event. Also included among the eleven symptoms were affective numbing, loss of interest in previously important activities, avoidance of reminders of events and difficulty concentrating. Other commonly noted PTSD-type symptoms are preoccupation with safety concerns, revenge fantasies and desensitization towards aggression (Meichenbaum 1999).

In addition to PTSD, several clinicians and researchers have found that traumatized children and adolescents are also likely to exhibit an array of other symptoms (Boney-McCoy and Finkelhor 1995a; Browne and Finkelhor 1986; Fletcher 1996; Kendall-Tackett, Williams and Finkelhor 1993; Meichenbaum 1999; Miller 1998; Perez and Widom 1994). Many children exhibit an increase in externalizing behaviors, such as aggression, noncompliance, risk-taking behavior, running away and sexual acting out. Other trauma-related symptoms include increased anxiety and phobias, problems with separation, sadness and depression, suicidal thoughts, guilt and shame, omen formation, low self-esteem and somatic complaints. Depending on the nature of the trauma, grief for the loss of family members and/or friends may also be evident. Difficulties in social competencies may also develop as evidenced by regressive behavior or loss of previously acquired skills, fear of rejection and difficulties maintaining friendships. Traumatized youth are also likely to exhibit cognitive and language delays, school problems and poor overall academic and intellectual functioning. Traumatic experiences can skew expectations about the world, the safety of interpersonal relationships, and the child's sense of personal integrity (Pynoos, Steinberg and Goenjian 1996).

The few studies on criminal victimization of children indicate that exposure to crime produces PTSD symptoms and other symptoms similar to those of non-criminally victimized children. Of six studies of children victimized by violent crime reviewed by McNally (1993), five indicated that exposure to criminal victimization produced rates of PTSD ranging from 27 to 100 percent. All of the studies reviewed by McNally (1993) evaluated children using either DSM-III or DSM-III-R criteria and the youth in the studies were exposed to kidnapping, sniper fire or the rape or murder of a parent. In general, the literature suggests that exposure to victimization involving violent crime triggers symptoms of PTSD in children more consistently than other traumatic events (McNally 1993; Miller 1998).

Unique to trauma associated with criminal victimization, there is often a link between judicial outcome and trauma symptoms (Pynoos and Eth 1985). Review of the literature indicates that children's participation in the court process can lead to secondary victimization. This is often a result of stressors such as pre-trial apprehension, preparation for trial, public exposure, facing the accused and cross-examination (Wolfe, Sas and Wilson 1987). Clinically, researchers have noted that the lack of an arrest or conviction may impede 'psychological closure' (Pynoos and Eth 1985).

Too few prospective long-term studies have been completed, thereby limiting the conclusion that can be drawn regarding the temporal course and prognosis for child and adolescent victims. Some researchers have found decreased incidence of symptoms over time, while others have found that high levels of symptoms persist over time (Fletcher 1996). Anecdotally, Terr (1983) noted that four years following a school-bus kidnapping, all of the twenty-five children who were involved exhibited posttraumatic symptomatology including trauma-specific fears, avoidance of thoughts of the event, repetitive nightmares and trauma-related repetitive play. Nader *et al.* (1990) found that many children continued to experience PTSD symptoms one year after a sniper attack at their school. Early childhood victimization is thought to increase a child's risk for criminal arrest during adolescence (Widom 1997), and retrospective studies of victims of childhood sexual abuse indicate that depression, self-destructive behavior, poor self-esteem, feelings of isolation and sexual maladjustment may persist into adulthood (Browne and Finkelhor 1986; Fletcher 1996).

Several researchers have discussed the need to identify moderator variables, risk indicators and resilience factors associated with childhood psychological distress. For example, researchers have suggested that the nature of the traumatic event (e.g., level of violence, degree of exposure, duration of trauma and evidence of multiple traumas), aspects of the social environment (e.g., familial reactions, parenting style, family cohesion, SES and social support), characteristics of the child or adolescent (e.g., gender, ethnicity, age, developmental stage, coping strategies, history of prior trauma, IQ and problem-solving capacity) and emotional and cognitive factors (e.g., helplessness, attributions and perceptions of the trauma) may moderate the nature and severity of trauma reactions. Level of exposure or physical proximity to the trauma was found to be strongly associated with the severity and course of psychological distress following trauma (Pynoos *et al.* 1996). Better parent–child relationships were found to be associated with fewer symptoms (Boney-McCoy and Finkelhor 1995b) and individual child resources such as self-esteem have been found to moderate the impact of trauma (Vicknair 1996). Some have suggested that younger children are more vulnerable to the effects of victimization, but it may depend on the nature of the trauma and specific symptom expression (Meichenbaum 1999). Theorists have only begun to apply developmental theory to the understanding and assessment of children's posttraumatic stress reactions (Fletcher 1996).

Variability in symptom levels

In reviewing this literature as well as in our own work with child and adolescent victims of violent crime, we have observed an interesting phenomenon. Despite the fact that child victims of crime have either experienced or been exposed to horrendous acts of violence, a surprising number of them report only minimal psychological distress. In fact, fewer than 20 percent of the children who sought treatment services through our program at the Victims' Resource Institute reported symptoms that were sufficient to warrant a DSM-IV diagnosis of Posttraumatic Stress Disorder. Other investigators have reported similar findings. For example, in their review of the literature on child sexual abuse, Kendall-Tackett *et al.* (1993) reported that researchers have found that between 21 percent and 49 percent of child victims of sexual abuse were asymptomatic.

This phenomenon could be accounted for in several ways. Differences in the nature and severity of psychological symptoms may be attributable to variability in children's psychological resilience. In addition, limitations of current assessment instruments for children, coupled with child and parent coping styles based on avoidance and minimization, may contribute to underreporting biases of the psychological impact of violence on youth.

Some children may be buffered from many of the detrimental psychological consequences of victimization. For example, psychologically resilient children with good premorbid adjustment, exceptional coping skills and a strong network of supportive resources may simply not experience clinical levels of distress. We know from the literature on children's psychological resilience that there is considerable variability in children's ability to cope with negative or stressful events, and some are relatively unaffected by experiences that are significantly harmful to most children (e.g., Reynolds 1998). However, the percentage of child victims of violence reporting virtually no distress are greater than would be expected from these findings, suggesting that other factors are involved.

Limitations in assessment measures for child populations may also account for the variability in reported symptoms. Many of the measures used in research with child victims are not normed for the youngest victims, who also have difficulty identifying and reporting internal emotional states. Self-report data are used almost exclusively in studies of child victims, with all the attendant methodological problems. In order to avoid the mono-rater bias problem, data from parents or other adults may be collected. Unfortunately, self-reports and parent reports of children's distress are often poorly correlated. For example, in the sample of child victims referred to our own treatment program, child and parent reports of child behavior problems were virtually uncorrelated (internalizing problems, r = 0.10; externalizing problems, r = 0.006). While lack of correspondence between child and parent reports of child behavior is common, our estimates are even lower than for other samples of clinic and non-clinic children, where the correlation between parent and child reports averages r = 0.22 (Achenbach 1991a). It is also noteworthy that when we compared parent and child reported measures of child psychological distress, mean parents' scores were consistently higher than children's scores.

It is not clear how to account for these discrepancies between child and parent reports of children's adjustment following victimization. It is possible that poor correspondence between child and parent reports of symptoms may reflect that children exhibit an avoidant coping style more often than parents. A defensive coping style based on cognitive and behavioral avoidance can effectively block out the majority of children's conscious distress, and probably results in inaccurately low estimates of child-reported symptoms that fall below clinical cutoffs. Unfortunately, since assessment data are typically not available from child victims prior to the trauma, it is impossible to compare their level of functioning post-trauma with their pre-trauma baseline. Even though individual children do not exhibit clinical levels of symptoms, they may exhibit a significant increase in symptoms compared to their own level of prior functioning. It is easy to see how such data could be misinterpreted. If the children do not report clinical levels of distress, one might falsely conclude that they have not experienced any adjustment problems associated with the trauma. Such misinterpretation of child victim data has resulted in strong controversy in response to an article suggesting that there are essentially no significant long-lasting effects from child sexual abuse (Rind, Tromovitch and Bauserman 1998).

In an attempt to explore factors that might account for variability in child reports of psychological symptoms following exposure to crime, we conducted analyses of our own data from child victims at the outset of their participation in one of our treatment programs. In a series of correlational analyses, Zygmuntowicz *et al.* (1997) examined how well one could account for child-reported internalizing symptoms by looking at children's self-esteem and their use of avoidance to cope with trauma. In this study, self-esteem was conceptualized as an individual resource variable like psychological resilience and avoidance was viewed as a negative coping strategy. Use of cognitive and behavioral avoidance in response to trauma may thwart a natural exposure process that could diminish the conditioned association between trauma stimuli and subjective distress. This assumption is implicit in the use of exposure-based treatments for survivors of trauma, including adult victims of sexual assault (e.g., Foa *et al.* 1991). Zygmuntowicz *et al.*'s (1997) results support this conceptualization, insofar as children who reported higher levels of self-esteem and lower levels of cognitive and behavioral avoidance experienced lower levels of emotional distress. Even though one must be careful not to make causal inferences from correlational data like these, the results are consistent with conceptualizing self-esteem as a protective factor and avoidance as a nonadaptive coping response to trauma. In subsequent analyses, consistent results were found when gender effects were controlled in the analyses, but not when parent reports were used as the index of child distress. When the results were examined for a subset of children who had been victims of sexual assault, as opposed to other violent crimes, self-esteem, but not avoidance behavior, was related to child-reported distress. Although the small sample size of sexually abused children (n = 23) may have worked against finding statistical significance, these follow-up analyses underscore the need for caution in making generalizations of the findings across subsamples of child victims and data sources.

In another VRI study of children's reactions to violent crime, Battle (1998) used structural equation modeling to examine the variability in child-reported distress following victimization. In this study, an effort was made to construct a scale of victimization severity, based on earlier research that linked specific aspects of a crime with the degree of victims' psychological distress. These crime characteristics included type of victimization, type of crime, relationship of perpetrator to victim, physical injury/life threat and number of incidents. Inter-rater reliability of the scale was quite good (r = 0.84), but only moderate internal consistency was obtained (Cronbach's alpha = 0.65). Battle (1998) then computed structural equations to test five models that posited a mediational role of child self-esteem in the relationship between severity of victimization and children's psychological distress. These data indicate that children who had higher self-esteem experienced less distress than those with lower self-esteem. Greater length of time since victimization was also linked to lower self-esteem, but severity of victimization was not related to either self-esteem or distress. The amount of time since victimization was not directly related to the levels of distress that children experienced, but was indirectly related through its relationship with self-esteem. Battle's (1998) findings support the role of self-esteem, conceptualized as an individual resource variable, in accounting for the variability of psychological symptoms in child victims who present themselves for treatment.

In addition to helping to understand the variability in initial symptom presentation of child victims, these findings have important implications for practitioners who work with child victims of crime. First, children with poorer self-esteem were much more likely to experience clinically significant distress following victimization than children with higher self-esteem. Furthermore, because the amount of time that had elapsed since victimization and low self-esteem was linked to greater distress, it may be especially important to initiate treatment with child victims of low self-esteem as soon as possible after a traumatic event. Second, since cognitive and behavioral avoidance appear to be related to children's distress in a general sample of child victims, interventions that help them gradually confront distressing stimuli through exposure may help diminish the conditioned arousal that has been associated with those stimuli.

Interventions for child victims of crime

In addition to documenting the nature, severity and correlates of children's psychological distress following criminal victimization, researchers have begun to develop and evaluate interventions designed to facilitate children's emotional recovery. As with the general area of research on child victimization, the treatment literature for child victims of crime relies heavily on intervention studies with adults. The best research on adult interventions has been done since 1990, and provides information about the effectiveness of various treatment strategies. Cognitive-Behavioral Therapy, Cognitive

Processing Therapy, Prolonged Exposure, Stress Inoculation Training and Supportive Psychotherapy have all been shown to reduce symptoms of PTSD and depression in adults significantly (Bryant *et al.* 1998; Foa and Meadows 1997; Foa *et al.* 1991; Resick and Schnicke 1992; Resick *et al.* 1988). The improvements seen in clients appear to be maintained over three to six month follow-up periods.

Although there is no clear superiority of one treatment approach over another in terms of impacting general psychological functioning, there are some indications of possible differential effectiveness on specific symptom clusters. For example, Foa *et al.* (1991) found that supportive treatment seemed less effective, compared to prolonged exposure and stress inoculation treatment, in reducing the *re-experiencing* and *avoidance* symptom clusters of PTSD, while being equally effective for depressive symptoms for adult victims of sexual assault. In contrast, Bryant *et al.* (1998) found cognitive-behavioral treatment superior to supportive therapy in reducing intrusive, avoidance and depressive symptoms.

Overall, the treatment literature for adult victims consistently reveals that several intervention strategies, including supportive treatment and cognitive-behavioral treatment, are effective in ameliorating the most common presenting problems of this population. Further, evidence suggests that these gains are maintained, at least over a period of several months. It is not clear, however, whether specific types of clients are more responsive to one treatment over another. Research that documents differential effectiveness across interventions would permit matching a specific treatment to a specific pattern of presenting symptoms, thereby maximizing both efficiency and effectiveness of treatment.

Compared with the treatment literature with adults, research on treatment for child and adolescent victims is at an earlier stage of development. For the most part, intervention techniques that appear promising for adults have been adapted for use with children. Many have questioned the appropriateness of this strategy and the generalizability of findings from these intervention studies. Unlike adults, interventions with children must be developmentally congruent with the cognitive, behavioral and developmental level of the client (Pynoos and Nader 1988). In addition, interventions with children must involve, to varying degrees, the child's caretakers (Gillis 1993).

Evidence of treatment outcome for child victims has generally been anecdotal in nature, and methodologically sound treatment outcome studies using comparative research designs are rare. The bulk of evidence on treatment outcome for child victims is based on single-case reports, which are useful at the earliest stage of investigation for providing some preliminary evidence of effectiveness. In general, these studies suggest that cognitive-behavioral treatment, similar to that used with adults, may also be effective for children and adolescents (e.g., Farrell, Hains and Davies 1998; Saigh 1987a, 1987b, 1987c, 1989a, 1989b; Yule 1998). Studies with larger samples, but without control groups, have been conducted with children victimized by natural disasters, crime, accidents and exposure to community violence. Cognitive-behavioral treatment, including exposure, and supportive therapy again appear to be useful in reducing both anxiety and depressive symptoms for children and adolescents (e.g., Deblinger, McLeer and Henry 1990; Galante and Foa 1986; Murphy, Pynoos and James 1997). Studies employing an untreated (non-randomly assigned) control group have reported similar findings in that cognitive-behavioral treatment and supportive treatment results in reduced anxiety and depression symptoms, compared to untreated children (Goenjian et al. 1997; Yule 1992). Studies using a treatment comparison outcome design (Cohen and Mannarino 1996, 1997; Harris et al. 1997) have yielded inconsistent findings. Cohen and Mannarino (1996) found cognitive-behavioral treatment to be more effective than supportive therapy for a sample of sexually abused preschoolers. Harris et al. (1997), working with a sample of juvenile victims of violent crime, found comparable effectiveness for cognitive-behavioral treatment and supportive treatment. In both of these studies, good methodology was used, including standardized assessment measures, random assignment to treatment conditions and manualized treatment.

Overall, the research literature on treatment of juvenile victims of crime is sparse but promising. Based on the few existing studies, the treatment strategies first identified for use with adults appear to be adaptable to youth, and equally effective. A stronger empirical base is certainly needed to confirm and extend these findings. Refinement of knowledge about treatment outcome with child crime victims is needed, especially with regard to possible differential impact of intervention by type of treatment, initial symptom presentation, developmental level of the client and involvement of the client's caretakers in treatment.

The Victims' Resource Institute's treatment programs

The Victims' Resource Institute at the University of Houston began development of a cognitive-behavioral and supportive treatment program for young victims of violent crime. The primary focus of treatment is the child, although parents or other family members are included in some facets of treatment. For purposes of case formulation and evaluation of treatment, comprehensive assessments are obtained from parents and children at the beginning and end of treatment, and weekly assessments of treatment process are collected from the child throughout treatment. Individualized treatment within the cognitive-behavioral and supportive intervention modalities is relatively long term, averaging twenty sessions in total.

Based on our review of the literature on youth victimization and our own clinical research experience, we have found that the variability in initial symptom presentation following violent victimization has important implications for individualizing treatment within each modality to meet client needs most appropriately. Two symptom clusters are common. *Symptomatic* children exhibit primary symptoms of heightened arousal, including high levels of intrusive and racing thoughts, hypervigilance, behavioral avoidance of trauma-related cues and intense anxiety or fear. *Asymptomatic* children evidence primary symptoms of avoidance and underarousal, including active avoidance of trauma-related stimuli, denial, emotion numbing, reluctance to communicate about the trauma and depressive symptoms. These clients often deny any adverse reaction to the trauma and may display minimal affect. We have found that within the general cognitive-behavioral and supportive treatment framework, different clinical techniques appear to be better suited to effective intervention with children exhibiting each symptom cluster.

Cognitive-behavioral treatment

The primary goal of the cognitive-behavioral treatment approach is to equip the client with a new set of skills to facilitate their psychological management of the traumatic event. Based on the presenting problem, treatment follows a specific plan focused on teaching the client new ways of regulating affective, cognitive and behavioral responses which interfere with daily functioning while optimizing general psychological adjustment. The therapist guides the content of the therapy sessions and provides homework to give the client opportunities to practice newly acquired coping skills. The client completes treatment having learned a variety of new skills that facilitate the management of memories and reactions to the traumatic event and associated stimuli.

The initial phase of treatment involves assessment of the client's current and past symptoms related to the traumatic event and the resources available to facilitate coping with other stressors, including participation in court proceedings associated with prosecution of the offender. During this phase, the therapist focuses on building rapport, educating clients regarding the normality of their reaction to the trauma and what they can expect (e.g., some memories will always be there in some form; it is normal to feel depressed or angry at times).

While recognizing that each child's response is unique and may involve a mix of the two common reactions, specific procedures have been developed for the symptomatic and asymptomatic subgroups. The treatment procedures for helping manage the elevated arousal exhibited by *symptomatic* children focus on decreasing the intensity of the arousal experienced by the client through the use of cognitive and behavioral techniques, such as controlled breathing, distraction, relaxation, systematic desensitization and exposure. The treatment procedures for underarousal or avoidance exhibited by *asymptomatic* children address the tendency to avoid dealing with the trauma and its consequences. The goal with these children is to intensify emotional responses while helping the client cope effectively with his or her reaction to the trauma and its consequences. This is accomplished through slowing down the process of recounting the traumatic experience to include greater details and refocusing the client's awareness on internal experiences both during the trauma and while recalling the events of the trauma. Once they are able to experience more fully their emotional reactions to the trauma, these clients can then benefit from learning more adaptive ways of managing their emotions using some of the same behavioral techniques that we have found to be helpful in managing hyperarousal.

Cognitive restructuring of client's appraisals of their traumatic experience is important to both subgroups. During the initial stages of treatment, therapists probe for cognitions related to beliefs of helplessness, personal responsibility for the trauma, how the event will affect the future, and clients' view of the self and the world. General steps involve increasing awareness of automatic thoughts and their impact on behavior and emotions, evaluating the thoughts and beliefs and 'testing out' the conclusions drawn from them, and increasing clients' awareness of their basic beliefs and working to alter maladaptive beliefs.

The next portion of treatment (tenth to fifteenth sessions) focuses on clients' interpersonal relationships and general coping style. Typically, these issues have already arisen during treatment; however, further assessment is conducted in this treatment phase as needed. In addition to helping clients access social and emotional support available from interpersonal relationships (i.e., family, friends and organizations), a problem-solving or re-educative approach is used to help clients formulate and implement a specific plan designed to remediate problems in this area.

The final portion of treatment addresses the generalization and maintenance of treatment gains. The goal at this stage of treatment is to solidify the progress that has been made and adequately prepare the client for potential difficulties that may arise in the future. The changes that have occurred across previous sessions are reviewed to highlight progress that has been achieved. Skills learned are reviewed and future stumbling blocks are anticipated. The final session is an opportunity to celebrate the client's self-confidence regarding mastery over the traumatic experience and a sense of moving forward in life.

Parents are also involved in treatment in order to mobilize supportive resources for the child as well as provide useful information about the child's psychological adjustment and response to treatment. We have also found it important to educate parents regarding their child's response to the victimization – by normalizing children's reactions and providing parents with insight into how children cope with trauma and how they can facilitate their children's recovery. Helping parents manage their own distress regarding their children's victimization is also necessary at times. Understandably, parents can become very distraught following their child's victimization, which may elevate their children's emotional distress or lead them to minimize the impact of the trauma in order to protect their parents' feelings. Occasionally, it is helpful to teach parents child management skills, especially when children manifest their distress through conduct problems and other forms of externalizing behavior. In addition to parents, siblings or other relatives may also be enlisted as therapeutic adjuncts. For example, siblings can be a valuable source of information regarding the client's reaction to the traumatization as well as a source of support for the client during the recovery process.

Supportive treatment

The second intervention strategy developed and evaluated by VRI is a supportive treatment. A key distinction between the cognitive-behavioral and supportive model of treatment is whether or not new emotional coping skills are taught. The primary goal of the supportive intervention is to identify and encourage the client's use of existing coping strategies.

Within the supportive treatment condition, different procedures are emphasized for the symptomatic and asymptomatic subgroups. In response to elevated arousal exhibited by *symptomatic* children, the focus is on coping with the intensity of affect experienced by the client through the use of techniques such as acceptance and normalization. The child's ability to tolerate and integrate intense emotional states is supported through self-exploration and the use of metaphors. The treatment procedures for underarousal or avoidance exhibited by *asymptomatic* children are designed to facilitate awareness of their emotional responses while providing a safe and supportive environment. This is typically accomplished through focused questioning about emotional responses, keeping the client's awareness on internal experiences both during and after the trauma. Therapist's emotional engagement with the client and provision of emotional support and nurturance during this phase is crucial.

For all children, the use of ego-supportive interventions encourages the client to express feelings surrounding the traumatic event and its repercussions. The therapist facilitates the client's progress towards self-realization by reflecting and validating the client's experiences and emotional reactions. The specific content of therapy sessions is determined primarily by the client. The client is encouraged to use already developed adaptive coping skills to reduce distress and to manage the memory of the traumatic event. The goal is integration of the new experience in a healthy manner.

This supportive therapy model is predicated on the assumption that emotional recovery following victimization results from the combination of consciousness raising and corrective emotional experiences that occur within the context of a genuine, empathetic relationship. Consciousness raising can be aided by educating the client regarding the predictable fear response to trauma and normalizing the symptoms being experienced. Emotional catharsis and empathetic exploration are also considered to be important. By discussing the event with a therapist who is empathetic and displays unconditional positive regard, clients are able to increase trust in their feelings and learn to value their own emotional experience. Ultimately, clients complete therapy feeling greater confidence in their ability to manage the memories and reactions to traumatic experiences. As with the cognitive-behavioral treatment, our approach to supportive treatment involves parents and other family members in order to facilitate the client's emotional recovery from victimization.

Evaluation of treatment effectiveness

A major goal of the Victims' Resource Institute has been to conduct research in order to empirically support promising interventions for child victims of crime. We have taken an incremental approach to establish treatment effectiveness. Guided by Paul's (1969) recommendations for the tactical use of research designs in outcome research on psychotherapy, this approach involves use of research designs of increasing complexity to help establish a causal relationship between participation in our treatment and observed changes in children's emotional reactions and behavior following victimization. At VRI, children are randomly assigned to the individualized cognitive-behavioral or supportive treatment conditions previously described. Therapy is conducted by advanced doctoral students in clinical psychology under the supervision of the clinical psychologists who designed the treatment protocols. In order to assess treatment outcome, a battery of well-validated standardized measures is administered before and after treatment and at six months following termination. Information is collected on alternating weeks about the current level of depressive symptoms, intrusive thoughts and behavioral and cognitive avoidance (see Table 8.1). Each measure has been used widely in studies of children in various clinical and non-clinical contexts. This battery assesses externalizing and internalizing behavior problems, the symptom criteria for clinical diagnoses and child reports of self-esteem. We have included both parent and child report measures that can be administered in a relatively brief amount of time.

Traditional outcome designs based on analyses of pre-, post- and follow-up assessments allow one to document the average treatment response across clients, with individual variability represented as a source of error (Francis et al. 1991; Willett 1989). Research designs that involve use of individual growth curve modeling of biweekly data allows studying the pattern of change at the individual level. At this stage of research, we believe that it is important to document possible differences in the patterns of change that are observed among individual children, in addition to changes aggregated at a group level.

Table 8.1 Treatment outcome measures

Pre-, post- and six-month post-treatment

1. *Diagnostic Interview for Children and Adolescents – Revised (DICA-R)* (Kaplan and Reich 1991) is a structured interview designed to identify diagnoses in children based on the *Diagnostic and Statistical Manual – Third Edition – Revised.*

2. *Child Behavior Checklist* (Achenbach 1991a) is a parent report questionnaire of child behavioral and emotional problems.

3. *Youth Self-Report* (Achenbach 1991b) is a self-report questionnaire designed to obtain reports of feelings and behavior from youth.

4. *Piers–Harris Self-Concept Scale* (Piers 1984) is a self-report measure designed to assess self-esteem in children and adolescents.

5. *Demographic Information Questionnaire* obtains information from the parent on education, race, income, marital status and living arrangements.

Biweekly assessments

1. *Impact of Event Scale – Revised* (Horowitz, Wilner and Alvarez 1979) is a child report questionnaire of trauma-related symptoms associated with intrusive thinking, cognitive and behavioral avoidance.

2. *Children's Depression Inventory* (Kovacs 1992) is a child report questionnaire of depressive symptoms.

Source: Vincent and Harris 1992.

We have selected two of the studies we have conducted thus far that illustrate our approach to studying the patterns of change and outcome of our treatment programs. In the first study, Vicknair (1996) examined changes over the course of treatment in children's trauma symptoms of avoidance and intrusive thinking. Individual growth modeling techniques were used to describe the pattern of change in each over the course of treatment at the individual and group level. Based on an interest in the role of self-esteem in children's recovery process, scores on the Piers–Harris Self-Concept Scale were used to predict the slope of change in trauma symptoms. In preliminary analyses of these data, Vicknair (1996) created an index of clinically significant improvement similar to that employed by Resick *et al.* (1988). Child clients were classified as improved if their score on the variable of interest declined at least 0.5 standard deviations from the beginning to the end of treatment. In analyses of those clients who had completed treatment at the time (n = 11), 73 percent demonstrated clinically significant change in one or both of the trauma symptom indices. When individual growth curve analyses were employed, Vicknair (1996) found considerable variability in the pattern of change across both clients and time. This suggests that, while the majority of children demonstrated clinically significant improvement through their participation in VRI's child-based treatment program, when examined as individuals, children exhibited patterns of change that differed considerably. Consistent with the analyses of clinically significant change, the individual growth curve analyses revealed that most of the children exhibited functional change in avoidance or intrusion, whereas some children exhibited either no treatment response, and one exhibited actual deterioration. In addition, the patterns of change for avoidance and intrusion were virtually uncorrelated, suggesting that different change processes may govern each variable. Post-hoc inspection of any striking increases that occurred in trauma symptoms mid-treatment were correlated with entries in therapists' progress notes. Short-term deterioration (sharp increases in trauma symptoms) often coincided with secondary trauma stimuli, such as meetings with police and prosecutors, or learning new information about the perpetrator.

In order to determine if children's self-esteem predicts treatment response, scores on the Piers–Harris Self-Concept Scale were regressed on the slope of change indices for each trauma variable. Controlling for length of treatment, children with higher self-esteem had greater rates of reduction for avoidance behaviors. Similar effects were not found for the rate of change in intrusive thoughts. Collectively, these analyses indicate that the treatment program for child crime victims is effective for roughly every three out of four clients who participated in treatment. The innovative use of individual growth curve analyses revealed that the patterns of change for individual children are unique. Variability in the change indices across client, outcome variable and time suggest that individual children recover from trauma in several ways; no single process appears to capture how they responded to treatment on a weekly basis. These findings have important implications for therapists' expectations concerning how treatment progresses across weekly sessions. Furthermore, the findings suggest that therapists may encounter greater challenges in effecting therapeutic change in child clients with low self-esteem who appear to relinquish trauma-based avoidance at a slower rate than children with high self-esteem.

In the second study, Merkel (1999) conducted a traditional outcome analysis based on pre-post changes in behavioral and emotional functioning of children who participated in treatment at VRI. The initial aim of this study was to assess whether or not there was an overall treatment effect in reduction of depressive symptoms and other internalizing problems in child victims of crime. Depression is a common presenting symptom among children referred to treatment at the Victims' Resource Institute, and other investigators have noted a high incidence of depressive disorders along with other symptoms among children who have experienced various types of trauma (Amaya-Jackson and March 1995). In addition, Merkel (1999) was interested in testing the possible differential treatment effects of the supportive and cognitive-behavioral treatment programs described above. In many ways, the study was modeled after similar treatment studies with adult rape victims, where supportive treatments were compared with various cognitive-behavioral modalities (e.g., Foa *et al.* 1991; Resick *et al.* 1988). Outcome was assessed in terms of pre-post assessments based on child and parent reports of internalizing behaviors. The fidelity of treatments was checked by blind ratings of a sample of client files. Analysis of these ratings demonstrated that the two treatments could be reliably differentiated in terms of the presence or absence of cognitive-behavioral treatment elements.

Preliminary analyses assessed group comparability on a number of relevant dimensions, including demographic variables, type of victimization and pre-treatment level of functioning. Children who participated in the supportive versus cognitive-behavioral treatment were comparable on virtually all of these variables. Marginally significant differences were noted, however. A shorter time period has elapsed since the crime for children in the cognitive-behavioral treatment condition, and parent-reported internalizing symptoms were higher at pre-treatment for children in the supportive treatment condition. Analyses of treatment effects revealed some interesting findings. Using two-way analysis of variance, an overall treatment effect for child-reported symptoms in both treatment conditions was found. Regardless of treatment modality, children reported fewer depressive symptoms and internalizing symptoms at the end of treatment than at the beginning. Parents also reported positive treatment effects, but only for children who received the supportive treatment. In general, no other differential effects of cognitive-behavioral and supportive treatment were found. Based on the possibility that confounding variables may have attenuated between-group differences, follow-up analyses controlling for the effects of treatment length, time since victimization and type of victimization were conducted. These results did not alter the original findings.

Merkel (1999) also addressed the clinical significance of findings using the method employed by Resick *et al.* (1988) and Vicknair (1996). Based on child-reported depressive symptoms, 60 percent of participants improved in the supportive condition and 82 percent improved in the cognitive-behavioral condition. Using child-reported internalizing symptoms as the index of change, an 83 percent improvement rate was found for children in the supportive condition and a 78 percent improvement rate was found for the cognitive-behavioral treatment. Similar results were found for parent reported change in internalizing symptoms: an 86 percent improvement rate for supportive treatment and a 70 percent improvement rate for cognitive-behavioral treatment. When aggregated across data sources, the fact that 76 percent of children evidenced clinically significant improvement in each condition attests to the value of treatment generally, but not to the superiority of one modality over the other.

Finally, Merkel (1999) examined children's self-esteem as a possible predictor of treatment response. Similar to Vicknair's (1996) study, scores on the Piers–Harris Self-Concept Scale were used to predict changes in child-reported depressive symptoms and internalizing symptoms reported by parent and child. After controlling for pre-treatment symptom levels, regression analyses found that self-esteem predicted reductions in child-reported depression, but not parent-reported internalizing symptoms. These results partially replicated Vicknair's (1996) earlier findings that children's self-esteem predicts their response to treatment, in this case when child-reported change in depressive symptoms was the index of treatment response.

Extrapolating the results of Merkel's (1999) study to the clinical setting, these findings support the notion that child victims may be responsive to treatments that differ in terms of specific technique, as long as the specific modality is administered competently by trained therapists. We are inclined to think that the most powerful ingredient in effective treatment with child victims of crime may be the presence and caring of an emotionally engaged therapist. Regardless of the specific tools that the therapist employs, effective treatments for child victims have in common the process of establishing a therapeutic alliance, sensitively exploring one of a child's darkest moments, and instilling hope about a brighter future. While clinical researchers like ourselves are often interested in finding technical elements that enhance the effectiveness of treatment, we are reminded not to overlook how to identify and train therapeutic expertise in cultivating an effective collaboration with clients.

Summary and future directions

In this chapter, we have discussed the current state of knowledge concerning the psychological effects of crime on children, interventions that are available to facilitate their emotional recovery and our approach to the development, evaluation and application of effective treatments. We believe that our approach exemplifies the effective partnership between research and practice, where experience in each arena can serve to inform the other. As we said at the outset, the state of knowledge concerning effective treatment for child victims is in an early stage of development. Tragically, given the current level of violence in many parts of the world, the need for effective services for child victims is on the rise. Our research will continue looking for risk and resilience factors that predict children's reactions to violence and conducting treatment outcome studies designed to identify the ingredients of effective interventions. We hope that our work will provide a model for other communities in establishing a comprehensive program of services that meet the needs of child victims of violence at all stages of their recovery process.

Author Acknowledgements

We wish to acknowledge the Ima Hogg Foundation and the Advanced Research Program of the Texas Coordinating Board of Higher Education for supporting research and treatment services for child victims at the Victims' Resource Institute. In addition, we wish to acknowledge the doctoral clinical psychology students at the University of Houston, who have been actively involved since the inception of the Victims' Resource Institute in 1992.

References

Achenbach, T.M. (1991a) *Manual for the Child Behavior Checklist/4–18 and 1991 Profile.* Burlington, VT: Department of Psychiatry, University of Vermont.

Achenbach, T.M. (1991b) *Manual for the Youth Self-Report and 1991 Profile.* Burlington, VT: Department of Psychiatry, University of Vermont.

Amaya-Jackson, L. and March, J.S. (1995) 'Posttraumatic stress disorder.' In J.S. March (ed) *Anxiety Disorders in Children and Adolescents.* New York: Guilford.

American Psychiatric Association (1994) *Diagnostic and Statistical Manual of Mental Disorders – Fourth Edition.* Washington DC: American Psychiatric Association.

Bard, M. and Sangrey, D. (1979) *The Crime Victim's Book.* New York: Basic Books.

Battle, J.V. (1998) 'Structural modeling of child and adolescent reactions to violent victimization: the mediational role of self-esteem.' Unpublished doctoral dissertation, University of Houston, Texas.

Bendek, E.P. (1985) 'Children and psychic trauma: a brief review of contemporary thinking.' In S. Eth and R.S. Pynoos (eds) *Post-Traumatic Disorder in Children.* Washington DC: American Psychiatric Press.

Boney-McCoy, S. and Finkelhor, D. (1995a) 'Psychosocial sequelae of violent victimization in a national youth sample.' *Journal of Consulting and Clinical Psychology 63*, 726–736.

Boney-McCoy, S. and Finkelhor, D. (1995b) 'Prior victimization: a risk factor for child sexual abuse and for PTSD-related symptomatology among sexually abused youth.' *Child Abuse and Neglect 19*, 1401–1421.

Bownes, I.T., O'Gorman, E.C. and Sayers, A. (1991) 'Assault characteristics and posttraumatic stress disorder in rape victims.' *Acta Psychiatrica Scandinavica 83*, 27–30.

Browne, A. and Finkelhor, D. (1986) 'Impact of child sexual abuse: a review of the research.' *Psychological Bulletin 99*, 66–77.

Bryant, R.A., Harvey, A.G., Dang, S.T., Sackville, T. and Basten, C. (1998) 'Treatment of acute stress disorder: a comparison of cognitive-behaviorali therapy and supportive counseling.' *Journal of Consulting and Clinical Psychology 66*, 862–866.

Bureau of Justice Statistics (1998) *National Crime Victimization Survey, Criminal Victimization 1998: Changes 1997–98 with Trends 1993–98* (NCJ 176353). Washington DC: US Department of Justice, Office of Justice Programs.

Cohen, J.A. and Mannarino, A.P. (1996) 'A treatment outcome study for sexually abused preschool children: initial findings.' *Journal of the American Academy of Child and Adolescent Psychiatry 35*, 42–50.

Cohen, J.A. and Mannarino, A.P. (1997) 'A treatment study for sexually abused preschool children: outcome during a one-year follow-up.' *Journal of the American Academy of Child and Adolescent Psychiatry 36*, 1228–1235.

Deblinger, E., McLeer, S.V. and Henry, D. (1990) 'cognitive-behavioral treatment for sexually abused children suffering post-traumatic stress: preliminary findings.' *Journal of the American Academy of Child and Adolescent Psychiatry 29*, 747–752.

Earls, F., Smith, E., Reich, W. and Jung, K.G. (1988) 'Investigating psychopathological consequences of disaster in children: a pilot study incorporating a structured diagnostic interview.' *Journal of the American Academy of Child and Adolescent Psychiatry 27*, 90–95.

Eth, S. and Pynoos, R. (1985) 'Interaction of trauma and grief in childhood.' In S. Eth and R.S. Pynoos (eds) *Post-Traumatic Disorder in Children.* Washington DC: American Psychiatric Press.

Farrell, S.P., Hains, A.A. and Davies, W.H. (1998) 'Cognitive-behavioral interventions for sexually abused children exhibiting PTSD symptomatology.' *Behavior Therapy 29*, 241–255.

Finkelhor, D. and Dziuba-Leatherman, J. (1994) 'Victimization of children.' *American Psychologist 49*, 173–183.

Fletcher, K.E. (1996) 'Childhood posttraumatic stress disorder.' In E.J. Mash and R.A. Barkley (eds) *Child Psychopathology.* New York: Guilford.

Foa, E.B. and Meadows, E.A. (1997) 'Psychosocial treatments for posttraumatic stress disorder: a critical review.' *Annual Review of Psychology 48*, 449–480.

Foa, E., Rothbaum, B., Riggs, D. and Murdock, T. (1991) 'Treatment of posttraumatic stress disorder in rape victims: a comparison between cognitive-behaviorali procedures and counseling.' *Journal of Consulting and Clinical Psychology 59*, 715–723.

Francis, D.J., Fletcher, J.M., Stuebing, K.K., Davidson, K.C. and Thompson, N.M. (1991) 'Analysis of change: modeling individual growth.' *Journal of Consulting and Clinical Psychology 59*, 27–37.

Galante, R. and Foa, D. (1986) 'An epidemiological study of psychic trauma and treatment effectiveness for children after a natural disaster.' *Journal of the American Academy of Child and Adolescent Psychiatry 25*, 357–363.

Garmezy, N. and Rutter, M. (1985) 'Acute reactions to stress.' In M. Rutter and L. Hersov (eds) *Child and Adolescent Psychiatry: Modern Approaches*, 2nd edn. Oxford: Blackwell.

Gillis, H.M. (1993) 'Individual and small-group psychotherapy for children involved in trauma and disaster.' In C.F. Saylor (ed) *Children and Disasters*. New York: Plenum.

Goenjian, A.K., Karayan, I., Pynoos, R.S., Minassian, D., Najarian, L.M., Steinberg, A.M. and Fairbanks, L.A. (1997) 'Outcome of psychotherapy among early adolescents after trauma.' *American Journal of Psychiatry 154*, 536–542.

Harris, G.E., Vincent, J.P., Gerasimova, Y. and Rizzo, L.P. (1997) 'Effectiveness of cognitive-behavioral and supportive treatments for juvenile crime victims.' Paper presented at the American Psychological Association, August. San Francisco, CA.

Horowitz, M., Wilner, N. and Alvarez, W. (1979) 'Impact of Event Scale: A measure of subjective stress.' *Psychosomatic Medicine 41*, 209–219.

Kaplan, L.M. and Reich, W. (1991) *Diagnostic Interview for Children and Adolescents – Revised (DICA-R) DSM-III-R Version*. Division of Child Psychiatry, St Louis, MO: Washington University.

Kendall-Tackett, K.A., Williams, L.M. and Finkelhor, D. (1993) 'Impact of sexual abuse on children: a review and synthesis of recent empirical studies.' *Psychological Bulletin 113*, 164–180.

Kovacs, M. (1992) *Children's Depression Inventory*. North Tonawanda, NY: Multi-Health Systems.

McFarlane, A.C. (1987) 'Posttraumatic phenomena in a longitudinal study of children following a natural disaster.' *Journal of the American Academy of Child and Adolescent Psychiatry 26*, 764–769.

McNally, R.J. (1993) 'Stressors that produce PTSD in children.' In J.R. Davidson and E.B. Foa (eds) *PTSD: DSM-IV and Beyond*. Washington DC: American Psychiatric Press.

Meichenbaum, D. (1999) 'Posttraumatic stress disorder: cognitive-behavioral approaches to treatment of children, adolescents and their families.' Presented at a workshop of the Los Angeles Center for Traumatic Stress and Sudden Bereavement, Los Angeles, CA, March.

Merkel, K.M. (1999) 'Effect of treatment of distress symptoms in child victims of violent crime: a comparison of supportive therapy and cognitive-behavioral therapy.' Unpublished doctoral dissertation, University of Houston, Texas.

Miller, T.W. (ed) (1998) *Children of Trauma: Stressful Life Events and their Effects on Children and Adolescents*. Madison, CT: International Universities Press.

Morgan, J. and Zedner, L. (1992) *Child Victims: Crime, Impact and Criminal Justice*. Oxford: Clarendon.

Murphy, L., Pynoos, R.S. and James, C.B. (1997) 'The trauma/grief-focused group psychotherapy module of an elementary school-based violence prevention/intervention program.' In J.D. Osofsky (ed) *Children in a Violent Society*. New York: Guilford.

Nader, K., Pynoos, R., Fairbanks, L. and Frederick, C. (1990) 'Children's PTSD reactions one year after a sniper attack.' *American Journal of Psychiatry 147*, 1526–1530.

National Institute of Justice (1997) *The Prevalence and Consequences of Child Victimization*. Washington DC: Office of Justice Programs, US Department of Justice.

Osofsky, J.D. (ed) (1997) *Children in a Violent Society*. New York: Guilford.

Paul, G.L. (1969) 'Behavior modification research: design and tactics.' In C.M. Franks (ed) *Behavior Therapy: Appraisal and Status*. New York: McGraw-Hill.

Perez, C.M. and Widom, C.S. (1994) 'Childhood victimization and long-term intellectual and academic outcomes.' *Child Abuse and Neglect 18*, 617–633.

Piers, E.V. (1984) *Piers–Harris Children's Self-Concept Scale: Revised Manual.* Los Angeles: Western Psychological Services.

Pynoos, R.S. and Eth, S. (1985) 'Children traumatized by witnessing acts of personal violence: homicide, rape or suicide behavior.' In S. Eth and R.S. Pynoos (eds) *Post-Traumatic Disorder in Children.* Washington DC: American Psychiatric Press.

Pynoos, R.S. and Eth, S. (1986) 'Witness to violence: the child interview.' *Journal of the American Academy of Child Psychiatry 25*, 306–319.

Pynoos, R.S. and Nader, K. (1988) 'Children who witness the sexual assault of their mothers.' *Journal of the American Academy of Child and Adolescent Psychiatry 27*, 567–572.

Pynoos, R.S., Frederick, C., Nader, K., Arroyo, W., Steinberg, A., Eth, S., Nunez, F. and Fairbanks, L. (1987) 'Life threat and posttraumatic stress in school-age children.' *Archives of General Psychiatry 44*, 1057–1063.

Pynoos, R.S., Goenjian, A., Karakashian, M., Tashijian, M., Manjikian, R., Monoukian, G., Steinberg, A.M. and Fairbanks, L.A. (1993) 'Posttraumatic stress reactions in children after the 1988 American Earthquake.' *British Journal of Psychiatry 32*, 407–416.

Pynoos, R.S., Steinberg, A.M. and Goenjian, A. (1996) 'Traumatic stress in childhood and adolescence: recent developments and current controversies.' In B.A. van der Kolk, A.C. McFarlane and L. Weisaeth (eds) *Traumatic Stress: The Effects of Overwhelming Experience on Mind, Body and Society.* New York: Guilford.

Resick, P.A. and Schnicke, M.K. (1992) 'Cognitive processing therapy for sexual assault victims.' *Journal of Consulting and Clinical Psychology 60*, 748–756.

Resick, P.A., Jordan, C.G., Girelli, S.A., Hutter, C.K. and Marhoefer-Dvorak, S. (1988) 'A comparative outcome study of behavioral group therapy for sexual assault victims.' *Behavior Therapy 19*, 385–401.

Reynolds, A.J. (1998) 'Resilience among Black urban youth: prevalence, intervention effects and mechanisms of influence.' *American Journal of Orthopsychiatry 68*, 84–100.

Rigamer, E.F. (1986) 'Psychological management of children in a national crisis.' *Journal of the American Academy of Child Psychiatry 25*, 364–369.

Rind, B., Tromovitch, P. and Bauserman (1998) 'A meta-analytic examination of assumed properties of child sexual abuse using college samples.' *Psychological Bulletin 124*, 22–53.

Russell, D.H. (1986) *The Secret Trauma: Incest in the Lives of Girls and Women.* New York: Basic Books.

Saigh, P.A. (1987a) 'In vitro flooding of an adolescent's posttraumatic stress disorder.' *Journal of Clinical Child Psychology 16*, 147–150.

Saigh, P.A. (1987b) 'In vitro flooding of a childhood posttraumatic stress disorder.' *School Psychology Review 16*, 203–211.

Saigh, P.A. (1987c) 'In vitro flooding of childhood posttraumatic stress disorder: a systematic replication.' *Professional School Psychology 2*, 133–145.

Saigh, P.A. (1989a) 'A comparative analysis of the affective and behavioral symptomatology of traumatized and nontraumatized children.' *Journal of School Psychology 27*, 247–255.

Saigh, P.A. (1989b) 'The use of in vitro flooding in the treatment of traumatized adolescents.' *Journal of Behavioral and Developmental Pediatrics 10*, 17–21.

Schwarz, E.D. and Kowalski, J.M. (1991) 'Malignant memories: PTSD in children and adults after a school shooting.' *Journal of the American Academy of Child and Adolescent Psychiatry 30*, 936–944.

Stallard, P. and Law, F. (1994) 'The psychological effects of traumas on children.' *Children and Society 8*, 89–97.

Stekettee, G. and Foa, E.B. (1987) 'Rape victims: post-traumatic stress responses and their treatment. A review of the literature.' *Journal of Anxiety Disorders 1*, 69–86.

Terr, L.C. (1981) 'Psychic trauma in children: observations following the Chowchilla school-bus kidnapping.' *American Journal of Psychiatry 138*, 14–19.

Terr, L.C. (1983) 'Chowchilla revisited: the effects of psychic trauma four years after a school-bus kidnapping.' *American Journal of Psychiatry 140*, 1543–1550.

Terr, L.C. (1985) 'Children traumatized in small groups.' In S. Eth and R.S. Pynoos (eds) *Post-Traumatic Disorder in Children.* Washington DC: American Psychiatric Press.

Terr, L.C. (1991) 'Childhood trauma: an outline and overview.' *American Journal of Psychiatry 148*, 10–20.

US Department of Justice (1994) *Criminal Victimization in the United States, 1992 (Special Report No. NCJ-145125).* Washington DC: Bureau of Justice Statistics.

Vicknair, J.A. (1996) 'Self-esteem as a predictor of reactions of child and adolescent victims of violent crime.' Unpublished master's thesis, University of Houston, Texas.

Vincent, J.P. and Harris, G.E. (1992) *Demographic Information Questionnaire.* Unpublished manuscript. Houston, TX: University of Houston.

Widom, C.S. (1997) 'Child victims: in search of opportunities for breaking the cycle of violence.' In *National Institute of Justice Perspectives on Crime and Justice 1996–1997 Lecture Series.* Washington DC: National Institute of Justice.

Willett, J.B. (1989) 'Some results on reliability for the longitudinal measurement of change: implications for the design of studies of individual growth.' *Educational and Psychological Measurement 49*, 587–602.

Wolfe, V., Sas, L. and Wilson, S. (1987) 'Some issues in preparing sexually abused children for court testimony.' *Behavior Therapist 10*, 107–113.

Yule, W. (1992) 'Post-traumatic stress disorder in child survivors of shipping disasters: the sinking of the "Jupiter".' *Psychotherapy and Psychosomatics 57*, 200–205.

Yule, W. (1998) 'Posttraumatic stress disorder in children and its treatment.' In T.W. Miller (ed) *Children of Trauma: Stressful Life Events and their Effects on Children and Adolescents.* Madison, CT: International Universities Press.

Yule, W. and Udwin, O. (1991) 'Screening child survivors for post-traumatic stress disorders: experiences from the "Jupiter" sinking.' *British Journal of Clinical Psychology 30*, 131–138.

Zygmuntowicz, R. (1999) 'Symptom variation among child and adolescent victims of violent crime.' Unpublished master's thesis, University of Houston, Texas.

Zygmuntowicz, R., Vincent, J.P., Harris, G.E. and Dominguez, J. (1997) 'Symptom variations in child and adolescent victims of violent crime.' Paper presented at the American Psychological Association meeting, August. San Francisco, CA.

The Contributors

Julia C. Babcock is an Assistant Professor of Psychology at the University of Houston in Houston, Texas. Dr Babcock received her PhD from the University of Washington in 1997. She conducts research in the areas of marriage, couples' therapy and domestic violence, focussing on the perpetrators of abuse towards their partners. Dr Babcock is currently conducting laboratory studies examining differences in emotional regulation between violent and non-violent men. She also collaborates with domestic violence treatment agencies, police and the courts to examine the effectiveness of coordinated community interventions.

Janette Cross is a clinical psychologist and Clinical Assistant Professor in the Department of Psychology at the University of Houston. She is the Research Coordinator for the Victims' Resource Institute. Dr Cross has over 10 years' experience in working with children, several of those years with criminally victimized children. In addition, Dr Cross' interests include treatment outcome research, program evaluation and treatment of anxiety disorders and other serious mental illnesses among both child and adult populations.

Elizabeth Ezell is a doctoral candidate in clinical psychology at the University of Houston. She has worked for five years in the area of domestic violence and children's adjustment. She has contributed to clinical and research efforts aimed at understanding and helping women and children in families marked by marital conflict, domestic violence and child abuse. She has participated in both the implementation and evaluation of Project SUPPORT.

John H. Grych is an Assistant Professor of Psychology at Marquette University. His primary research interests are in studying family processes related to the development of psychopathology in children. He has published numerous articles examining the effects of interparental conflict, family violence and divorce on children and recently edited a book (with Frank Fincham) on the impact of interparental conflict on child development. He is on the editorial board of the *Journal of Family Psychology* and serves as an editorial consultant for other professional journals dedicated to the study of children and families.

Gerald E. Harris is a licenced psychologist and Research Associate Professor in the Department of Psychology at the University of Houston. He is also the Executive Director of the Victims' Resource Institute. Dr Harris has extensive experience in working with children and adolescents. In addition to directing several research initiatives focusing on violence, aggression, and the prevention and treatment of victims, Dr Harris has published work in the areas of divorce, prevention/ intervention of child conduct problems and child aggression. For many years, Dr Harris has been involved in forensic psychological work involving both perpetrators and victims.

Amy Holtzworth-Munroe is a Professor in the Psychology Department at Indiana University. For 15 years, she has conducted research on the problem of husband violence, including studies comparing the social skills of violent and nonviolent husbands and examining the marital interaction behaviours of violent couples. Her recent research focuses on the identification of subtypes of male batterers. She has led batterer treatment groups and, working with her local domestic violence taskforce, has set up a new batterers' treatment program. Through writings and workshops, she is involved in educating marital/family therapists about husband violence. She serves on a variety of journal editorial boards, is an Associate Editor of the *Journal of Consulting and Clinical Psychology*, and a past Editor of *Cognitive Therapy and Research*.

Ernest N. Jouriles is Professor of Psychology at the University of Houston. His research interests center around understanding and ameliorating the negative effects of marital conflict and violence on children. He has published numerous scientific articles in the areas of marital conflict and child adjustment, domestic violence and child maltreatment. His research has been supported by grants from the National Institute of Mental Health, the Interagency Consortium on Violence Against Women and Violence in the Family Research, the National Institute of Justice, the Texas Higher Education Coordinating Board, the George Foundation, and the Hogg Foundation for Mental Health. Dr Jouriles received an early career award from the Association for Advancement of Behavior Therapy for his research on marital and child problems.

Jaslean J. La Taillade is currently a Carolina Minority Postdoctoral Scholar in the Department of Psychology at the University of North Carolina at Chapel Hill. Dr La Taillade received her degree in clinical psychology from the University of Washington in Seattle, WA. She has written and presented research related to African American inter-racial couples, domestic violence, couple therapy and treatment of African American couples and individuals.

Rennee McDonald is Assistant Research Professor of Psychology at the University of Houston. Since 1988, she has been developing and evaluating service programs for battered women and their children and conducting research on the effects of domestic violence and child abuse on children. She is director of the Family Interaction Project, a research project designed to improve our understanding of children's exposure and responses to marital conflict and violence toward their mothers. She currently co-directs Project SUPPORT, an NIMH-funded research project evaluating an intervention designed to reduce conduct problems among children of battered women, and is also co-directing an evaluation of an intervention designed to reduce risk for child abuse among domestically violent families referred to child protective agencies. In addition to her research and publishing activities, Dr McDonald has served as a consultant to women's centres and agencies providing assessment and service programs for battered women and their children.

Anu Palapattu is a doctoral student in clinical psychology at the University of Houston. She has worked with victimized children and their families for several years through the Victims' Resource Institute as a therapist and as a research assistant. In addition, she has interest and experience working in the areas of childhood conduct problems, adult trauma and behavioural medicine.

Nanette Stephens is Assistant Research Professor of Psychology at the University of Houston. She received her BA from the University of Texas and her PhD from the University of Houston. Dr Stephens is a co-director of Project SUPPORT, a program for women and children departing from battered women's shelters.

Cris M. Sullivan is Associate Professor of Ecological Psychology at Michigan State University, and Director of Evaluation for the Michigan Coalition Against Domestic and Sexual Violence. Dr Sullivan has been an advocate and researcher in the movement to end violence against women since 1982. Her areas of expertise include developing and evaluating community interventions for battered women and evaluating victim services. Dr Sullivan has served as a consultant for numerous local, state and federal organizations and initiatives, including the National Resource Center on Domestic Violence, the Pennsylvania Coalition Against Domestic Violence, the Department of Justice's Violence Against Women Office, the Institute for Law and Justice, the Urban Institute, the National Research Council, and the Battered Women's Justice Project.

Cynthia N. Vincent is a licenced attorney and Research Assistant Professor in the Department of Psychology at the University of Houston. She is also the Co-Director of the Victims' Resource Institute. Ms Vincent has worked extensively with juvenile crime victims who must testify in court. In addition to her leadership role in developing programs to assist young victims of crime, she has been active in promoting the dialogue between psychologists and attorneys. Her published work addresses prevention/intervention strategies for child and adolescent victims of crime.

John P. Vincent is Professor of Psychology at the University of Houston and Chairman of the Department of Psychology and is co-founder of the Institute for Family Treatment. For the past six years Dr Vincent has served as Director of the Victims' Resource Institute, whose mission is the design and implementation of effective programs of prevention and intervention for victims of violence. He has edited a five volume series, *Advances in Family Intervention, Assessment and Theory*, served on the editorial boards of numerous professional journals and has published extensively on the assessment and treatment of marital and family problems as well as childhood hyperactivity, health psychology and victimization of children. In addition to his practice in clinical and forensic psychology, Dr Vincent has served as a consultant to major corporations and governmental organizations regarding violence prevention and intervention.

Subject Index

Author Index